The Origins of Modern Japanese Philosophy

Bloomsbury Studies in World Philosophies

Series Editor:
Monika Kirloskar-Steinbach

Comparative, cross-cultural and intercultural philosophy are burgeoning fields of research. Bloomsbury Studies in World Philosophies complements and strengthens the latest work being carried out at a research level with a series that provides a home for thinking through ways in which professional philosophy can be diversified. Ideal for philosophy postgraduates and faculty who seek creative and innovative material on non-Euroamerican sources for reference and research, this series responds to the challenges of our postcolonial world, laying the groundwork for a new philosophy canon that departs from the current Eurocentric sources.

Titles in the Series:
Andean Aesthetics and Anticolonial Resistance, by Omar Rivera
Chinese Philosophy of History, by Dawid Rogacz
Chinese and Indian Ways of Thinking in Early Modern European Philosophy, by Selusi Ambrogio
Indian and Intercultural Philosophy, by Douglas Berger
Toward a New Image of Paramārtha, by Ching Keng
African Philosophy and Enactivist Cognition, by Bruce B. Janz
Interrelatedness in Chinese Religious Traditions, by Diana Arghirescu
The Metaphysics of Meditation, by Stephen Phillips
The Origins of Modern Japanese Philosophy, by Richard Stone

The Origins of Modern Japanese Philosophy

Nishida Kitarō and the Meiji Period

Richard Stone

BLOOMSBURY ACADEMIC
LONDON • NEW YORK • OXFORD • NEW DELHI • SYDNEY

BLOOMSBURY ACADEMIC
Bloomsbury Publishing Plc, 50 Bedford Square, London, WC1B 3DP, UK
Bloomsbury Publishing Inc, 1359 Broadway, 12th Floor, New York, NY 10018, USA
Bloomsbury Publishing Ireland, 29 Earlsfort Terrace, Dublin 2, D02 AY28, Ireland

BLOOMSBURY, BLOOMSBURY ACADEMIC and the Diana logo are
trademarks of Bloomsbury Publishing Plc

First published in Great Britain 2024
This paperback edition published 2026

Copyright © Richard Stone, 2024

Richard Stone has asserted his right under the Copyright,
Designs and Patents Act, 1988, to be identified as Author of this work.

For legal purposes the Acknowledgments on p. ix constitute an
extension of this copyright page.

Series design by Louise Dugdale
Cover image © Olga Kurbatova/Getty Images

All rights reserved. No part of this publication may be: i) reproduced or transmitted in
any form, electronic or mechanical, including photocopying, recording or by means
of any information storage or retrieval system without prior permission in writing from
the publishers; or ii) used or reproduced in any way for the training, development or
operation of artificial intelligence (AI) technologies, including generative AI technologies.
The rights holders expressly reserve this publication from the text and data mining
exception as per Article 4(3) of the Digital Single Market Directive (EU) 2019/790.

Bloomsbury Publishing Inc does not have any control over, or responsibility for,
any third-party websites referred to or in this book. All internet addresses given
in this book were correct at the time of going to press. The author and publisher
regret any inconvenience caused if addresses have changed or sites have
ceased to exist, but can accept no responsibility for any such changes.

A catalogue record for this book is available from the British Library.

ISBN: HB: 978-1-3503-4679-6
PB: 978-1-3503-4683-3
ePDF: 978-1-3503-4680-2
eBook: 978-1-3503-4681-9

Series: Bloomsbury Studies in World Philosophies

Typeset by Integra Software Services Pvt. Ltd.

For product safety related questions contact productsafety@bloomsbury.com.

To find out more about our authors and books visit www.bloomsbury.com
and sign up for our newsletters.

Contents

Preface	vi
Acknowledgments	ix
List of Abbreviations	x
Timeline of Events	xi
Introduction: Nishida Kitarō and the Beginning of the Modern Japanese Philosophical Canon	1
1 The Middle Path and Pure Experience: A Re-evaluation of the "Beginning" of Modern Japanese Philosophy	19
2 Direct Experience and the Problem of Meaning: Motora Yūjirō, Nishida Kitarō, and Takahashi Satomi	41
3 Individualism and Pure Experience: Interpreting the Early Nishida's Ethics with Reference to the Theory of Self-Realization	69
4 Revisiting the "True" Self in *An Inquiry into the Good*: As Seen from the Perspective of Meiji Organicism	95
Conclusion: Continuities and Discontinuities with the Meiji Era—Nishida Kitarō as a Turning Point	123
Notes	136
References	167
Index	175

Preface

This book is based on my doctoral thesis, "How Original Is Nishida Kitarō's Philosophy in *An Inquiry into the Good*? A Critical Investigation of Japan's 'First' Philosophy." My thesis was submitted to Hokkaido University in March 2021. I remember the process in which I gradually decided to write on this topic quite vividly. In my early years in the master's program at *Hokudai*, I was fascinated with Tanabe Hajime's *Philosophy as Metanoetics* and was slowly familiarizing myself with the entirety of the Kyoto School. Whenever Nishida's name had come up in conversation, particularly with Japanese friends or colleagues who were only vaguely familiar with the history of philosophy in Japan, the response was always the same. *Oh, yes, Nishida, he was the first original philosopher in this country, you know.* I saw multiple academic writings on Nishida somehow—tacitly or otherwise—affirming this description. The more I heard this title, the more I started to wonder how it was possible to know so precisely when and how philosophy started in an entire linguistic community (and why nobody seemed to really question the notion in the first place).

This was the seed of doubt that led me to investigate if there was really nothing before Nishida. The more I investigated the matter, the more convinced I became that his reputation as the starting point of Japanese philosophy was malignant for anyone who wanted to understand either Nishida's philosophy or Japanese intellectual history as a whole. This eventually led me to shift my doctoral studies toward an investigation of Nishida and the Meiji period. My goals were self-centered, considering that the seeds of doubt that grew this investigation came from my own inability to understand that most researchers who write that Nishida was the first philosopher in Japan do so with the implicit disclaimer that, *yes, there were other philosophers before him, but Nishida was the first to create something intellectually robust enough to capture the imaginations of philosophers around the globe for over a century.* Moreover, it should go without saying that there are more than a few scholars who are critical of this reputation and my lack of knowledge on this point is a testament to my early ignorance. Still, considering that there are probably more than a few confused young scholars in a similar situation to me and that there is currently no systematic attempt to account for Nishida's relation to philosophy in the Meiji period available in English at the moment, I do not feel ashamed of my decision to publish my findings. Rather, I feel now more than ever that questioning Nishida's place in the Japanese philosophical canon and seeing what came before him is a necessary task.

Since this project started in earnest back in 2018, I have noticed two important changes gradually taking place. The first change is external. Each passing year, it seems that interest in Japanese philosophy continues to grow. The ongoing success of new academic societies like the International Association of Japanese Philosophy (IAJP) and the European Network for Japanese Philosophy (ENOJP) is a sign of this fact. Amidst this growing international interest in Japanese philosophical thought, the number of thinkers who are critically researched continues to increase, connections between traditions—Japanese or otherwise—become clearer, and gaps in our knowledge of Japanese intellectual history continue to close. Still, even as this process of widening the circle of Japanese philosophical research continues, it remains a fact that Nishida and his Kyoto-school contemporaries are still the most widely researched figures in Japanese philosophy. In this regard, I feel this monograph to be timely, given that it will aim to both expand the circle of Japanese philosophical studies further by investigating several figures who are frequently overlooked, and show their connections to the Japanese philosopher who has garnered the most critical attention from scholars.

The second change is an internal one. I must confess, when this research first started, I was skeptical of the idea that Nishida's title as modern Japan's first philosopher could be justified in any way. When I began this project, I did so with the intention of writing an exposé, showing that Nishida's philosophy was secretly a creatively bankrupt copy of his Meiji predecessors, and that it was only a lack of historical knowledge that kept readers interested in his early work. The more I read *An Inquiry into the Good*, however, the more I started to find key differences in not only content between Nishida and his predecessors, but also how his arguments were laid out. In this regard, even if it may be easy to misunderstand my position, I do not wish to disparage anyone who has described Nishida as the origin of modern Japanese philosophy. To the contrary, at some point I started to agree with this general line of thought. At the same time, however, I remained steadfastly convinced that the influence of his predecessors should not be dismissed in any facile way. Hence, somewhere along the line, my goal shifted sharply from showing how this reputation is not deserved to critically exploring what we mean when we say that Nishida is modern Japan's first philosopher by analyzing the continuity and discontinuity between him and his predecessors.

Regarding the construction of the book itself, quite a bit has changed since my doctoral thesis. Chapters 1, 3, and 4 are all roughly based on my thesis but have been re-written in some way or another. Chapter 3 features more content than it did in my doctoral thesis, owing partially to my continually growing interest in the work of Onishi Hajime. Almost everything in the introductory and concluding chapters as well as the entirety of Chapter 2 is new. Generally, my overall position has remained the same as my doctoral paper. I argue that Nishida's title *can* be meaningful if we look at his philosophy as the final product of a gradual process of methodological refinement and, thus, an impetus for us to find new questions and avenues for philosophical dialogue. I find this to be true in the sense that Nishida's work was the point of departure for many influential philosophical trends in thought in Japan, as well as the fact that his work presents similar insights to his predecessors in a manner rigorous enough to raise questions for all readers, regardless of their intellectual background. While this core thesis remains largely the same, I have tried to avoid straying too far from the task at hand and making broad claims about the nature of originality or the meaning of words like "modernity" or "philosophy" that I cannot responsibly back up in this book. In this sense, the biggest difference between this book and my doctoral thesis is likely my willingness to remain agnostic on important topics that need more attention to be handled in an appropriate way.

I am sure that there will be some who disagree with my claims about Nishida's place in Japanese intellectual history (whether it be because I relativize his originality too much or because I do not thoroughly debunk the "myth" that he was modern Japan's first philosopher). I am also certain that some will not be interested in the question as I frame it. However, I do not think this will pose a problem for anyone, insofar as I believe this book can be profitably read regardless of one's view of the desired scope of Japanese philosophy or any of the secondary questions that arise when thinking about Nishida's connection to the Meiji era. I believe this study will be useful for anyone who wants to know more about Nishida's philosophy, overlooked members in the modern Japanese philosophical canon, or the overall scope of Japanese intellectual history. Nishida's place in the Japanese canon is the starting point of this investigation, but in the end there a multitude of other points that will arise as we continue along. Because I mention these points in much more detail in the introductory chapter, I will not focus on them anymore here, but I do want to stress that this text will (hopefully) have something even for those who do not agree with any of my conclusions or are not interested in questioning the Japanese philosophical canon.

Acknowledgments

Both this general project of finding out what it means to say that Nishida was the first original philosopher in Japan and the list of people who supported me in my efforts to work through this project have become quite long. Hence, I will not be able to thank everyone who helped me along the way, but I will try my best below:

First, I wish to offer my gratitude to *The Journal of East Asian Philosophy* (Springer Nature) and *The European Journal of Japanese Philosophy* for allowing me to reprint material published in these respective journals for this book.

I must also thank my advisory professor at Hokkaido University, Taguchi Shigeru. Professor Taguchi not only refused to give up on teaching me how to be a philosopher during my seven-year-long struggle in graduate school, but also offered crucial insights about both Nishida and philosophy in general that made this thesis possible. While no phenomenologist's name came up in this thesis, I like to think that the phenomenological attitude that I witnessed in Professor Taguchi's work is apparent in my reading of Nishida.

I must also thank Andrea Altobrando (University of Padua), who gave excellent advice and insightful comments. Andrea's constant advice and willingness to read my unfinished drafts were immensely helpful as I attempted to muddle through this process from start to finish.

I also thank Morisato Takeshi (University of Edinburgh) for, among other things, recommending me to publish my work in this series. That push was enough for me to take action and prepare this book for publication with Bloomsbury Academic's Studies in World Philosophies Series. As an extension, I would also like to thank all the series editors and everyone at Bloomsbury for their incredible patience and insight throughout the process.

I am also grateful for the help I received from all my friends from Hokkaido University throughout the years. I offer special thanks to Sawasaki Takahiro (National Institute of Informatics of Japan), Hara Kenichi (Kanazawa Institute of Technology), Kobayashi Kazuya (Hokkaido University), Inohara Jirō (Hokkaido University), and Kobayashi Chie (Yokohama National University) and many others who shared many great philosophical insights and conversations with me throughout the years.

I would like to thank my family. I am especially grateful to my younger brother, Jesse Stone, and my mother, Corrine Stone, for constantly checking in on me.

List of Abbreviations

IG: Nishida Kitarō. *An Inquiry into the Good*, Translated by Masao Abe and Christopher Ives. New Haven, CT: Yale University Press, 1990.

NKZ: Nishida, Kitarō (西田幾多郎). *Nishida Kitarō Zenshū* (西田幾多郎全集), 24 volumes. Tokyo: Iwanami shoten, 2003–9, 24 vols.

IES: Inoue Enryō (井上円了). *Inoue Enryō Senshū* (井上円了選集). Tokyo, Toyo University Press, 1987–2004, 25 vols.

OHS: Onishi Hajime (大西祝). *Onishi Hajime Senshū* (大西祝選集). Tokyo: Iwanami Bunko, 2013, 3 vols.

Timeline of Events

To aid our investigation, I have included a timeline of how Western philosophy was introduced into Japanese society leading up to the publication of Nishida's *Inquiry*. This timeline will be brief and will only aim to organize the events referenced in this book. This will necessarily omit several key moments in the history of Japan's relation to Western learning and philosophy. Additionally, this timeline will not handle theoretical questions of whether there was philosophy in Japan before the influence of the West or what philosophy means. Instead, we will merely provide the context necessary to orient ourselves as we discuss Nishida's relation to his philosophical predecessors:

1612: Tokugawa Ieyasu (徳川家康, 1543–1616) formally bans the worship of Christianity in 1612 and orders the deportation of missionaries in 1614. Ties with European countries are gradually severed over the course of the 1630s. By 1639, the only European nationals permitted to trade with Japan were Dutch traders coming through Dejima in Nagasaki. This is the beginning of the so-called "Sakoku (鎖国)" era, which severely limited Japanese scholars' access to Western philosophical resources. Christianity is referred to as the "wicked learnings (邪宗)" of Westerners and "Fumie (踏絵)," the practice of stomping on Jesus Christ's image to prove that one is not Christian, is commonplace by the mid-seventeenth century.

1825: Aizawa Seishisai (会沢正志斎, 1782–1863) writes his "New Theses (新論)" and shows a change in attitude toward Western culture. Save for a few isolated incidents, Japanese scholars showed only sporadic interest in Western philosophies or religions in the eighteenth century. This attitude changes as news of nineteenth-century European imperialism slowly enters Japan. For example, Aizawa argues that the Japanese need to be wary of the Western barbarians – especially the British and the Russians – insofar as they utilized trade and religion to spread their ways of life and muscle into foreign shores.

1835: Takano Chōei (高野長英, 1804–50) releases his "Theories of the Western Sages," a schematic overview of Western philosophy from the pre-Socratics to Christian Wolff (1679–1754). The basis for the writing seems to be a Dutch text on the history of Western philosophy. Chōei is later arrested in 1838 for criticizing the Shogunate's policies on foreign ships and strict attitudes against Western learning. Chōei escapes prison in 1844 and lives as a fugitive until 1850, wherein he commits suicide.

1839: Concerns about the possibility of Japan being overrun by Western barbarians accelerate after news of the Opium War (1839–42) comes in the late 1830s and early 1840s. While it is agreed by many that Western military technology is necessary to survive, the general distrust of Western morality, religions, and thought we mentioned with Aizawa Seishisai continues to prevail throughout the 1840s and 1850s.

1853: Matthew Perry (1794–1858) finally arrives in 1853. This initial approach from Perry was rebuffed, but his second attempt in 1854 was successful in establishing a trade agreement between the United States and Japan soon after. The major European forces of the day would follow with their own trade treaties.

1854: Sakuma Shōzan (佐久間象山, 1811–64) writes his *Seikenroku* and expounds his thesis that Japan needed "Western Technology and Eastern Morality (西洋芸術、東洋道徳)." This idea that Japan needed to attain Western technology while retaining Eastern spirit would remain a dominant trend among Japanese intellectuals until the 1860s.

1859: In 1859, the Tokugawa Shogunate dispatched its first diplomatic mission to San Francisco, which took Fukuzawa Yukichi (福澤諭吉, 1835–1901) abroad. Fukuzawa subsequently released his famous *Conditions in the West* (西洋事情) over the course of several volumes from 1866 to 1870. These volumes recorded what Fukuzawa had seen abroad and helped guide Japanese readers who had no image of what life was like in the West.

1862: Nishi Amane (西周, 1829–97) and Tsuda Mamichi (津田真道, 1829–1903) are sent out as the first Japanese students to study in Europe. The two study under Professor Simon Vissering (1818–88) at the University of Leiden in Holland from 1863 to 1865. The two learned about Western legal studies, economic theory, and philosophical theory. Tsuda translated Vissering's lectures on law while

Nishi translated his notes on the philosophy courses. The focus of the philosophy lectures seems to have been on positivistic authors like Auguste Comte (1798–1857) and J. S. Mill (1806–73).

1868: Dissatisfaction with how the Shogunate handled interactions with Westerners (among other economic or agrarian concerns we cannot delve into here) leads to the Emperor's "restoration" to power in January 1868, thus marking the end of the Shogunate's rule in Japan. The fledgling Meiji government hit the ground running, making controversial changes like banning swords and doing away with the domain system in the early years of its rule.

1870: Nishida is born in Unoke village at the start of the Meiji period. Around this time, widely read Japanese translations of texts like J. S. Mill's *On Liberty* and Samuel Smiles's (1812–1904) *Self Help* are released from Nakamura Keiu (中村敬宇, 1832–91) in 1871 and 1872, respectively, thereby showing that access to Western philosophical texts is picking up as Nishida is born.

1873: Signposts prohibiting Christianity are taken down in 1873. The founding of Kyoto's Doshisha English School in 1875 by Niijima Jō (新島襄, 1843–90; also known as Joseph Hardy Neesima) and the influence of Western teachers preaching Christian ideals to students (like William Clark's [1826–86] trip to Sapporo Agricultural College in 1876 or Leroy Lansing Janes [1838–1909] convincing many young students at the Kumamoto School for Western Studies to convert to Christianity in 1875) start to foster a Christian community of scholars and philosophers in the Meiji.

1874: The first issue of the Meiji Six Journal (*Meiroku Zasshi*; 明六雑誌) is released in the sixth year of the Meiji period (1874). Fukuzawa Yukichi's *An Outline of a Theory of Civilization* is released in the following year. The connecting point between these works is that they emphasized the need to reform Japanese lifestyles, adopt certain ideas from the West, and pursue a higher level of civilization. By the 1870s, many scholars emphasize that Western modes of living, morality, and philosophy were necessary for Japanese progress.

1877: Tokyo University is founded in 1877 and is subsequently renamed to Tokyo Imperial University in 1886. Ernest Fenollosa (1853–1908), the American philosopher, came in 1878 and lectured on the history of Western philosophy, economic theory, and politics, emphasizing the importance of Hegel and Spencer while doing so. Students receive lectures on "Indian Philosophy" from Hara Tanzan (原坦山, 1819–92), who was at least partially responsible for the widespread Meiji tendency to merge Buddhist thought with Western metaphysics. The first Japanese professor of Western philosophy was Inoue Tetsujirō. Tetsujirō himself learned at Tokyo University before going to Germany to study philosophy and experimental psychology from 1884 until 1890. Upon returning to Japan, he was named professor of philosophy. Also, three of our main focuses in the coming chapters, Inoue Enryō, Onishi Hajime, and Miyake Setsurei, spent time studying at Tokyo University under Fenollosa and/or Inoue Tetsujirō as well.

1881: The first philosophical dictionary is released in 1881. Up to this point, few philosophical terms had set translations. Nishi Amane alone is often credited with coining translations for terms like subject (主体; *shutai*), object (客体; *kyakutai*), logic (論理; *ronri*), concept (概念; *gainen*), consciousness (意識; *ishiki*), philosophy (哲学; *tetsugaku*), and more. While it would take until the twentieth century for most standard translations to settle down, this dictionary helped establish the terminology needed to discuss Western philosophy.

1889: The Meiji emperor promulgates the constitution in 1889. This would be followed up in 1890, wherein the Japanese Ministry of Education released the "Imperial Rescript on Education (教育に関する勅語)," a document that affirmed loyalty and filial piety (忠孝) as the central virtues of the Japanese Empire. Both documents lead to a surge in nationalistic pride and mark an ideological shift in the main currents of Meiji thought. Instead of intellectuals primarily emphasizing the adoption of Western spirit, there is now a tendency to stress the need for a unified sense of Japaneseness in the now budding empire.

1891A: Nishida Kitarō enrolls in Tokyo Imperial University as a special auditing student in 1891. There, he takes classes from Inoue Tetsujirō, Motora Yūjirō, Nakajima Rikizō, and others. Fenollosa, the influential teacher of many early philosophers, is gone. In his place is the new foreign professor of philosophy, Rafael von Koeber (1848–1923), a German professor who emphasized the importance of classical philosophy. Nishida studies a broad array of Western philosophical sources and writes his graduation thesis, "Causality in Hume (ヒュームの因果法; NKZ 11: 23–34)." After graduating, Nishida plans to write a treatise on the work of T. H. Green (1836–82) before ultimately cooling off on his work.

1891B: The Uchimura Disrespect Incident (内村鑑三不敬事件) takes place in 1891 as famous Christian scholar and advocate Uchimura Kanzō (内村鑑三, 1861–1930) refused to bow before the "Imperial Rescript on Education" at the First Higher School in Tokyo. Inoue Tetsujirō leads the charge to accuse Christians like Uchimura of being untrustworthy, given that their loyalties will always lie with their religion (and thus not with the nation) in the end. Christian scholars like Onishi Hajime, Ebina Danjō (海老名弾正, 1856–1937), Yokoi Tokio (横井時雄, 1857–1927), and others defend Uchimura and Christianity. This incident sparks far-reaching debates about the limits of individual freedoms and need for religious tolerance.

1894: Japan engages in war with China in 1894 and ultimately emerges victorious in 1895. Public opinion has shifted thus that many in Japan and abroad view the Japanese Empire as the pinnacle of Asian politics. More importantly for us, though, is that many major Western philosophical works have been translated into Japanese and there is a growing familiarity with Western philosophical terminology. Titles like Inoue Enryō's *An Outline of Philosophy* (1886) and translated textbooks like Francis Bowen's *History of Modern Philosophy: From Descartes to Schopenhauer and Hartmann* (published in English in 1877, translated into Japanese as *Kinsei Tetsugaku* 『近世哲学』 in 1884) also provide descriptions of Western philosophical history in the Japanese language. Many Japanese thinkers begin to posture that the age of "playing catch up" is over and that Japan has managed to establish herself as one of the world's civilized countries.

1904: The Russo-Japanese War begins in 1904. Japan emerges victorious in 1905. In the background of this event, one finds a new emphasis on how Japan has "awakened" as a major world power—as evidenced by texts like Okakura Tenshin's (岡倉天心, 1863–1913) *The Awakening of Japan* in 1904—capable of meeting Western criteria for civilization and providing novel contributions to the world through her uniquely Asian aesthetic and intellectual traditions. Amidst the general chaos, we find those like Nishida, who lost family members in the war or become lost in the rapid modernization project.

1906: Nishida publishes the first articles that will become *An Inquiry into the Good*. He publishes "On Reality" and "Ethics" in 1906. These two papers would respectively go on to become the second and third sections of *Inquiry*. The first and fourth sections of *Inquiry* are written in 1908 and 1909, respectively. The reputation from these articles helped earn Nishida his position at Kyoto University in 1910, where he would stay until his retirement in 1928.

1911: *An Inquiry into the Good* is published and our story starts in earnest.

Introduction

Nishida Kitarō and the Beginning of the Modern Japanese Philosophical Canon

Nishida and the Meiji Period: A Non-trivial Starting Point

Nishida Kitarō (西田幾多郎, 1870–1945), the alleged father of philosophy in modern Japan, was born in the village of Unoke right after the Meiji era (1868–1912) began. The young Kitarō grew up alongside many important transitions in Japanese social, educational, and technological practices following the reopening of Japanese borders to Western powers and the collapse of the last pro-Shogunate forces in 1869. It was only sixteen years before Nishida's birth that Matthew Perry (1794–1858) had finally managed to break Japan's self-imposed period of national isolation and instigate the changes that would lead to the restoration of the emperor to power. This was a dynamic time and a true revolution, with the fledgling Meiji government working to relearn not only how to interact with potentially dangerous Western powers during the colonial era, but also how to create a modern nation state, complete with a constitution, rights, and everything else needed to thrive in the nineteenth century. This was the background in which Nishida's thought was forged.

Now, while this biographical fact may sound like a trivial bit of flavor text to interest readers in the coming pages about Nishida's unique place in world philosophy, the truth is that his life in the Meiji period has often been taken as a key element in explaining his philosophical brilliance. Indeed, the *zeitgeist* of this dynamic time, it has been said, can be felt in almost all aspects of Nishida's life and work. This is evidenced by the fact that some of his earliest photographs in his high school days show scenes of him celebrating the promulgation of the Meiji Constitution with friends or posing with a newly admitted foreign teacher for English classes (despite the fact that, only three decades prior to the picture being taken, there was not even a Japanese-English dictionary, let alone foreign teachers providing instruction on the language).[1] Nishida grew up in an environment where things like trains, universities, a centralized postal service, and—importantly—translations of Western literary and philosophical works were becoming increasingly more common.[2] As an early graduate at Tokyo Imperial University's Philosophy Department as a special auditing student (選科生) in 1894, Nishida embodied these generational changes, showing a mastery of both the Eastern classics he had studied from a young age and the Western philosophy he learned about during his university years. After his graduation, he spent time teaching at various high schools and engaging with Zen Buddhist meditation. During the early years of the 1900s, he experienced loss (as did many others after the Russo-Japanese War ended in 1905).[3] The accompanying existential questions of living in this tumultuous era continuously brought him back to Western philosophy, Buddhist Meditation, or, to some extent, even Christianity as a means of pursuing a truly life-changing "soul-experience."[4] That is, Nishida used these various footholds to aid in his quest of thoroughly rethinking the nature of true reality. The culmination of Nishida's unique philosophical acumen, existential concerns, and exposure to Western and Eastern thought was his novel rethinking of philosophy's great problems outgoing from "pure experience (純粋経験)," i.e., experience that stands prior to even distinctions between the individual subject and its object of cognition, the world it lives in, or even other minds. This was the worldview he put forth in what has widely been regarded as modern Japan's first work of original philosophy, *An Inquiry into the Good* (1911).

Some readers may remain unconvinced that this information is relevant or interesting. After all, nothing stated above sounds new in any substantial sense (even if not everyone would agree with this simplified narrative). The idea that Nishida was a sort of genius who popped up amidst the turbulent Meiji times to offer the first original and, importantly, authentically Japanese work of philosophy as specifically *Tetsugaku* (哲学) has long been accepted as true to some degree by many for good reason and is likely a familiar enough story to anyone who has heard his name before.[5] This very word to denote philosophy done in the Western style as *Tetsugaku* was first coined by Nishi Amane (西周, 1829–97) slightly before the Meiji period started, so it makes sense that philosophy in Japan took off in earnest several decades later.[6] Moreover, while there were researchers before Nishida who introduced Western philosophical concepts to the Japanese public, it has been frequently stated that much of their work was either "translational" or "syncretic." That is, it has often been asserted that many pre-Nishidian Meiji era philosophers limited themselves to either translating Western thinkers for Japanese readers or showing how they could be reconciled with traditional Eastern ideas instead of expressing their own thoughts. In all likelihood, it was this perceived lack of originality or theoretical rigor that prompted the famous writer Nakae Chōmin (中江兆民, 1847–1901) to lament at the beginning of the twentieth century that "from antiquity to the present day, there has never been any philosophy [i.e., *Tetsugaku*] in Japan" (Cited in Blocker and Starling 2001: 1).[7] However, as readers of *An Inquiry into the Good* (henceforth shortened to *Inquiry*) will certainly know, the sort of complaints made by those like Chōmin cannot so easily be applied to Nishida's philosophy of pure experience, which remains a testament to the heights a philosopher working out from both the newest Western philosophical sources and traditional Eastern thought can reach.

As far as I can tell, this story remains the "standard" view of Nishida's place within the modern Japanese philosophical canon to this day. Though there are some scholars who are skeptical of this narrative, it remains common for Nishida to be presented to new audiences in this way.[8] There may be good reason for this—there is at least a kernel of truth in everything written above. Yet, I cannot shake the feeling that treating Nishida as the embodiment of Meiji ingenuity or the "starting point" of modern Japanese philosophy misses something. This could be true in many senses. First, I have glanced over the controversial distinction between "philosophy" and "traditional Eastern thought" that so many scholars have critiqued in recent years. I have also taken it for granted that Japan was only exposed to Western intellectual resources after Perry's arrival, a claim which is also not as obvious as one may think.[9] But perhaps the biggest issue of all would be the rather surprising fact that portraying Nishida as the quintessential Meiji man, appearing out of his unique struggle with classical Western and Eastern resources to present something new, ends up rather *obscuring* our vision of just how deeply ingrained in the Meiji era he actually was. Put briefly, the narrative I have laid forth of Nishida's place in Japanese philosophical history paradoxically prevents us from seeing just how deep the connection between Nishida's philosophy of pure experience and the philosophical world of the Meiji period goes.

Although Nishida has often been described as Japan's first "original" philosopher—going back to long before his work was ever appreciated outside of Japan[10]—it has been an open secret of sorts among his researchers that the influence he received from his predecessors goes deeper than the above offered story shows. Nishida took classes at Tokyo Imperial University from prominent philosophical writers like Inoue Tetsujirō (井上哲次郎, 1856–1944) or Motora Yūjirō (元良勇次郎, 1858–1912) and their influence can be felt in Nishida's views on meaning and selfhood in pure experience. Nishida professed his profound respect for authors he did not directly study under, like Onishi Hajime (大西祝, 1864–1900), Tsunashima Ryōsen (綱島梁川, 1873–1907), or Kiyozawa Manshi (清沢満之, 1863–1903). This respect, moreover, seems to have left a mark on his early ethical and religious thought, most specifically on his writings about the nature of self-realization and religious ecstasy. And, as we shall discuss in more detail soon, the reason that he chose to study philosophy in the first place seems to partially be due to his early reading of Inoue Enryō's (井上円了, 1858–1919) *An Evening of Philosophical Conversation*—and his appreciation of the non-dual ontology presented therein. Thus, as many experts of his philosophy are already aware, Nishida not only learned from these figures, but he seems to have also accepted many of their philosophical concerns, premises, and strategies. Or, rather, it is likely safer to say that there is virtually no element of *Inquiry* that does not relate to debates going on around Nishida as he grew up alongside philosophy as a concept in the Meiji period.

At this point, there arises a rather simple question: how can Nishida at once be the *beginning* of philosophy in modern Japan while also being thoroughly influenced by *previous* philosophers in the Meiji era? It would be one thing to take him as the father of philosophy in Japan if he was literally responsible for the first and only attempt to state his own ideas in the format of Western philosophy. But things seem to get murkier when we simultaneously admit that philosophers who came before him (those who we have typically assumed to be merely "syncretizing" East and West or "translating" certain ideas from Western authors) not only presented similar ideas themselves, but likely had absolutely no intention of merely repeating other thinkers' words. So, again, what do we mean when we take Nishida as the "starting point"? While this question brings with it difficult issues relating to the nature of what Japanese philosophy is as a discipline, our task is simple. That is, to better understand the formative process of Nishida's philosophy—as well as what precisely we mean when we discuss Nishida's alleged originality or place in Japanese intellectual history— we must have a solid understanding of his relation to his predecessors in the Meiji era. What continuities do we find between Nishida and his predecessors like Onishi Hajime or Inoue Enryō? How did the philosophical concerns of such Meiji-era writers color Nishida's work? And what—if anything—sets him apart from his contemporaries in the Meiji period? In this investigation, we will face these questions by digging into the relation between Nishida Kitarō's earliest philosophy in *Inquiry* and his Meiji era predecessors and thus come away with a better understanding of both Nishida's philosophy and the formative process of philosophy itself in modern Japan.

Delimiting the Aim and Scope of This Investigation

Before we answer any of the questions presented above, we must take a step back and clarify the precise scope and aims of the investigation at hand. Even after only the brief introduction to Nishida's place in the Japanese philosophical canon, there are already plenty of potential objections in front of us. Why have we been so willing to implicitly accept the distinction between "modern Japanese philosophy" and "pre-modern Japanese thought"? Alternatively, why are we so interested in specifically *Japanese* philosophy in the first place? Should we not look at Nishida in a larger world narrative? Or, perhaps, is there no possibility of falling into mere orientalism by fetishizing the notion of the first "unique Japanese" philosophical system? Why are we so interested in Nishida's relation to the Meiji period in the first place? In order to indirectly answer these kinds of questions—as well as to help orient ourselves—I would like to more rigorously spell out the problem at hand.

Let us begin highlighting the scope of this investigation. As I mentioned before, this work will focus on Nishida's relation to other key philosophers in the Meiji period. Naturally, this leaves plenty of questions about Nishida's work and the influences it received from both philosophical resources from outside of Japan and traditional Japanese Buddhist/Confucian insights. After all, it is undeniable that studies of Nishida's connections with thinkers like William James (1842–1910), Immanuel Kant (1724–1804), G. W. F. Hegel (1770–1831), Dōgen (道元, 1200–1253), Kūkai (空海, 774–835), or Confucius (孔子, 551–479 BCE) can play, and in reality have played, a key role in helping us understand his thought. However, due to both the limitations of what can be responsibly handled in one academic investigation and the need to fill in what I believe to be a relative blind spot in contemporary Nishida studies, I will not be able to touch upon these other influences in detail. To make any kind of academic progress and question how we view the development of Nishida's philosophy and its role in Japanese intellectual history, I will forego any intensive studies on this topic and leave his relations to non-Japanese or "pre-modern" Japanese Buddhist and Confucian thinkers in brackets for the moment. In this investigation, we shall only attempt to critically assess the common narrative that Nishida's *Inquiry* was the first original philosophical work in modern Japan by addressing his oft-overlooked relation to his Meiji era predecessors.

One may be tempted to insist that our goal implies an assumption that all of Japan's pre-Perry intellectual traditions are not philosophy and that this could lead us to accept the undesirable premise that philosophy is a purely "Western" pursuit. In response to this doubt, I can only say that—although I recognize the severity of the issue—I will have to stay decidedly agnostic on the topic of whether philosophy existed in Japan before the coining of the word *Tetsugaku*. Entailed within this agnosticism is an admission that there almost certainly *was* philosophy in some non-trivial sense of the word, but that I do not have the time nor space to make any concrete attempt at demarcation here. Considering the plurivocal nature of the idea of Japanese philosophy (or, really, the notion of philosophy in general), coming to any kind of conclusion about whether Dōgen is a philosopher or "just" a thinker whose ideas have a massive philosophical value is a question that I cannot responsibly engage with in this current work.[11] Addressing the political concerns that come with this question is equally impossible right now.[12] However, we do not need to tackle these questions for our current project to make sense. Our only goal for the moment is to investigate how philosophy grew and developed in early modern Japan, as delineated by the coining of the word *Tetsugaku* and growing interest in American and European philosophical resources. In other words, we are interested in what it means to say that Nishida is the first original philosopher in modern Japan, tentatively understood as beginning alongside the Meiji era. Hence, the only assumption that I must ask the reader to hold at this point is that there is a non-arbitrary reason to look at the beginning of the Meiji period as a milestone or turning point during a transitional period in Japanese thought.

For some readers, this may be a bigger ask than I am letting on here. Consider that even during the end of the so-called *Sakoku* period (roughly 1612–1854)[13] interest in and concern about Western nations was already present. Mito School authors like Aizawa Seishisai (会沢正志斎, 1782–1863) warned against Westerners using trade and Christian worldviews to brainwash the Japanese masses by as early as the 1820s.[14] Such concerns increased after news about the Opium War (1839–42) reached Japan. Debates about how to balance the evident need for Western technology (especially military equipment) with traditional Eastern concepts of morality were a lasting theme from the 1840s through the 1860s.[15] Both expeditions to the United States and the dispatch of students like Nishi Amane and Tsuda Mamichi (津田真道, 1829–1903) to learn Western legal and philosophical theory in Holland had taken place before the restoration occurred in 1868 as well.[16] However, even while recognizing the truth of this information (and that there is thus no absolute line between Meiji history and what took place beforehand), I still believe the Meiji period is a *non-arbitrary turning point* in Japanese history. The change in government, the abolition of the class system (and subsequent opening of educational opportunities to more of the Meiji youth), the rapid increase in translations for Western resources, and the opening of universities and colleges all attest to the intellectual dynamism that exploded in the Meiji era. Even if the roots of all of these changes may have taken hold well before 1868, my point is this: any historical investigation has to start *somewhere* and the beginning of the Meiji period signals an important shift in Japanese cultural and political concerns. In this sense, while it is not an absolute borderline, I think that the Meiji period is a non-trivial "cut" in Japanese history (in addition to being the environment that the 1870-born Nishida grew up in).

Now, as one final point of clarification, this investigation will primarily concern Nishida's earliest philosophy of pure experience as it is outlined in *Inquiry*. In the main text we will not discuss Nishida's other core philosophical positions (i.e., his logic of place, action-intuition, absolute contradictory self-identity, etc.) in detail. This may seem like a questionable choice, given that Nishida himself recognizes that even later discussions of historical reality are an attempt to make good on what is called pure experience in his early philosophy.[17] So, why leave aside concepts in his later philosophy? There are several reasons, but the following two stand out as important:

A) **Proximity:** While it may seem obvious, Nishida's intellectual debt to the Meiji era can be felt most strongly in his earliest philosophy. This should make sense, given that *An Inquiry into the Good* was written and published before the Meiji period had even ended.[18] The connections in terminology, philosophers cited, and intellectual concerns with his predecessors can likely be felt much more clearly at this stage of his career. Indeed, even if the core of Nishida's goal stayed the same over the years, identifying the connections between this core and his Japanese predecessors becomes substantially more difficult after Nishida becomes more interested with the trends that defined the early to mid-twentieth century (e.g., Neo-Kantianism, Phenomenology, etc.).[19]

B) **Precision:** Following from this prior point, we can further understand that Nishida's philosophical enterprise may have been working toward one goal from start to finish, but this does not make his philosophy a monolith. The tools that he relied on to express this philosophical vision, the ethical consequences and offshoots of his thought, and the logical corroboration for his arguments all evolved over the course of his career. Nishida's own characterization of himself as a miner, constantly sifting for ore and letting anything unnecessary flow down the metaphorical river, is apt for precisely this reason.[20] Hence, for the sake of maximizing precision, we will not treat Nishida's entire career as interchangeable and shall instead opt to focus specifically on pure experience in the main text.

Naturally, some readers may not be convinced. Depending on how one understands the development of Nishida's career, it may be possible to say that even his earliest work can only be understood fully by referencing his last work. I will hold off on any further debate on this topic for now and merely mention that how influence from the Meiji era can be felt in his more mature philosophy will be a core theme of the concluding chapter.

There are still many potential objections about how the investigation will proceed that remain untouched. However, addressing every potential critique is not possible or useful. What is more important is that we have limited ourselves to a specific domain of Japanese intellectual history and more clearly established the scope of our work. That is to say, we are specifically trying to understand what it means to say that Nishida Kitarō's *An Inquiry into the Good* is the starting point of modern Japanese philosophy. This does not entail a denial of the existence of pre-modern philosophy, any assumptions about how his philosophy developed, nor do I ask the reader to make any presuppositions about whether this title of Nishida's is valuable in any practical sense. We will only concern ourselves with how Nishida's philosophy developed within the context of the Meiji era and what it means to say he is the "starting point" of modern Japanese philosophy as opposed to those who came before him, including Onishi Hajime, Inoue Enryō, Inoue Tetsujirō, or other such thinkers. Anything outside of the Meiji will thus be left in brackets for another occasion.

Why Worry about a Canon? Historical and Philosophical Motivations

Now, before more concretely discussing how we will try to understand Nishida's place in the Meiji era and who we will compare him with, there is one last poignant critique that deserves contemplation. Namely, we have yet to establish *why* we should care about Nishida's connection to the Meiji era. Yes, perhaps it is a bit odd that Nishida has historically been accepted as the starting point of modern Japanese philosophy despite the evidence that there was a historical process leading up to his work, but also this view does not seem to be damaging to Nishidian scholarship. For decades now, this idea that Nishida is a good beginning for those looking to learn about philosophy in modern Japan has likely helped many new scholars orient their studies (not to mention the fact that most researchers who describe Nishida as the starting point of Japanese philosophy only do so with the implicit recognition that "original" is a relative term). Keeping this in mind, I believe there are three main motives for continuing with an investigation of Nishida's relation to the Meiji era:

Historical Concerns: Keeping in mind what we have said up to this point, we can see how this investigation can be of interest to intellectual historians discussing how philosophy developed in Japan. While a complete investigation of how the notion of *Tetsugaku* was understood among Meiji authors or what this could mean when thinking about how to understand the impact that Western philosophy had on intellectual discourse in Japan in the nineteenth century elude us, getting a better grasp on how Nishida's work developed and what marks him as different when compared to his Meiji predecessors is an invaluable step toward thinking about such problems.

Though considerations of how philosophy developed in Japan may not sound particularly important within the bigger picture of Meiji history, I must confess that I find questions of how *Tetsugaku* was conceived as similar or different, commensurate or incommensurate with traditional Japanese thought to be a riveting topic. Was philosophy a thoroughly Western discipline that the Japanese were as-of-yet too uncivilized to master?[21] Was it a universal enterprise that was shared between the sages of the East and the West?[22] Or was *Tetsugaku*—literally the study of wisdom—something that could only be achieved by the classical Confucian sages of yore?[23] All of these answers were present throughout the Meiji period and all of these answers brought with them significant political baggage and questions about how to understand Japanese identity and uniqueness (in contrast with both new Western resources and classical Chinese and Indian inspirations). Exploring said answers thoroughly goes beyond the scope of our investigation, but understanding the formative process leading up to Nishida's work and what—if anything—set him apart from the philosophers (*Tetsugakusha*) before him is a good step in unpacking these issues.

Philosophical Concerns: In addition, these kinds of historical issues can help offer us several important case studies for understanding the notion of philosophy itself—as well as what makes it "valuable" or "original." Rarely do we have a chance to analyze the "first original philosopher" in a given linguistic community with such a treasure trove of saved letters, writings, or lecture notes. I would daresay that the fact that Nishida's reputation has survived for decades is proof that there is some kind of intuitive appeal to the claim that he was somehow more philosophically "original" than writers like Inoue Enryō or Onishi Hajime. If, in comparing these predecessors with Nishida, we can get a more clear understanding of what that "spark" of originality is (or otherwise what makes his work more philosophically "rigorous"), then it stands to reason that we can gain valuable insights about what it is we philosophers are doing, what makes philosophy out as philosophy, and how we can properly integrate alternative voices and resources into our own philosophical contemplations to reach greater heights.

Nishidian Concerns: Perhaps, though, the simplest reason to pursue this investigation is purely because of how much we can learn about Nishida's career by investigating how deep the connection between his thought and his Meiji era predecessors goes. As we shall see clearly over the course of this book, if one takes Nishida's alleged originality to mean that his work appeared from nowhere but his ingenious understanding of Western philosophy and unique Eastern perspective, then one will have completely disregarded a core element of what makes Nishida who he is as a thinker. Now, one may say that this is not what we mean when we say that Nishida is modern Japan's first philosopher. But then we are left to ask what this originality amounts to in the first place. Decades of research undertaken by philosophers across the globe show that *something* in Nishida is worthy of our attention, but why do we pay attention to *Inquiry* if similar ideas were developed decades before Nishida even started writing the manuscript? By asking these questions, I am not attempting to imply that Nishida is not as original as we think. Instead, I am driving home the very limited point that we can likely understand much more about what makes Nishida's philosophy tick by investigating it critically alongside his predecessors.

Crucially, I believe there will be plenty to gain from this investigation even for readers who are only interested in learning more about Nishida as a philosopher. There are plenty of hints for understanding Nishida's work that can be found by looking at his thought within its historical context. Ideas that have been typically attributed to Nishida may have had their start much earlier than we assume and, by comparing Nishida with such preceding thinkers, we can better establish the nuances that make his work more exciting and fruitful than those who had similar ideas (assuming these nuances exist). Thus, given that this book will be the first systematic attempt to work out Nishida's relation to the Meiji era in the English language, there should be plenty for those who simply wish to engage with Nishida's philosophy to grapple with. [24]

Keeping the above three motives in mind, I believe a thorough exploration of the relation between Nishida and his predecessors in the Meiji can impact—or at least offer an interesting case study for—various avenues of philosophical and historical research and, as such, can be of interest to a diverse set of scholars.

Plan and Overview

With our premise, aims, and motivations established, we are finally ready to dig in and explore Nishida's connection to the philosophical world of the Meiji era. At this point, though, one may start to realize that—although I have insisted that we limit the scope of our investigation to the greatest extent possible—the scale of this project is still too huge to be taken seriously. The Meiji period lasted for almost fifty years and no sane person would even dream of documenting every aspect of philosophy in this era in one monograph, let alone how it developed with Nishida's complex work in mind. As this is the case, we must come up with a more concrete method for achieving our goal. The best answer that I have come up with is to highlight the core elements of Nishida's philosophy and show how they relate to one key intellectual movement or another in Meiji philosophy.

To be specific, I believe that the most expedient way of assessing Nishida's connection to his predecessors in the Meiji era is to analyze key philosophical works in the Meiji period as they relate to each section of *Inquiry*. As readers of Nishida know, the book is divided into four sections. The first section establishes the psychology and epistemology of pure experience, the second section highlights the ontological implications of pure experience as the one true reality, the third section introduces the ethical implications of this worldview, and the fourth section is Nishida's first major contribution to the philosophy of religion. In accordance with these divisions, I will split this book into four main chapters, each showing a glimpse of how each topic relates Nishida with one of his relevant predecessors. Although the precise question I will approach for each of these sections will be different, the general method will remain the same. In each case, I will first demonstrate the historical context of the early Nishida's work before seeing how (or, in some cases, if) Nishida differs from his contemporaries' efforts to express similar ideas. A brief outline of each of these four chapters can be found below.

In Chapter 1, we will start by analyzing the cornerstone of Nishida's early philosophy (and, possibly, his entire philosophical career): his theory of pure experience as the one true reality. A look at the history of this theory will reveal the basic paradox that lies at the heart of Nishida's relationship to Meiji philosophy, as well as introduce some core themes of this investigation. We will explore the basic issue in which Nishida's philosophy of pure experience is treated as both an unparalleled and unprompted start to original philosophy in Japan and the final incarnation of a staple in Meiji period's theory of "phenomena-*soku*-reality." As the name implies, this theory looked to provide a view of reality in which conscious phenomena are immediately one with (*soku*; 即)[25] reality itself. To see how this theory—which has also been associated with such authors as Inoue Tetsujirō, Kiyozawa Manshi, and Miyake Setsurei—relates to Nishida's philosophy of pure experience, we will conduct a minimal genealogical investigation focusing on the relation between Nishida and a key predecessor of his, Inoue Enryō. By means of evaluating the similarities and differences between how these thinkers interpreted reality, two things will become clear. First, we will be able to clearly see that there are substantial overlapping claims in both of their theories. This will allow us to reasonably state that Nishida's philosophical originality ought not be pursued in the philosophical intuitions he portrays as much. However, we will also see a critical difference between the ways that these two authors approach philosophy, and what they expect of philosophical argumentation. This will open the way for us to see one basic claim I wish to make: Nishida's philosophical originality is not necessarily to be found in only the ideas he espouses. Rather, we must look carefully at his methodology and his attitude toward philosophical argumentation.

In Chapter 2, we will flesh out one key point that arises in Chapter 1 and will be helpful for understanding Chapters 3 and 4: Nishida's ontology of meaning in *Inquiry*. In Chapter 1, it will become clear that one key element of Nishida's early work is his attempt to explain how meaning is able to form in pure experience. This makes sense not only in terms of Nishida's desire to explain the true nature of reality in concrete terms, but also to show that pure experience is inherently laden with some kind of values or meanings. At the same time, however, this will likely appear strange to us, given that pure experience is often equated with the dimension of experience that precedes any kind of reflective consciousness or cognitive subject to confer meaning onto experience. Here, we must ask: how can experience be meaningful without a subject to provide meaning? To better understand this key element of Nishida's work, we shall look at Nishida's ontology of meaning in comparison to his old teacher and early Japanese psychologist, Motora Yūjirō. As we shall see, while both thinkers were influenced by prominent psychologists like Wilhelm Wundt and William James in their respective quests to show how individual experiences can formulate meaning without presupposing a transcendent subject, we will also come across a sharp difference between the two. That is, while Motora endorses a psychologistic account of meaning, Nishida instead attempts to make an ontological leap by taking pure experience itself to be the concrete universal that renders meaning possible. We will then attempt to critically inspect Nishida's project by revisiting one of the earliest and most important critiques of *Inquiry* at the hands of Takahashi Satomi (高橋里美, 1886–1964), thereby putting ourselves in a position to better grasp the strengths and weaknesses of his work.

In Chapter 3, we will explore the historical background of Nishida's ethics. As authors going back to the aforementioned Takahashi have claimed, Nishida's ethics appear to be the comparatively "least" original or valuable aspect of his early philosophy (see Takahashi 1912/2001: 298). In order to evaluate if this commonsense understanding is accurate, we will take another look at Nishida's ethical theory as it is situated within the critical discourse concerning individualism in the Meiji period. In other words, to clarify the meaning of Nishida's contribution to modern Japanese ethical discourse, we must accomplish the following two goals. First, we will establish the framework in which Nishida's ethics formed. That is, we must make clear what problems he faced and what matters were of considerable import to thinkers in his generation. Only after we have done so can we move on to our second goal: establishing what—if anything—Nishida contributed to ethical discussions in the Meiji period. Here, I will make the following two claims. The first will be that Nishida's ethical thought ought to be understood within the progression of thinkers starting from early efforts to assert the need for "independent" and "self-sufficient" individuals such as Fukuzawa Yukichi (福澤諭吉, 1835–1901), which later progressed to what was referred to as the theory of self-realization. The second will be that, although there are significant flaws with Nishida's ethics, the consistency of his ethics with his ontological views provides a theoretical grounding for many Meiji iterations of similar ideas that had yet to receive complete and rigorous foundations.

In Chapter 4, we will approach the religious aspect of Nishida's thought as it relates to Meiji philosophy. To do so, we will focus on the concept that is perhaps the most appealing notion in his earliest work: the True Self (真の自己). In *Inquiry*, Nishida often discusses our individual selves as though they were merely parts of a greater, "true" self. Despite the intuitive appeal such a reading may carry, I question whether it can be justified within the framework of his philosophical project (or if it is even an accurate depiction of what he is trying to express). Keeping this in mind, we will attempt to understand how Nishida uses this term, and what possible influence the historical background of his work could have had on this possibly misunderstood term. To accomplish this task, we will move in the following order. First, we will contextualize the spread of the phrase personality in the context of what Inoue Katsuhito (2016) has referred to as Organic Philosophy. Put better, we will see that frameworks employing a "small self" and "great self" were often treated as a bridge between the individual's consciousness and a larger consciousness (i.e., the nation, humanity). As our representative of this organic tradition, we will take up the work of Miyake Setsurei in *The Cosmos* (1909). For Miyake, the universe was not just *comparable* to an organism—it *was* an organism. Our individual selves, as part of this organism, needed to find harmony with this larger consciousness. Although in many respects this appears commensurate with how Nishida describes the relation between individual and universe or self and God, I believe that reading him along these lines raises unanswerable questions and fails to get at the heart of what Nishida was hoping to achieve. In this chapter, we will attempt to provide a non-organic reading of Nishida's theory of self that cannot be spoken of in terms of the relation between small self and big self and—in the process—rethink his related conceptions of religion and God. While doing so, we will consider how to understand the relationship between Nishida and his organic predecessors like Miyake.

Methods and Themes

To perform an academically permissible level of analysis in each of these four chapters, it is paramount that we find some footholds to help us along the way. The Meiji era was a long stretch of time and was the stage for many intellectual developments. Identifying all lines of thought that influenced Nishida, highlighting how they fit in with the bigger picture of Japanese intellectual history, and exhaustively discussing what lessons can be learned from their study are clearly impossible for us to achieve in one investigation. As such, we will pursue our goal here under the following methodological principles and themes:

1. While the main goal of each chapter will be comparison, we will typically try to avoid only looking at textual differences between Nishida and his predecessors. In other words, we will not conduct philosophical comparisons between authors independently of their historical context. To the contrary, to make any such comparison conceivable, I believe it is

generally useful start by articulating the framework that led up to the state of philosophy as it was in 1911. As such, we will generally try to clarify the intellectual concerns in the background of Nishida and his predecessors. This effort to highlight the framework of Meiji debates and the context they were held in will be our primary method of avoiding making arbitrary comparisons between Nishida and the large number of possible candidates that his philosophy could be grouped together with.

2. It must be stressed that we will not cover all possible lines of comparison in this project. Meiji philosophers like Nishi Amane, Nakae Chōmin, or Kiyozawa Manshi (just to name a few examples) all deserve more space than they receive here. Indeed, one could convincingly draw lines between—just as an example—Kiyozawa's discussions of a philosophy of Other-power to Nishida's religious philosophy in the fourth part of *Inquiry*. Additionally, although his presence will be felt to some extent in every chapter, we will not make a dedicated comparison between Nishida and Inoue Tetsujirō. As I have stated previously, we will focus only on the direct themes of each overarching section of Nishida's *Inquiry* as they relate to a small number of the philosophers I feel most closely relate to the topic at hand. This is done for the sake of not only avoiding redundancy when discussing popular trends in Meiji philosophy (e.g., not having a separate chapter for Nishida's ontology with respect to both Inoue Enryō and Inoue Tetsujirō), but also providing greater clarity and more detailed textual analysis of Nishida's predecessors (hence allowing us to get more familiar with one of them than we would be if we rushed to deal with several in a single chapter). While it is unfortunate that many great philosophers worthy of further investigation will not get the attention they deserve, it is necessary that we save analyses of their work for a later occasion. This will allow us to do justice to the writers handled here and save these unmentioned writers from having their work oversimplified.

3. When making these comparisons, it will be important to not only see *if* there are differences between Meiji philosophers and Nishida, but also to see what the nature of such differences amounts to. For instance, are there sufficient differences in content that make it impossible to even treat Nishida's work in the same light as other Meiji philosophers? Are the differences just a matter of Nishida discussing more topics than his predecessors, rather than a more "substantial" or "essential" difference in the world view both are trying to defend? In short, what is it that we mean when we say that Nishida is different?

As a running theme in this work, I will provide the following proposal: The most profound sense of originality that can be found in *Inquiry* must be understood in terms of Nishida's *methodological* rigor in comparison to any other philosopher in the Meiji era. Put differently, while many nineteenth- and early-twentieth-century Japanese thinkers attempted to state similar claims to Nishida, I believe that none of them were as systematically thorough as what we find in *Inquiry*. Indeed, Nishida's capacity to establish a fundamentally sound and thorough basis for his thought allows him to substantiate his ideas more thoroughly and ask more questions than his predecessors. To my mind, this act of thoroughly substantiating his thought and providing standards expound upon and develop the theory of pure experience is, in and of itself, a stride forward in modern Japanese philosophy. In this sense, while I disagree with any characterization of Nishida that portrays him as a genius who came out of thin air, I believe that looking at Nishida's work within the context of a process of methodological refinement can help us find something in his work that is substantially different from his predecessors (and, as we discuss in the concluding section, at least partially responsible for many key trends in modern Japanese thought).

Additionally, one other running theme we will see is the importance of "the problem of life (人生の問題)" as it relates to the construction of Nishida's philosophical system. Although Nishida's interest in the existential capacities of philosophy is hardly a new finding, I believe that there are two aspects of this concern with the problem of life that have not been sufficiently documented. The first is possibly the more obvious: Nishida was hardly the only young man educated in the mid-Meiji period interested in the problem of life. Certainly, some early Meiji writers were more dismissive of existential worries, but this was not the case when Nishida began his career (a point we will discuss as our thoughts develop). To the contrary, it is possible that Nishida was instead the poster child for a new generation of writers disconnected from the academic benefits of philosophy or literature and more interested in looking at how it could be related to his own life.

The second, and likely more important, point is that this concern is not separate from Nishida's methodology. It may be easy to think of the relation between philosophical attitudes and methodological rigor as an arbitrary affair—or, perhaps, one may even assume that "academic" philosophy is more likely to perform stringent and thorough investigations in comparison with those doing philosophy for personal or existential reasons. To reiterate a key point that will arise throughout the book, though, I believe that Nishida's philosophical attitude called for a level of rigor that went beyond contemporary academic standards and pushed him to develop his philosophy in tandem with the more formal methodological principles he adopted. Indeed, I think that looking at Nishida within the context of Meiji philosophy will help drive home just how crucial his demand for thoroughgoing answers that do not stop in either the realm of academism or political interests was to his overall philosophical enterprise.

Now that we have covered the basic methodological and hermeneutical points necessary to proceed, we will begin our investigation of Nishida's relationship with Meiji philosophy while keeping these principles in mind. In doing so, we will hopefully grasp a novel picture not only of how we can understand Nishida's philosophical ventures, but also how to look at the development of philosophy in Japan in and of itself.

1

The Middle Path and Pure Experience

A Re-evaluation of the "Beginning" of Modern Japanese Philosophy

Introduction

To recap our claims in the introduction, many common-sense understandings of Japanese philosophy accept Nishida Kitarō's theory of pure experience as the beginning of original philosophical thought in modern Japan. As the story goes, in comparison with the largely translational or interpretive work being done by philosophers in Meiji Japan (1868–1912) before him, Nishida's theory of pure experience in *An Inquiry into the Good* (1911) was a demonstration of his own independent thought. While Nishida's pure experience may have been influenced by William James's concept of the same name, the result of the ideas in *Inquiry* can only be taken as his own unique contribution to philosophy in Japan. More specifically, it is said that Nishida's attempt to return to a level of pure or direct experience that stands prior to the subject–object distinction, and has thus yet to be tainted by the fabrications of our thought, gave him a novel view of reality. According to the early Nishida, insofar as philosophy must be conducted only outgoing from what can be justified by appealing to such pure experience, our presumed conceptions of an independent objective reality or a pre-individuated subject can never be taken as anything more than dogmatic fabrications made to ease our minds. (IG: 38) True reality could thus never be merely subjective or objective, nor could it be described in terms of "extreme" positions such as idealism, materialism, or any form of dualism. Instead, as Nishida finds, such apparent dualities between internal and external,

---

This chapter is a revised version of the following paper: Stone, Richard (2021) "The Middle Path and Pure Experience: A Re-Evaluation of the 'Beginning' of Modern Japanese Philosophy," *The Journal of East Asian Philosophy*, vol. 1: pp. 15–29.

mind and matter, or self and other can arise only within the underlying unity of pure experience. No particular perspective or outlook on pure experience could ever be "more real" than another. To borrow Nishida's example, the poet's "subjective" view of the night sky is every bit as real as the astronomer's "objective" scientific analysis (IG: 49). Hence, rather than attempting to do away with such oppositions by proclaiming one more fundamental than the other, Nishida instead embraced them as a necessary aspect of an overarching unity (IG: 56). It is thus impossible to look at reality in terms of the usual—ism's and oppositions that we usually rely upon, given that they are all only representations of the interpenetrating aspects of reality that actually exist as a more comprehensive unity. As one hundred years of scholarship on his work can report, it was this view of reality that sparked the momentous occasion of Japanese thinkers finally overcoming the mere importation and translation of philosophical thought, allowing them to breakthrough and provide their own original contributions to world philosophy.

However, an almost immediate threat to this narrative arises when we consider another apparently uncontroversial claim: Nishida's theory of pure experience can, and likely should, be situated within the critical continuity of what has come to be referred to as the concept of "phenomena-*soku*-reality (現象即実在論)." This theory, which has been chiefly associated with Buddhist philosophers like Inoue Enryō and Inoue Tetsujirō (and tangentially with those such as Miyake Setsurei and Kiyozawa Manshi), appears to share the core components of Nishida's view of reality as a non-dual and interpenetrating unity between mind and matter or subject and object in which neither of the two could ever be "more real" than the other. Moreover, it is clear that Nishida was influenced by (or at least familiar with) the teachings of all major proponents of this theory. Thus, in this first chapter, I would like to look at the author I find to be both most influential on Nishida—and most likely to challenge the notion that he is the undisputed first philosopher in modern Japan—Inoue Enryō (井上円了, 1858–1919). In doing so, I will take Inoue as a potential forerunner to Nishida's work and see how he set the stage for the philosophy of pure experience.[1]

Founder of the first philosophical journal in Japan, member of the *Seikyōsha* publishing group, expert debunker of superstitions and ghost stories, noted Buddhist reformer, and critic of Christianity, Inoue Enryō played a central role in many Japanese intellectual circles in the nineteenth and twentieth centuries.[2] However, possibly due to sheer breadth of his thought, it seems that his work as a philosopher in particular has not always been properly recognized for its importance. In extreme cases, Inoue has even been accused of "deploying" philosophy with the intent of using it as a mere tool to legitimize his claims in other practical debates (specifically those concerning Buddhism as a philosophical religion). Additionally, his philosophy has at times been treated as mere syncretism. In other words, Inoue's work has sometimes been treated as little more than a theoretically incomplete sketch that attempts to synthesize ideas in Buddhist thought and Western philosophy.[3] Yet, a closer inspection of Inoue's thought shows that the role he played in the development of philosophy in modern Japan cannot be so easily dismissed. This is true not only in terms of his work in introducing Western philosophers (or, indeed, the concept of philosophy itself) into Japanese society,[4] but also in terms of providing novel arguments that stimulated later philosophers, including Nishida. Despite the comparative lack of attention his metaphysical thought has received, I believe we can find in Inoue a worthy attempt to describe reality in its most raw form that resonates with many of Nishida's goals. More specifically, I believe that Inoue's attempt to do so by pursuing the "middle-path (中道)" or "perfect completion (円了)" between extreme positions such as idealism and materialism offered several insights that played an important role in early modern Japanese philosophy and (to at least some degree) helped give shape to Nishida's philosophy.

Keeping this in mind, we shall reconsider the development of critical and non-dual philosophy in modern Japan by comparing Inoue and Nishida. To do this, we will first establish the background information needed to assess claims that Inoue merely deployed philosophy for political purposes. In the second section, we shall provide a reconstruction of Inoue's position while focusing largely on the first section of *An Evening of Philosophical Conversation* (哲学一夕話). In the third section, we will show both how Inoue's efforts link to Nishida's early philosophy of pure experience and, perhaps more importantly, how his struggle against materialism and idealism left Nishida with the challenge of finding a way to give a *positive* account of reality in its most concrete state without reducing it to abstract or biased positions. Once we have done this, we will move on to explore the methodology behind the philosophy of pure experience and demonstrate how it allowed Nishida to achieve a more thoroughgoing positive description of this non-dual conception of reality than Inoue had initially achieved. In the conclusion, we will explore the possibility that differing attitudes toward philosophy among Inoue's and Nishida's respective generations played a role in their philosophical methods.

The Background of Inoue Enryō's Theory of the Middle Path—Inoue's Historical Background and Conception of Philosophy

Now, if we are going to properly evaluate Inoue's philosophy as something more than an unfinished sketch or uncritical syncretism, we must address the most serious concerns that surround his philosophy. In particular, the proverbial elephant in the room we face when discussing Inoue's career as a thinker is the relationship between his metaphysics and his assertions concerning Buddhism as a modern religion for the Japanese people (and his subsequent denial that Christianity could play a similar role in Japanese society). The critic who has most clearly criticized Inoue for mixing one with the other, Judith Snodgrass, levels the following charges against him:

> [B]y denouncing it [i.e., Christianity] from the supposedly impartial stance of philosopher, Inoue enlisted the support of an audience beyond Buddhists. He did not simply dismiss it as evil but analyzed it as irrational, conceptually untenable, prescientific, deleterious to Japan. By taking the title 'philosopher' Inoue was able to promote Buddhism and undermine Christian influence from a pedestal of rationality and objectivity.
>
> (Snodgrass 2003: 141)

The charges pressed against Inoue here are simple. To promote Buddhism and drive away Christianity, Inoue deployed "rigorous and logical" Western philosophy as a tool to dictate what is and is not rational. As we may expect, what was written in the Christian Bible was generally deemed irrational by Inoue, although Buddhism could be stripped of its superstitions while maintaining the religious truths at its core. If what Snodgrass is saying is true and Inoue's interest in philosophy was only as an aid to justify these conclusions, then the deployment thesis can help us make sense of the notion that Inoue is not a philosopher as critical or valuable as Nishida, given that his career would be little more than an attempt to legitimize his claims about religion. Hence, we will briefly look at the background of Inoue's philosophy and question the degree to which this characterization is accurate.

Before going any further however, we should step back and provide context for the critique leveled against Inoue. First, the alliance between Buddhism and Western science was not a coincidence. While Buddhism was struggling to stay afloat at the beginning of the Meiji period, many Buddhist thinkers responded by attempting to "scientize" or "rationalize" Buddhism. In other words, although Buddhism spent much of the nineteenth century facing criticism as a "superstitious" and old-fashioned religion, some thinkers foresaw the possibility of a new Buddhism that was capable of coexisting with modern values and science. Or, rather, as some Meiji Buddhists (including Inoue himself) attempted to demonstrate, Buddhism—as a "study of causes"—was just as capable of coexisting with modern science as any other competing doctrine.[5] Crucially, it appears that one of the earliest thinker to label Buddhism as philosophy, Hara Tanzan (原坦山, 1819–92), relied on precisely this appeal to the rationality of philosophy in his discussions of Buddhism. A physician and Buddhist monk by trade, Hara argued that Buddhism was a philosophy of the mind (心性哲学) that had to be distinguished from a set of superstitions or even religion in the Western sense (Watabe 1998: 94–8). This use of philosophy to rationalize Buddhist thought earned him the prize of lecturing on "Indian Philosophy" at the newly established Tokyo University, where he would teach students such as the young Inoue.[6]

That these influences existed in the background of Inoue's work and that he was deeply interested in such issues himself is not debatable. Rather, after his graduation from Tokyo University in 1885, he became perhaps the leading figure in this attempt to pioneer a rational view of Buddhism as a philosophical religion (i.e., a religion capable of meeting the standards of philosophical scrutiny). This he did most clearly in *An Introduction to the Vitalization of Buddhism* (1887). In this work, Inoue begins with his now famous formulation that one must love the truth to defend their country, and would certainly understand they must defend their country if they love the truth (put as a slogan, we can use Inoue's phrase *gokoku airi*, 護国愛理). To genuinely love the truth (and become a learned and productive member of the nation), according to Inoue, included recognizing the spiritual truths of religion. Yet, it was not enough to merely accept any religion. Rather, it was necessary to seek out a religion whose spiritual truths could mesh with the physical truths of science. That is, spiritual and material truths posed here should not conflict with each other, even if they cannot be reduced to their counterpart. Christianity offered spiritual and emotional comfort, certainly, but conflicted with science in crucial ways (e.g., Christianity's claim that the world was created in 7 days, Jesus Christ being the son of God, etc.).[7] Japanese Buddhism was not only spiritually refined to the point that it was not inferior to any other religion, but could also be freed of such conflicts, insofar as it did not require one to assume any kind of transcendent, empirically unverifiable God.[8] Thus, speaking from the fair and impartial (公平無私) standpoint of the philosopher, Inoue was able to claim the superiority of Buddhism as a religion for the Japanese people. It is here that previous critics substantiated the claim that Inoue engaged in the strategic "deployment" of philosophy to promote a specific agenda.

While the claim of deployment made by critics like Snodgrass may appear sound at first glance, I believe that a more careful recognition of two important points can lead us to a more fulfilling alternate conclusion. The first point seems obvious enough and has been largely accepted by many interpreters: Philosophy is taken by Inoue as the fair and impartial pursuit of truth and, as such, can serve as the measuring stick that judges the scientific rationality of various specific doctrines. As one can glean from the previous discussion alone, such a description of Inoue's outlook on philosophy is not by any means a mistake. Importantly, such an interpretation highlights how Inoue believed philosophers or academics could reconcile their pursuit of the truth with the necessary drive to give back to the nation, as Inoue insisted they be able to do in *An Introduction to the Vitalization of Buddhism:*.

> To love the truth is, in other words, to defend the nation. I may be unlearned, lacking in potential, and not deserving of the position of scholar, but a part of me silently expects that I can merely pursue the truth and somehow [still] do my best for the nation. Thus, I am putting my love of the truth first and defending the nation second. Nevertheless, this love of the truth is, in all actuality, none other than one way of defending the nation.
>
> (IES 3: 332)

The entirety of *An Introduction to the Vitalization of Buddhism* is rife with such descriptions of how scholars' and philosophers' scientific quests for truth are inherently tied up with their status as citizens who must defend their nation. In other words, by shining light on more academic or metaphysical questions that come with a pursuit of the truth, academics can cause a trickle-down effect into practical disciplines. The practical benefits derived from these insights offer invaluable technological, moral, and political benefits to the nation-state. In light of both this stance toward philosophy and his emphasis on Buddhism being a religion that can be aligned with such a philosophical view, it would appear hard to deny that Inoue's conception of philosophy was, indeed, shaped by practical concerns and his desire to argue for Buddhism as the religion that best fit the Meiji Japanese people.

With that said, we must not ignore that Inoue also mentions in the previous quote that—in doing philosophy—he is prioritizing the truth. Doing so can help us avoid merely assuming that Inoue believed philosophy's pursuit of the truth to be defined *only* in terms of its practical capacity to contribute to building a stronger nation or that its practical capacities somehow weighed more heavily than its inherent desire for truth.[9] Inoue clearly stated in multiple lectures and works that philosophizing was a fundamental aspect of our humanity.[10] The argument is thus not that philosophy's *only* value is found in its ability to help us construct a strong state. As far as Inoue was concerned, the philosopher's inherent desire to pursue the truth and his or her need to give back to the state ought to be considered as the "front and back" sides of the same entity (IES 3: 332). To be more precise, Inoue seemed to believe that—perhaps even problematically—there were no conflicts between philosophy's pursuit of the truth and its role as arbiter in practical disputes. To the contrary, for Inoue, the theoretical and practical moments of philosophy fed into one another. Indeed, as Inoue explains, the "upward" movement of philosophy is a "skillful means (方便)" for addressing practical issues (IES 2: 416). While this point does not negate the previous paragraph's conclusion that Inoue's philosophy was at least partially shaped by practical concerns, it should lead us to accept the fact that Inoue simultaneously believed in the value of philosophical pursuit *for its own sake*.

This recognition leads us to the second point: that Inoue's apparent usage of theoretical philosophy to make practical arguments can likely be flipped on its head, i.e., we can likely look at the practical arguments made here as a window into his metaphysical interests. To be more specific, Inoue's practical claims concerning the importance of Buddhism as a philosophical religion in *An Introduction to the Vitalization of Buddhism* hint at a deeper concern with the relation between *mind and matter*. Buddhism was interesting not only because of the practical benefits of reconciling the physical or material sciences and the spiritual truths of religion, but because it could handle the metaphysical issues that stand at the core of these difficult questions. More generally speaking for Inoue—as one can glean from the fact that neither science nor religion could remain fully independent of or subsume the other—neither the spiritual nor the physical aspects of our lives could be primitive to or more important than the other. Inoue's basic intuition concerning the relation between mind and matter is spelled out in rather dense language below:

> To determine the substance of mind and matter, it is first necessary to take the standpoint of the rational form (理体) of neither matter nor mind. This rational form is called Suchness (真如). Suchness is matter but not matter. It is mind but not mind. It is neither matter nor mind, and at the same time it is both matter

and mind. This is called the middle path of "neither existence nor emptiness as well as existence and emptiness." [...] They are in a relation of neither one nor two.

(IES 3: 367)[11]

Here, one can see evidence of a more difficult metaphysical problem that cannot be reduced to Buddhist apologetics, i.e., the claim that mind and matter are not independent of, nor reducible to, one another. While Inoue himself does elect to connect this worldview to his praise of Mahayana Buddhism as a philosophical religion in *An Introduction to the Vitalization of Buddhism,* this seems to be indicative of a reciprocal relationship between both his philosophical conscience and his convictions about Buddhism as a religion for the modern Japanese people.[12] Indeed, it is not by accident that Inoue spent the back-half of the same text arguing for taking this "middle-path" to philosophy that would not take "extreme" or "biased" positions such as idealism or materialism, which would unduly favor either subjective-mind or objective-material. In this sense, when Inoue makes claims to the effect that both Buddhism and Hegelian philosophy are the most "perfect" forms of thought, he is doing so within the context of a specific intuition that only such positions have managed to avoid these naïve attempts to pigeon-hole reality into the kind of merely spiritual or merely physical worldviews we deemed insufficient in the previous paragraphs.

Thus, I would propose an alternative thesis to the notion that Inoue's deployment of philosophy was conducted solely for the sake of propagating Buddhism and—in much truer fashion to Inoue's own arguments on the nature of philosophy—admit that his practical interest in Buddhism fed into his metaphysical concern to avoid extreme or biased claims (and vice versa). This admission is important for two reasons insofar as it provides grounds to explicitly deny the possibility that philosophy before Nishida was deployed or imported purely for the sake of substantiating arguments about practical issues (and that Inoue specifically never developed any significant philosophical insights in virtue of his attachment to the propagation of Buddhism). Hence, an investigation of this philosophical intuition could likely provide a useful foothold with which to look over the development of philosophy in Japan. Now, even if we say as much, what exactly Inoue means by a middle-path that sees mind and matter as "neither one nor two" (or how he could justify this insight beyond vague appeals to Western philosophy and Buddhist dogma) is still far from clear. Keeping this in mind, we will attempt to get a closer look at what Inoue was attempting to do philosophically irrespective of his relation to Buddhism in the next section by looking at one of his most creative texts, *An Evening of Philosophical Conversation*.

Inoue's Philosophy of the Middle Path—Focusing on *An Evening of Philosophical Conversation*

An Evening of Philosophical Conversation was written in three pamphlets released between 1886 and 1889. In addition to being a favorite book of the young Nishida, this work has been taken by some historians as the first full-fledged instantiation of the broader tendency toward theories that have been referred to under the umbrella of "phenomena-*soku*-reality."[13] As the name implies, this theory looked to provide a view of reality in which conscious phenomena are immediately one with (*soku*; 即) reality itself. Perhaps more importantly, however, the work presents a crucial counterexample to assumptions that pre-Nishidian Meiji philosophical efforts were universally translational or limited to interpretations of Western texts. The central premise of the work is that it presents a dialogue between two and four discussants representing logical extremes who inevitably end up falling into unsolvable aporias. The various parties face off in three different sections, respectively covering the topics of ontology, God, and truth. In the first section, which is both the basis for Inoue's work in the remainder of the dialogues and likely the foundation of his philosophy, a "materialist" and an "idealist" find themselves determined to show that reality is entirely reducible to physical material and conscious phenomena, respectively.[14] The two combatants take turns pushing forward their own agenda, only to ultimately end with unanswerable questions (and thus fail to justify their positions). Considering not only the fact that the first section of *An Evening of Philosophical Conversation* is the basis of Inoue's ontology, but also the fact that it offers us the key to understanding the problem he left for later philosophers in Japan, I would like to start with a brief introduction to this dialogue.

The dialogue starts innocently enough. The idealist, Ryōchū (了水), remarks that no matter how vast the universe may be, it can only be as vast as we grasp it to be in our minds. Everything we perceive, no matter what it is, is only available to us in the human mind. Certainly, one may *assume* that there is a world far beyond what we perceive in our individual minds. Yet, to speak of anything that we cannot have a mental experience of would be far too speculative, given that we have no way of perceiving any such mind-independent objects. Even when his materialist opponent, Enyū (円山), fires back that it is equally speculative to assume that there is nothing beyond the mind, Ryōchū is prepared to answer. For Ryōchū, the very act of distinguishing between any object (including whether something is "in" or "outside" of the mind) is a mental act. To be more precise, not knowing is every bit as mental of an action as knowing is. In this sense, both that which we do know and that which we do not know (that which is assumed to exist outside consciousness) must share the same space in the mind. Ryōchū's theory here goes up in scale, revealing itself to be an indiscriminate monism based on a singular mind, which then articulates itself into a definitive form through discriminatory mental acts (i.e., the act of identifying an object as an individual separates it from the whole to which it primordially belongs). However, just as soon as Ryōchū attempts to expound upon this theory, Enyū points out that this notion makes a mockery of the fact that they are two distinct persons who are having a conversation precisely because they do not share the same mind and that, at any rate, Ryōchū has failed to account for how this discriminatory process of individuation occurs. Ryōchū gives up, stating that he still needs to study this point.

Ryōchū's defeat is followed by Enyū's own attempt to describe his materialist (or, in some sense, dualist) position. As far as Enyū is concerned, the world is made up of physically discrete individual things. Regarding how to account for the mind, Enyū chooses to make a sharp distinction between spatially discrete individual material things and consciousness. After Ryōchū presses him on the topic of death and the possibility that spatial differences between individuals are only a temporary state, Enyū attempts to evade this problem by claiming that the annihilation of physical distinctions does not imply the total loss of distinctions between physical things (and, curiously enough, seems to imply that the immortality of the soul is the reason that these distinctions are still possible). Although Ryōchū points out that this is an unjustified assumption, Enyū replies by saying that—even if some individuals are annihilated—there will always be physical differences left between material objects. Yet, in the end, when Ryōchū further asks him what will happen when the universe itself meets its inevitable end and there is no longer any possibility to account for physically distinct individuals, Enyū is unable to come up with a means to keep his worldview from collapsing in on itself and admitting the possibility of an indiscriminate whole. Enyū thus repeats Ryōchū's line, insisting that he needs to study this point further.

It is here, once both idealism and materialism have reached an impasse in trying to describe the true nature of reality, that both students attempt to appeal to the authority of their teacher: Enryō (円了). As one can surmise by looking at the names of all participants, *Enryō* serves to unite the fragmentary truths provided by *Enyū* and *Ryōchū*.[15] Upon being provided with a summary of their debate, Enryō does not side with either of the two students. Rather, he chides the two of them, stating:

> Ryōchū knows non-discrimination but knows nothing of discrimination. Enyū knows discrimination but knows nothing of non-discrimination. Neither of you have escaped from being biased toward one side or the other. This is the reason that both of you are able to [so easily] doubt the other's explanation. You are both convinced that non-discrimination and discrimination and the entity [body; 体] they make up are entirely different. Ryōchū's so-called non-discriminatory mind is the same thing as Enyū's discriminatory mind, and Enyū's discriminatory mind is the same thing as Ryōchū's non-discriminatory mind. They both make up one part of the same entity.
>
> (IES 1: 43)

In this quote, we find the core premise of Enryō's philosophy. Neither materialism nor idealism is entirely wrong. Materialism—as a worldview in which the world is composed of physically distinct individuals—must exist in a relation of immediate interdependence (expressed throughout Inoue's work as the logic of "*soku*") with idealism—as a worldview in which individuals emerge from a non-discriminate whole through mental acts. Indeed, according to Enryō (and thus Inoue), they both represent one fundamental moment inherent to reality in its most complete state. When we try to reduce reality to either extreme or take one as fundamental to the other, we end in absurdity. This declaration on the part of Enryō-*sensei* (as well as some more or less helpful metaphorical explanations to help the reader grasp the middle or perfect path) marks the end of the first section of *An Evening of Philosophical Conversation*.

Now, before moving on, there are two salient points about Inoue's middle path that deserve attention. First, Inoue's middle path is not a static entity that houses both mind and matter (or, otherwise, discriminate individuals and a completed whole) as two separate entities. To the contrary, they are both part of the same dynamically changing complex. Or rather, as Inoue emphasizes, "Non-discrimination develops itself into discrimination, while discrimination merges into non-discrimination" (IES 1: 45). For Inoue, non-discrimination (expressed initially by idealism) and discrimination (represented by materialism) exist in a relation of ebb and flow, feeding into one another. While attempting to express this interplay directly is bound for failure or contradiction, it is a fact of reality that the myriad of things around us is at once interconnected even though we can undoubtedly distinguish between them and demarcate them as individuals. In this regard, we should recognize that Inoue's middle path is not a completely different alternative to materialism or idealism, but instead as the *originary* activity that stands at the basis of this interplay between these two seemingly different perspectives and makes such distinctions possible in the first place.

The second point we must recognize is that, although the arguments the discussants provide are often shrewd and the connection between discrimination/non-discrimination and the mind/matter problem is interesting, the structure of this pamphlet is likely of even greater interest to us than any of its content. When reading this text, it is important that we avoid a crucial mistake and *do not* look at Enryō's lectures as an immediate or mystic revelation of the truth of the middle or perfect path to his hapless students. To do so would be to ignore the dialectical development in which both combatants systematically negate each other and gradually become indistinguishable over the course of their own dialogues. It is only once these individual positions have collapsed into one another that Enryō-*sensei*, as the representative of the middle path, can point out to his students a fact that should have already become clear from their own discussion: any attempt to reduce reality to one particular entity (and thus do away with other positions) was bound to become nothing more than a hollow abstraction. Given this fact, any such attempt to pigeon-hole reality as being precisely this, that, or the other will necessarily reveal itself to be incomplete when taken to its extreme.

Considering what we have mentioned above, it seems that Inoue's argument in *An Evening of Philosophical Conversation* is hardly reducible to the creatively bankrupt syncretism that less generous interpretations have saddled upon him. Indeed, insofar as I can tell, these dialogues are best looked at as a kind of internal struggle to do philosophy without resorting to the seemingly inevitable fate of extreme or biased positions.[16] While we will not take up the matter in any great detail here, it is worth noting that the development between discussants presented here matches his unique view on the development of the history philosophy as an oscillation between—and attempt to escape from—such extreme or biased positions.[17] Perhaps more than any form of historical speculation, though, the performative nature of Inoue's dialogues in *An Evening of Philosophical Conversation* can help the reader catch a glimpse of reality that cannot be reduced to any one particular position or entity. In this way, Inoue's work presents (and poses a mostly negative solution to) the question of how it is possible to describe reality without falling victim to bias and abstraction. In the next section, we will briefly review how these questions connect him to Nishida's attempt at a philosophy of pure experience.

From Inoue to Nishida: Similar Ideas and Unanswered Questions

To begin, although our introduction of Inoue's philosophy has been on the brief side of things, ignoring both his later works and his more systematic analyses of how philosophy relates to other disciplines, readers of Nishida's philosophy have likely seen enough to identify how some of the core themes in his work overlap with many ideas in *Inquiry*.[18] First, Inoue's decision to take the middle path to show that subjective consciousness and objective materiality form "true reality" as two interpenetrating aspects of one encompassing whole resonates clearly with central ideas in Nishida's philosophy. Indeed, similarly to our outline of Inoue's philosophy, even a cursory analysis of pure experience shows that Nishida also claims that such oppositions or contradictory moments exist as necessary aspects of an overarching unity. Or, to be more precise, in both systems, the constant dynamism of this unity, i.e., Inoue's middle path or Nishida's pure experience, is taken as the *originary* source of the various differences in perspectives and contexts that allow us to designate one aspect of this underlying unity as being either the individual's subjective consciousness or objective material. To this extent, to imply that one is "more real" or fundamental than the other is arbitrary at best, and the source of needless theoretical conflict at worst. As Nishida states, these distinctions are no more than differing perspectives on pure experience.[19]

Rather than focusing solely on similarities in content, however, I believe it is more important to note that Inoue helped point later philosophers like Nishida to an important formal problem. As the previous section likely made clear, Inoue's philosophy offered a glimpse into what Robert J. J. Wargo has referred to as the "problem of standpoints" (Wargo 2005: 11). Indeed, the dialogues in *An Evening of Philosophical Conversation* serve as an efficacious reminder that all attempts to pigeon-hole reality into one—*ism* or another, or otherwise to attempt to do away with other perspectives by accounting for a purely materialist/idealist world separated from its counterpart—were bound for failure. Considering this fact, Inoue attempted to show a way toward accounting for the underlying (and not directly describable) unity between the various perspectives presented in these debates without absolutizing any of them. Indeed, for Inoue both mind and matter were admitted as valid perspectives that comprise a more comprehensive unity. This attempt to describe reality in its most concrete state by capturing the difficult relation between the multiplicity of relative perspectives and the unity between them, then, is a crucial project left by Inoue and likely inherited and developed by Nishida.

However, there are crucial differences between the two in how they approach this problem. In this sense, it is important that we remain aware of the fact that Inoue did not exactly "solve" the issue at hand. More specifically, as several authors have pointed out, the matter of *how* one can provide a non-dual account of reality raises important questions that remain unanswered (or, perhaps, unanswerable by design) in Inoue's dialogue. Consistent with what we have seen in *An Evening of Philosophical Conversation*, Inoue seemed to prefer a negative approach to accounting for the middle path. In other words, the middle path can only be glimpsed in the negation of extreme positions and metaphorical images to help one grasp a concept of reality that is otherwise ungraspable. Yet, although the arguments designed to show that extreme positions cannot be absolutized or cut-off from other perspectives are enlightening, Inoue's dialectic never provides a clear or systematic account of what the middle path is or how it should be characterized. To be more precise, the skeptical claim that reality can only be approached negatively denies the possibility of positive description. Still, while Inoue's reasons for avoiding a positive characterization of the middle path may be clear, this point still opened him to various criticisms going back to the initial publication of the pamphlet. Indeed, Inoue's attempt to explain through Enryō how mind and matter are at once the same and not the same was decried as an unjustified acceptance of contradictions (as one of his earliest critics, Onishi Hajime put it, Inoue seems to have merely mixed oil and water).[20] Even as Inoue's career progressed, it would appear as though he never developed a serviceable account of how mind and matter or subject and object go about distinguishing themselves from one another.[21] In the end, as Wargo correctly states in regard to Inoue's ontological theory, the claim that reality was non-dual was seemingly posed as the solution to all of philosophy's problems. However, as he also points out—insofar as there is no substantial attempt to provide a theoretical foundation for this non-dual ontology—this assumption is incorrect.[22]

Several authors have used such potential criticism as evidence to state that there is a gap in philosophical rigor between Inoue and Nishida.[23] Although we have just seen that Inoue's metaphysics has been criticized for not providing a systematic foundation to accept his non-dual ontology, such criticism hardly seems applicable to Nishida's philosophy of pure experience. To the contrary, one could likely go so far as to say that the matter of how a fundamentally unified reality is capable of constantly changing, developing, and differentiating itself into apparent dualities was the core of Nishida's early thought (and, possibly, the driving force of his career as a philosopher).[24] While we do not have space here to give a total explanation of the dynamic of Nishida's system, even the briefest look at his philosophy shows how his analysis of the way that the structures of thought and will unite the gaps that open in pure experience as it constantly changes, thereby giving us a positive insight into the true workings of reality.[25] In this sense, there appears to be a fundamental difference between Nishida and Inoue.[26]

For clarity's sake, I believe we should not look at this distinction as devaluing Inoue's philosophical project in any way. After all, one could hardly say that Inoue failed in *An Evening of Philosophical Conversation*. To the contrary, insofar as he led his readers to the point at which only the middle path remained, one could look at his endeavor as a success. Additionally, in response to the critics we have referred to above, one could argue that his negative approach was the only viable conclusion to his investigation (or, more poignantly, one could argue that any attempt to put reality into non-metaphoric words is ultimately doomed to fail). More importantly than his theoretical insights, though, Inoue pointed to a crucial methodological problem for later philosophers in Japan: *how* could one provide an account of the reality we live in given that any attempt to grasp it in its entirety would be doomed to failure as an externalized abstraction that takes into view only one part of the bigger picture? I believe that this question helped set the stage for Nishida's more systematic endeavor to describe pure experience. Keeping this in mind, in the next section, we will briefly look at how Nishida attempted to positively and systematically describe pure experience without falling prey to abstractions.

Nishida's Early Methodology: Changing the Starting Point of Philosophy

As readers of *Inquiry* will be aware, pure experience is taken to be concrete reality as it is given to us in our most direct or obvious experiences. As Nishida explains from the outset of this work, such direct experience reveals that there is no intrinsic distinction between subject and object or mind and matter.[27] Yet, as we have seen in the previous section, recognizing the fact that reality cannot be reduced to one or the other does not constitute a systematic philosophical understanding of it. Paradoxically, then, while pure experience was that which is given to us in our most obvious and direct experiences, it is also that which we need to clarify and structuralize. Using Nishida's own words, it is the "alpha and omega of our thought" (IG: 16). Put differently, for Nishida, pure experience was both the *point of departure* and the *final goal* of philosophical contemplation. While this may seem like a banal fact, this difference in starting point is evidence of a crucial *methodological* difference between Nishida and Inoue insofar as it allowed for the possibility of claiming that positive descriptions of pure experience were possible without abstracting what was concretely given. Here, we will briefly review Nishida's notion of pure experience as a critical methodology and thus show how it contributed to facing the problems set forth in the previous section.

So, what does it mean to talk about the philosophical methodology of pure experience? Borrowing from Nishida, we can see a succinct explanation of how the philosophy of pure experience can be understood in the following quotation:

> To understand true reality and to know the true nature of the universe and human life, we must discard all artificial assumptions, doubt whatever can be doubted, and proceed on the basis of direct and indubitable knowledge.
>
> (IG: 38)

Regarding what he means by direct knowledge, Nishida then specifies as follows:

> It is knowledge of facts in our intuitive experience, knowledge of phenomena of consciousness. A present phenomenon of consciousness and our being conscious of it are identical; they cannot be divided into subject and object. Since facts are not separated even a hair's breadth from knowing, we cannot doubt this knowledge.
>
> (IG: 39)

The idea is simple enough. To do philosophy is to doubt all that can be doubted, discard all assumptions, and return to pre-reflective, lived experience. Through this practice, we can come to grips with reality in its most raw form before subject and object have been split apart and allowed themselves to be manipulated by inferences, linguistic infidelities, and fabrications of reflection. Yet, despite the superficial simplicity of this quasi-Cartesian outlook, a more careful look reveals that this change in starting point entails two crucial differences in how we approach philosophical argumentation.

The main difference we must account for in Nishida's methodology is obvious enough. In addition to establishing pure experience as what is given to us—our new starting point, as it were—we also gain a methodological foundation of sorts with which to both make observations about pure experience and *corroborate* said observations. In this sense, although Nishida's view of pure experience may indeed be discussed in similar terms as Inoue's middle path, the metaphorical explanations provided by Enryō-*sensei* are nowhere to be found in Nishida's early philosophy. In their place, Nishida provides a structural account of the workings of thought and the will and how they allow for us to develop the meaning or context necessary to distinguish varying perspectives within pure experience. Thus, while Inoue's support for his notion of the middle path was based on the mutual negation of relative positions (and thus lacked any positive elucidation), Nishida's arguments in his early philosophy aimed to illuminate the structures of reality based on what could be corroborated by pure experience. The goal of pure experience as a methodology, then, was to start from direct experience and provide a faithful account of it without devolving into the kind of abstract or external standpoints that Inoue had already deftly shown to be insufficient.

Still, one may doubt whether (1) Nishida's conception of pure experience itself is not a mere fabrication of reflection or (2) whether such a direct attempt to put pure experience into words itself presents his non-dual ontology in a merely abstract form. Indeed, the question of if and how Nishida managed to avoid the "myth of the given" is one that is still raised by modern interpreters and a matter that will remain relevant in the next chapter.[28] Otherwise, one could ask how it is possible to make any kind of faithful judgment about pure experience when—by definition—it stands prior to the distinction between a reflecting subject and her object of reflection. In response to these problems, it is important to recognize how Nishida attempted to develop a theory of meaning that is "internal" to pure experience. Although at times (similar to Inoue's skeptical outlook) Nishida states during *Inquiry* that pure experience itself is not immediately or fully graspable by language,[29] this is only true insofar as individual conscious experiences are mute without their proper context. Thus, crucial to Nishida's attempted solution is his explanation of how experiences can be bestowed with meaning by their relations with other experiences.

> Assuming that pure experience is endowed with discriminations, what are the meanings or judgments added to it and how do they relate to pure experience? People usually argue that when pure experience is connected to objective reality it generates meaning and takes the form of judgments, but from the perspective of my theory of pure experience, we cannot leave the sphere of pure experience.

> Meanings or judgments derive from the connection of a present consciousness to past consciousnesses; meanings and judgments are based on the unifying activity in the great network of consciousness. They indicate the relation between present consciousness and other consciousnesses, and therefore merely express the position of present consciousness within the network of consciousness. For example, when one interprets an auditory sensation to be the sound of a bell, one has merely established the sensation's position relative to past experiences.
>
> (IG: 9)

To paraphrase, meaning and judgments are generated in pure experience by allowing one experience to connect with other experiences (in this case, one's present experience of hearing a bell is made possible by having heard bells before in the past). Once conflicting or contradictory information enters our stream of consciousness, the initial unity between subject and object is lost. This gap between them allows for the implicit relations between such experiences to be made explicit in judgment.[30] In this case, the question "what was that noise" is answered by referencing our previous experiences of hearing similar sounds, resulting in the answer, "it was just a bell."

There is much more to be said on the topic, but for now all we need to note is that meanings and judgment do not derive from the mental act of an epistemic subject that stands outside of pure experience. Instead, they derive from the event of implicit patterns and connections between individual conscious moments making themselves explicit when a gap between subject and object arises in pure experience. Put differently, if we follow along with Nishida's early methodology, then judgments about pure experience must arise from *within* pure experience. Now, one may wonder here how it is possible to determine if these judgments are true without presupposing an external standard with which this internal position is correlative to. Nishida solves this by claiming that whether judgments were true or false was also determined by the systematic relation between experiences:

> Which ideas are true and which false? We always believe that what is most powerful, greatest, and deepest in a system of consciousness is objective reality. Whatever fits with it we consider true, and whatever conflicts with it we consider false.
>
> (IG: 15)

In this way, judgments, meanings, and truth could only be corroborated by their conformation or coherence with the systematic progression of what was given in the stream of consciousness. Extending these principles, we can extrapolate that the philosopher's job—in their quest to describe pure experience as the sole reality—was to make explicit the structures of this network of consciousnesses from an *internal* position, without abstracting only one aspect of it or relying on empirically unverifiable suppositions of a mind-independent material world or pre-individuated conscious subject. The workings of the will, the workings of thought, and the intellectual intuition revealing the inherent unity between subject and object could all only make themselves known as they reveal themselves in consciousness.[31]

To drive this point home, we can once again say that Nishida's attempt in *Inquiry* was to make judgments about the nature of reality while standing *within* the flow of lived experience. Taking pure experience as an external object of academic consideration would make philosophy easier, but it would also be self-defeating. Doing so would abstract us, the living self conducting the investigation, out of the picture and thus fail to achieve philosophy's goal of concretely detailing reality. In this sense, making judgments about reality outgoing from the "patterns" that instantiate themselves in each individual moment of experience offered Nishida a path to describing pure experience in a positive sense, offering descriptions of the structures of pure experience while appealing only to what has been "fulfilled" in intuition. By following this plan, Nishida presented an alternative to Inoue's negative descriptions and offered a path for positive philosophical reflection on a non-dual ontological framework that, by nature, defies external characterization.

I do not wish to claim here that Nishida's early methodology was necessarily sound. There are more than a few doubts one could pose to these explanations about how meanings and judgments form within experience. As we shall discuss over the course of the next chapter, the relation between the "facts" and "meanings" we find in pure experience is one of the most difficult topics to make sense of in Nishida's early philosophy and there are non-trivial reasons to believe that Nishida ends up not being able to make any distinction between what is given in the facts of pure experience and their meanings. Yet, these questions remain secondary for now. Despite his potential shortcomings, we find in Nishida's early philosophy a key change in directions from Inoue (and likely any of his predecessors) that contributed greatly to later trends in twentieth-century Japanese philosophy: a path to logicizing a conception of reality that cannot be reduced to one position and can accommodate the dynamic interplay between the various conflicting, relative positions that constitute our lived experience.

Concluding Remarks—A Shift in Attitudes as the Basis for a Shift in Methodology?

Over the course of this chapter, we started by comparing Nishida's work to that of Inoue Enryō. As we have seen, although it may perhaps sound trivial at first glance, the difference in starting points between Inoue and Nishida proved to be an important step in providing a more systematic account for exploring this conception of reality. Indeed, while Inoue's dialectic stops once it reaches a nondual account of reality referred to as the middle path, Nishida instead attempts to provide a systematic and detailed analysis of the structures of his similar ontological worldview. To be clear, this difference between the two does not indicate a failure on Inoue's part. However, it is still noteworthy that Nishida's use of pure experience as a thoroughgoing methodological principle to provide a comprehensive account for these ideas did provide an alternative method to describe similar ideas in a more direct way. In this sense we could say that if there is a noticeable difference between Nishida and Inoue, it likely is not found in the general picture that they are painting. Rather, the greatest steps Nishida took would be his fixation on providing—crucially—positive descriptions to develop ideas already present in Meiji philosophy.

As one final idea to consider before departing from our comparison between Nishida and Inoue, I would like to suggest that the adoption of these comparatively radical methodological principles may have been urged on by different expectations for philosophical argumentation between Inoue's and Nishida's respective generations. While, as we have seen in the first section, Inoue demanded that the pure or theoretical sides of philosophy be returnable to society, things seem slightly different in Nishida's case. Take, for instance, the following quotation from his notes:

> Philosophy is not necessary for those who have never met with suffering in life, or otherwise those who do not look for something deeper in life even after meeting with adversity. However, anyone who has ever met adversity or wondered about life in its entirety will surely have felt some kind of anguish. They will certainly try to find a new meaning in life, or to be reborn into a new one.
>
> (Cited in Stone 2018: 48)

Inquiry may have taken up metaphysical issues in the first half of the book but was centrally concerned with the problem of human life (IG: xxx). As one may grasp from the quotation above, this does not mean that there were two separate themes, but rather that even seemingly purely metaphysical questions stem from existential suffering Nishida mentions above. What's more, such existential worries were not posed in terms of their role as one side of a dual-sided structure of pursuing the truth *and* contributing to national strength or addressing particular social issues. I believe this difference in attitude may be crucial for understanding the methodological differences between them for the following two reasons.

Though at first blush this change in attitude may appear unrelated to Nishida's "technical" success in articulating a non-dual view of reality, I do not think this is the case. To the contrary, such a thirst for existential or religious peace of mind could never be quenched by purely academic or uncritical philosophy by Nishida's standards. Metaphysical doubt concerning one's life and one's place in the universe could not be solved by common-sense explanations, proverbial wisdom, or the mere repetition of what previous philosophers have already stated.[32] Philosophy had to be so thorough that it did not permit any unexamined dogmas to fester in the background of our thought and haunt us. In this sense, it is no coincidence that philosophy is described above in the language of rebirth in the quotation given above. What these two changes offer us, in the end, is a simultaneous change in what is expected of a philosophical argument and the philosopher making said argument between Inoue and Nishida. Regardless of whether Inoue's worldview was driven solely by his views on Buddhism (a contentious view anyway), any confusion between potentially dogmatic political claims and philosophical arguments we addressed in the first section was *not possible* in Nishida's case. Nishida's attitude toward philosophy precluded him from stopping even once he had provided convincing motivation for his theory of pure experience. An honest exercise in the philosophy of pure experience assumed that the author would leave any predisposed worldview behind and provide an empirically founded and thoroughgoing account of reality in its most concrete state. Naturally, one could conceivably twist what they have found in their analysis to match with their political views, but to do so would be tantamount to missing the very point of doing philosophy. The transformative potential of pure experience, as a radical opportunity to totally evaluate one's life within the vast expanse of the universe, was an integral aspect of Nishida's earliest philosophy and helped make his methodological advancements possible in the first place.

The second point worth mentioning about Nishida's attitude toward philosophy is that it can potentially offer us a means to situate his work in the broader flow of the development of Meiji philosophy. Indeed, while much has been made of Nishida's existential interests from a biographical standpoint, it would be unfortunate to overlook the fact that this shift in interests (from looking at pure philosophy as a "skillful means" to contribute to practical social issues to looking at philosophy purely in terms of its existential capacities) stands in line with popular trends around the beginning of the twentieth century. While the earliest uses of Western philosophy were in many cases—as one can see when looking at the roots of the notion of a "Buddhist philosophy"—practically minded attempts to drive forward the modernization process, we can see that philosophy had found a new calling as a means to evaluate the problem of human life by the end of the Meiji. While *Inquiry* may have been the most important example of such an effort, Nishida was hardly the only member of his generation who started to look at philosophy as an endeavor in exploring the existential problems left for his generation. To the contrary, the end of the nineteenth and beginning of the twentieth centuries ushered in a wave of troubled young men who looked for something more from philosophy than an academic exercise done in the name of practical interests.[33] As we shall discuss at the end of Chapter 3, this shift in philosophical outlooks was likely an important factor for spreading Nishida's philosophy beyond just academic circles and into the lives of troubled young men in the Taisho period.

Still, although this historical background gives some credence to the idea that Nishida's notion of pure experience was the first original Japanese philosophical theory, we must not overlook the contributions made by the previous generation of early Meiji philosophers in making this shift possible by ignoring their contributions to philosophical argumentation in Japan. Even if one may be able to create a meaningful distinction between the two authors in terms of rigor, Inoue's philosophical enterprise was not necessarily the much-maligned syncretism that it has often been painted as, nor was it solely driven by any politically charged agenda to foist Buddhism on the Japanese public. To the contrary, a look at texts such *An Evening of Philosophical Conversation* reveals that, even as early as 1886, clever and original philosophical works were present in Japan. It is, indeed, not without reason that young philosophers like Nishida were charmed by the work of those like Inoue and the potential for independent thought that it showed them. Hence, we cannot merely accept Nishida's supremacy by saying that he was the beginning of original thought insofar as there had been nothing similar before that point. He was, instead, likely the final step of a process in which philosophy continuously separated itself from practical or political trappings, pursuing instead existential truths.

2

Direct Experience and the Problem of Meaning

Motora Yūjirō, Nishida Kitarō, and Takahashi Satomi

Introduction

As has become clear in the previous chapter, the way Nishida tackled problems related to language, meaning, and judgment was crucial to his overall project in *An Inquiry into the Good*. This is true in a technical sense, given that his ability to make positive descriptions of a concrete reality that stands prior to static categories like mind or matter was tied up with his acrobatic attempt to describe how judgments and meaning could be generated *within* pure experience. While predecessors like Inoue Enryō also attempted to tackle such problems by describing this notion of reality in a negative sense, Nishida refused to do so and instead offered a unique philosophical methodology that hinted at how meaning and veridical judgments could be made about such a reality without falling back on the typical abstract categories that look at reality from an "external" position. Hence, by offering at least a worthwhile attempt at responding to this issue of how we can make judgments about direct experience, Nishida seems to have pointed toward something different than what could be found in Inoue Enryō's philosophy.

Perhaps more importantly, though, is how this quest for meaning in direct experience relates to a topic that came up at the end of the previous chapter: the problem of human life (人生の問題). Indeed, as Miikael-Adam Lotman (2020) has—in my mind, correctly—argued, Nishida's pursuit of a grounds for the generation of meaning in pure experience was not merely an academic problem. To the contrary, it was an existential demand to know who we are and what our place in this universe is. Given this, insofar as pure experience was taken as the one true reality, the possibility that said reality was either (i) completely beyond any kind of description or knowledge or (ii) itself entirely meaningless loomed as an existential specter over Nishida's earliest philosophy. If direct experience did indeed stand prior to meaning or judgments and was truly the ultimate reality that we must aspire to, we would have no other conclusion to reach than the idea that the universe we live in—that entity which our true self can only exist in continuity with—is *itself ultimately devoid of meaning*. In this case, Nishida's claims throughout *Inquiry* that philosophy can help us address matters of religion and existential qualms would end in an absurd conclusion.[1]

Keeping both these technical and existential concerns in view, we will delve deeper into a topic we briefly touched upon in the previous chapter: the ontological dimensions of *how* meaning is generated in pure experience and what impact this has for the early Nishida's vision of what philosophy is. Put differently, we will ask how Nishida is able to explain the position we have ascribed to him so far by addressing questions about meaning in pure experience that were only introduced in the last chapter. What is the difference between pure experience, i.e., moments in which we experience no separation between ourselves and the world, and reflective or judgmentive experience? Does an experience of meaning not imply that we have left the realm of pure experience? This would seem to go against our conclusions in the previous chapter. But if this is not the case, then does this mean that pure experience itself is inherently meaningful? How could Nishida justify such a claim? Otherwise, is our return to pure experience not the opposite, i.e., proof that reality itself is actually meaningless? The answers to these questions have wide-ranging methodological and existential implications for Nishida's project and, thus, should not be ignored.

However, we will not look at Nishida's work in a vacuum when addressing these questions. Indeed, considering that such technical questions of how direct experience can generate meaning are deeply intertwined with the history and importation of the newest Western psychological resources of late nineteenth and early twentieth centuries that attempted to answer precisely the same question of the relation between meaning and direct experience, this background could help offer us a foothold for dealing with Nishida's ideas on the matter. Hence, to get a more complete vision of this relation between direct experience and meaning—and, frankly, to get a picture of what kind of conclusion Nishida was trying to avoid—we will introduce the work of his former university professor and famed psychologist, Motora Yūjirō (元良勇次郎, 1858–1912) as a foil to Nishida. Considering both the shared influence of late-nineteenth-century psychologists (most notably, the work of Wilhelm Wundt and William James) and a mutual concern with finding a concrete grounds for analyzing experience, Motora serves as a useful comparison to Nishida's attempt to develop a philosophical view based on direct experience. As we shall see over the course of this comparison, although there are similarities between the two, Motora's willingness to accept a purely psychologistic view of the development of meaning illustrates precisely the trap that Nishida was *trying* to avoid. By distinguishing Nishida's view of meaning in direct experience from Motora, we will be able to identify the strong ontological claims that Nishida makes about meaning in pure experience and better understand his project.

Our operation will proceed in the following order. First, to ensure that the stakes are clear, we will show precisely why the relation between "direct" or "pure" experience and meaning is problematic with some general preparatory remarks. Upon establishing the problem at hand, we will then move back in time to see how this issue was framed in the work of Motora Yūjirō. Focusing principally in his writings on the generation of meaning through the interconnection of different "incomplete experiences," we shall see how Motora's attempt to develop what he had found in the work of psychologists like William James (1842–1910), George Herbert Mead (1863–1931), and Wilhelm Wundt (1832–1920) led to a view of meaning that appears similar to Nishida. However, we will then show how certain psychologistic tendencies in his work led to key differences between them, given that Motora's perspective ultimately could not provide the ontological grounds for meaning that Nishida was looking for. We will follow up on this basic discussion to see how Nishida avoided both taking an externalized position *and* any situation in which direct experience as ultimate reality would be rendered meaningless. In doing so, we will focus more deeply on his conception of the concrete universal, asking how this notion could fit within the framework of his philosophical methodology. Finally, to better grasp what Nishida was attempting to do in *An Inquiry in the Good*, we will revisit the critique of the first author to recognize the connection between Motora and Nishida, Takahashi Satomi (高橋里美, 1886–1964), to question the relation between meanings, values, and the facts of pure experience. In doing so, we will be able to understand not only one of the lynchpins of Nishida's early philosophy—his ability to account for direct experience without losing sight of logical judgment—but also how his ability to handle these questions ties in with the overall picture presented at the end of the previous chapter.

Direct Experience and Meaning

As should be evident by now, in *Inquiry*, Nishida attempted to rethink the nature of true reality and the concrete life of the self living it by looking back to how this reality is in its most concrete state, i.e., in pure or direct experience. We find out the true nature of our lives by looking back to our self before it has been distorted or twisted by language and concepts into something cut off from the rest of the world and the experience of others. As we have also seen in the previous chapter, this entails—to at least some degree—a sense of existential relief. That is, there seems to be for Nishida a deeper *meaning* to this act of returning to pure experience and finding the spiritual catharsis promised at the outset of his investigation. And yet, something seems odd about this premise. Consider, for instance, Nishida's first description of pure experience at the outset of *Inquiry*:

> To experience means to know facts just as they are, to know in accordance with facts by completely relinquishing one's own fabrications. What we usually refer to as experience is adulterated with some sort of thought, so by *pure* I am referring to the state of experience just as it is without the least addition of deliberative discrimination. The moment of seeing a color or hearing a sound, for example, is prior not only to the thought that the color or sound is the activity of an external object or that one is sensing it, but also to the judgment of what the color or sound might be.
>
> (IG: 3)

While there seems to be an evident tendency in Nishida to attach to pure experience a religious or ethical value (discussed in deeper detail in the following chapters), one may wonder how such values are possible in the kind of experience described above. A superficial application of the logic at play in *Inquiry* not only seems to lead us to the conclusion that pure experience stands prior to any kind of meanings and values (as the state of experience before we judge a flower to be blue or a cookie to be delicious), but it even seems to render such meanings and values as *utterly untenable* (i.e., as a delusion of reflective consciousness that stands in contrast to the true reality of experience as existing free of any such values or meanings). Presumably, this would include any form of ethical or religious meaning and values as well, thus rendering Nishida's ethical and religious project incoherent.[2]

Considering how problematic these issues would be for Nishida if they were to hold true, we should take a closer look at precisely where they come from, and why Nishida might struggle to overcome them. If we were so inclined, we could write off these problems and say that Nishida is merely giving an account of what the world is like before pure experience is "broken" by reflection and meaning is ascribed to it by the epistemic subject. It may be true that at this state of pure experience we have no thematic notion of a flower as blue or a cookie as delicious at the moment prior to the separation of subject and object, but this need not be a problem for Nishida. After all, the sense-data needed to make that judgment is provided as it is, in its most clear state, for us to impress the correct concepts or names upon after the fact of pure experience. As Nishida states, a veridical judgment does not "add" anything that is not already present in an experience (IG: 9). So, in theory, could not Nishida—like some of the empiricists of lore—just shrug off any distinctions between pre-reflective and "meaningless" experience and meaning-laden judgments by appealing to some notion of applying the correct concept or name to what is already given in sensual experience? Certainly this would not be possible in pure experience, i.e., the state in which subject and object are joined together, but after this state has been lost and individuated self-consciousness arises, what is to stop us from making judgments or applying concepts or names to it after the fact? Perhaps, in the end, could we not say that the only difference between Nishida and, for instance, George Berkeley's (1685–1753) nominalist position, would be that Nishida attempts to more thematically focus on the importance of said pre-reflective states of experience and, in doing so, account for experience before we have applied the proper names to what has appeared before us? The answer to both questions is "no" for two reasons I will outline below.

First, while it may seem to make sense to ascribe to Nishida some theory or other of what is "given" as a basis for explaining how meaning can be generated outgoing from mute pure experience, it is not entirely clear what that would entail (or if we "see" the same scenery in pre-reflective pure experience and after making such judgments). Indeed, among all of the difficult questions hidden with *Inquiry,* the matter of precisely *what* is given in pure experience has often gone overlooked and, thus, remains murky. Is pure experience a "snapshot" of things precisely as they are? That is, could we not think of it as a pristine view of sense data that is far too rich to be captured by mere concepts or language?[3] It certainly seems as though many interpreters have viewed Nishida in this light.[4] Or, alternatively, is pure experience a chaotic and anonymous flux that we cannot grasp? Nishida's infatuation with William James's psychology has been well-documented, and he provides similar examples of pure experience in which we find a "that" prior to a "what."[5] For instance, Nishida clearly describes the consciousness of an infant as "a chaotic unity in which even the distinction between light and darkness is unclear" (IG: 6). Keeping in mind that there is no decisive textual evidence for one or the other, we are left with several questions when considering what is given in pure experience. Can these two visions of pure experience fit together somehow? Is there another way of conceiving what is given in pure experience aside from either of these two options? Would any theory of what is given in pure experience provide an answer as to where meaning comes from? There is likely a kernel of truth to both of the views introduced here (or, rather, there seems to be a dialectical relation leading from pure experience as a chaotic flux to a pristine state of how things are), but this alone does not in any way make it obvious what is given in pure experience or how it differs from the kind of vision we have of the world in reflective and thematic self-consciousness.

The second, and more important point, is that a schematic in which the sense-data given in pure experience is thematized by a cognitive subject *is not actually possible* under Nishida's scheme for ontological reasons. Indeed, for many philosophers in the empiricist tradition, the thematization of pre-reflective sense data was not impossible, insofar as there is a *subject to which experience is given* that has the capacity to bestow concepts upon the things that they have been looking at or put them into relation with one another. As we have confirmed multiple times already, Nishida has already exorcised the notion of an independent subject capable of performing this action from his philosophy. In other words, our typical view of a flower gaining its status as blue because I, the epistemic subject looking at it, have judged it to be so, falls apart at a much earlier stage. For this explanation to work, we would either have to explain how such an individuated self-consciousness is able to stand "outside" of pure experience until it is called upon to make a judgment, or we will have to rethink how meaning can be generated without presupposing a subject-as-substance that can serve as such a repository of meanings.[6] In short, without an independent subject capable of serving as a manifold of sorts, not only do we fail to explain *how* such an act of judgment takes place, we also lose the most expedient source of bestowing meaning unto pure experiences that are said to stand prior to such concepts. All of this leads us back to the most fundamental question of Nishida's early philosophy: How can there be *any* meaning generated in pure experience without supposing an external subjectivity and, in the process, spoiling Nishida's most fundamental principles?

Given these discussions, we have two options available to us at this point (presuming that we are still willing to follow Nishida's philosophical methodology, of course). The first would be to simply dismiss anything related to meaning as a delusion of sorts and look at our return to pure experience as an awakening to the true vacuousness of our reality. In other words, we could realize that our individual self and all of the judgments it made were but a temporary impression that was made upon an otherwise indifferent reality. Our moral values, our connections to others, and our religious aspirations are all naught but a delusion brought about by the mistaken belief that there is anything in this reality aside from the fleeting moments that disappear from our view as quickly as they arise. The second would be to more precisely illustrate the ontological principles that explain how pure experience generates meaning *within* itself, without pre-supposing any kind of primordially given subjectivity to do this job. At any rate, the problem is clear. Nishida's philosophical methodology seems to lead us to the conclusion not only that there is a dimension of experience that stands prior to meaning, but also that (insofar as this dimension is "true reality") anything we conceive of as meaningful is actually a delusion. Hence, in the following sections, we will try to see how one could avoid this odd conclusion.

Motora Yūjirō and Direct Experience: Direct Experience, Meaning, and Inference

Before seeing Nishida's solution, though, it would likely be helpful to contextualize our investigation by clarifying both what kinds of ideas were in the background of these philosophical adventures and what precise conclusions Nishida wanted to avoid. Luckily, we can establish both points by appealing to Nishida's relationship with one of his most surprisingly overlooked forerunners (and an important figure in the history of clinical psychology on Japanese shores), Motora Yūjirō. Motora deserves a special place in our considerations not only due to his status as one of Nishida's teachers during his university days, but also because of the multitude of shared goals between himself and Nishida. Indeed, while his well-known pursuit of a "logical foundation" for his work later on in his career may often obfuscate this critical fact, the fact remains that Nishida professed in the days leading up to *Inquiry* that he initially hoped to establish his own philosophy on psychology.[7] This, along with Nishida's interest in authors like Wundt and James (presumably thinkers he learned about in Motora's classes), seems to indicate that there is some overlap in the resources and goals that he and Motora had while considering the relation between direct experience and meaning.

While Motora is best known for his contributions to clinical psychology in Japan—introducing psychophysics (i.e., explanations of psychological phenomena through physiological explanations) as a concept and conducting various clinical psychological experiments on attention and cultivation of personality—his achievements go well beyond the field of psychology. Motora was a baptized Christian who was educated in Confucian classics, and had formative experiences with Zen Buddhism in the mid-1890s.[8] He studied at Johns Hopkins University with G. Stanley Hall (1844–1924) from 1883 to 1888, learning not only about psychology, but also about the social sciences.[9] He commented on various societal issues and showed an affinity with early Japanese socialist movements.[10] He became professor at Tokyo Imperial University in 1890, lecturing on psychology until his death in 1912.[11] Most importantly, Motora has been described as a philosopher of sorts, with his student Fukurai Tomokichi (福来友吉, 1869–1952) calling him "a philosopher who took the form of psychologist" (cited in McVeigh 2017: 84).

Indeed, far from only engaging in experimental psychology, Motora's primary research motivation seems to have been his interest in how to conduct psychological research in the first place. While Motora may be best known for his introduction of psychophysics into Japanese academia, this does not mean that he would adopt a purely materialistic or behavioralist view of the mind. Rather, a great deal of his career seems to have been dedicated to rethinking the different "positions (系統)" one could take on psychological or scientific research, whether it be from an "introspective or subjective position (内観的系統・主我的系統)" or a "natural position (自然的系統)."[12] In contrast with certain trends one can find in the early clinical psychology of his day, Motora maintained a strong intuition throughout his career that the two positions, i.e., subjective introspection and objective or external observation of behaviors, were necessarily reconcilable.[13] Yet, while it may sound appealing to assume that what we see subjectively could ultimately be reconciled with objective observation from without, we are left to wonder how he can make this assumption. Is it really impossible to reduce psychology to purely external observations about behavior? Or could we not merely understand the human mind through good old-fashioned introspection? Most pointedly: what is the relation between our own internally accessible conscious lives and the externally observable actions or behaviors we take and, ultimately, can the two be reconciled with one another?[14]

For Motora (as was also the case for Nishida), a close inspection of experience thus ought to show us a clear picture of how the subjective elements relate to the "external" or "objective" elements of our lives. In search of such a concrete method of rethinking experience, Motora appeals to "direct" experience; a level of experience that stands before we have made any abstractions or assumptions about it. The following definition of direct experience will likely feel rather familiar to readers of Nishida:

> Anything that appears in our consciousness is an experience. Yet, in cases in which we see experiences as they are without any added abstractions, inference, etc., this is a direct experience [直接経験]. For instance, when I feel red as red, feel heat as hot, or feel hardness as hard, [these are examples of direct experiences].
>
> (Motora 1915: 316)

Indeed, those who have given *Inquiry* even a cursory reading will likely have noticed a striking similarity to the first few lines of Nishida's work. Direct experience is things "as they are (その儘)." In contrast, for Motora, inferences and judgments, which rely on concepts and meanings, are given as examples of *indirect* experience. We see the flower before we have made any judgment that it is blue, so we experience its blue-ness without any conceptual filtration or any extra-experiential signs or symbols. Alternatively, after we have stepped away from gazing at the flower and are asked to say what color we think it is, we are able to say that it was blue, even though it is not directly in front of us. More importantly, whether it be for Nishida or Motora, analyzing concrete, direct experience is posed as the goal for their respective studies and, for both, distinctions between subject and object are *secondary* to such abstractions. This implies that spirit and nature cannot only be reconciled with one another, but that views based in mind–matter dualism need to be reconsidered.[15]

This general distinction between direct and indirect experiences itself shows both a common starting point with Nishida and the overlapping influence of Wilhelm Wundt between them.[16] But perhaps more crucially for our purposes, this "starting point" is not the end of the discussion. Indeed, we see in Motora a lack of satisfaction with any simple distinction between direct and indirect that leads to a crucial problem. First, allow us to clarify what difficulties come with merely distinguishing between direct and indirect experience:

> While distinctions between direct and indirect experience may seem extremely clear at first, when we try to think of how they are different from a psychological perspective, we realize that this is not necessarily as clear as we [initially] believe. The reason why is because even if we say that inferences are indirect experiences, we still have a direct experience of inferring. We still have a direct experience of imagining [as another example of a seemingly indirect experience] wherein we

still feel red as red or hear a sound as a sound and thus cannot find a distinction between them [i.e., direct and indirect experiences]. In the end, these so-called direct experiences are things directly as they are while indirect experiences are the meanings referred to by these experiences.

(Motora 1915: 317)

This statement may sound fine at first, but we reach a significant problem when we look at both ideas presented in this quotation in tandem with what was mentioned in the preceding paragraph. If we follow Motora in admitting that there are direct experiences that stand prior to conceptual content or meaning and that, ultimately, even seemingly "indirect" experiences are actually given directly in *some* sense or another, we are left with a familiar question: How do indirect experiences, as those "meanings," even form at all? In the end, is not everything a direct experience? And if so, would not all experiences be "meaningless" in some sense?

Motora, not unaware of the problem this presented to him, chose to tackle this issue by massaging the distinction between direct and indirect experience in a series of papers published in 1906 (and later collected in his *Outline of Psychology* in 1915).[17] While Motora himself admits that his revision of this formula is influenced by both William James's notion of pure experience[18] and Mead's description of direct experience as experience we are having in the present moment,[19] his solution is ultimately a novel one. For Motora, this distinction between direct and indirect experience must be replaced by *complete experience* (自全経験) and *incomplete experience* (不全経験). Motora explains the difference by complete experiences as "moments that are able to exist on their own, without relating to any other experiences" (Motora 1915: 315–16) we have had so far, while incomplete experiences cannot be made sense of only by what is given in that moment and rely on a connection to something that has previously happened, will happen, or goes beyond what is presented intuitively. While this all sounds difficult, an example will help make sense of the idea:

Suppose that there is a desk with flowers on it and I have a visual perception of it [lit., I have a perception of it with my eyes]. At this time, when I vaguely perceive the entirety [of the flowers] and experience it as such, we could say this is a complete experience. The reason is that I have an experience that does not rely on any other experiences and can stand on its own. Nevertheless, if at this time I were to add an act of inference and judge that this flower exists objectively beyond my body, then this would be an incomplete experience. The reason why is because the existence of the flower and the distance between the flower and my body have not yet been fully experienced; these judgments are inferred through suggestions [示唆] found in my experience up to this point [経験中]. Moreover, determining the validity [of these judgments] is not possible through vision alone; for they rely on the movement of my body to measure out the distance [between myself and the externally existing flower], and my sense of touch for proof of [the flower's objective] existence.

(Motora 1915: 580-1)

For now, we will put aside the physiological descriptions mixed into Motora's ideas here and note that the mere fact of seeing red flowers on a desk, i.e., my acquaintance with the flowers, is something that requires nothing else to substantiate it. It is what it is, so to speak. But suppose I want to prove that the flowers are not a hallucination or a hologram and that they exist in the world beyond my vision of them. I would have to rub my hands up and down the stem, look at them from behind, etc. In other words, as opposed to mere acquaintance with flowers, making some kind of inference that these flowers exist beyond my mind requires connections between experiences that cannot possibly be complete in and of themselves.

There is plenty more that could be done to analyze this distinction and the ways it can be applied. However, what is important for our purposes is that Motora consistently claims that meaning can *only* be established through incomplete experiences relating to one another. The mere moment of witnessing the redness of the flowers before me in and of itself does not "mean" anything per se. Indeed, we can likely follow Motora in saying that a mere impression of a desk with flowers with no prior context or linguistic reference to what I have just seen does not seem to mean much of anything to a newborn. Yet, when I am trying to *recall* what color the desk I just saw was, or when I *think* about where I can put my paper for writing, or when I *imagine* how I could reorient my office's layout when I buy new chairs, then it seems natural to think of that mere appearance as a "desk" in relation to the other experiential elements present before me. In short, when we think of a particular object as "meaning" a desk, we can only do so after it has been put into relation with other experiences and the linguistic symbols formed therein. It is these relations that allow us to recognize and abstract the elements that constitute a desk from our experience, recognize it as an external object, and discuss it as a concept even when it is not present before our very eyes.[20]

So, the crucial point we have seen is that what we refer to as meanings are essentially abstracted relations between different elements of incomplete experiences (i.e., experiences that could not stand on their own). Yet, how do those "relations" form in the first place? Why do we not merely have one meaningless image passing into the next? Motora gives a two-pronged answer to this question. First, Motora argues that concepts are none other than the "relation of similarity or commonality between representation and representation" itself (Motora 1915: 371). In other words, concepts are none other than associations between different elements of experience that register similarly to our perceptual capacities (the concept of "horse," for instance, is the relation of similarity between the different horses we have come across to this point).[21] There are plenty of questions we could ask about what constitutes this similarity (some of which might not be answerable), but the idea is intuitive.[22] Elements of experience that register to us as similar are associated with one another. When these associations become regular, we abstract a relation of similarity between them. This relation itself constitutes what we could call a concept.

Second, regarding why these experiences would come into relation with one another in the first place (the pre-condition for us to abstract anything like a concept from experience), Motora offers a rather Jamesian view. Consider, for instance, the following description of complete and incomplete experience:

> Complete experience is something that does not rely on anything else but is self-subsistent; since it does not allow for any acts of inference nor expectation whatsoever it is a pure experience or a so-called "fact." In contrast to this, incomplete experience possesses a *fringe* and points to something else. Moreover, since the means that constitute its necessary conditions for development are naturally distinct and vary depending on its purpose, incomplete experience can, at times, take the form of *judgements, techniques [i.e., technology, 技術] or imagination*.
>
> (Motora 1915: 884)[23]

In the same way that James did before him, Motora finds experiences *connecting to themselves* through the dynamic process of moving to see what is on the *fringe* of our experiences. Again, I do not just see the table as a static snapshot. There are edges that deserve further exploration, an underside to be looked at, and various angles that I could take to gaze upon it. I can imagine it somewhere else or move it to another room. In short, there's always "something more" to the table that leads from one view to the next. Hence, rather than just having one meaningless snapshot appear one right after another, we are in a process of moving on from what we have seen to what waits for us next. Whether it be by touch, sight, or anything else, the exploration of these fringes of experience allows us to identify certain objects, recognize their future potential, or recognize the similarities between them and other experiential elements that we have seen in the past. In short, meanings and judgments form within experience by incomplete experiences coming into relation with one another.

To tie things up, let us consider one possible example. I am sitting at my desk, mindlessly staring at the red flowers in front of me. From the other room, my mother asks me if I have seen her favorite roses. I answer back that I have moved them onto the desk in the study before she comes into the room and takes them away to be displayed in the living room. Now, for this judgment that the roses my mother is looking for are right before me, we need to assume the following criteria are met:

i. I am currently having an experience of red flowers before me.
ii. I have had a previous experience of the same flowers in another room.
iii. I can recognize the flowers as belonging to the conceptual category of red roses. In other words, I see these flowers as possessing enough similarities with other "roses" that I can perceive them as such.
iv. I can abstract these roses from the whole of my present experience and imagine or think of them as being in other situations, such as on the kitchen table instead of in the study.

The idea for Motora, as far as I can tell, is the following: Insofar as my experience of seeing the flowers or having seen the flowers holds up regardless of whether my mother calls out to me or if I ever stop to think about what I am seeing, they are bare facts (complete experiences). However, to make a judgment that puts two facts together (that there *are* flowers before me and that they *are* the flowers my mother is looking for), I need more than what can be found in just *this* moment. I must connect two separate moments together (e.g., my current view of the flowers and my memory of their previous location) while relying on some kind of conceptual knowledge of what roses are and how they appear. These "concepts" do not come from beyond or outside of experience. Rather, they come from the different relations hinted at within experience itself; by the relations we find when we are compelled to explore the fringes of objects and gradually find out more about them, establish similarities between them and other like objects, and ultimately see what more we can do in experience. In short, we must suppose that this state of affairs was made possible by incomplete experiences being put into relation to one another before being made complete again in judgment.

Along these lines, we come to an interesting method of explaining how individual moments that are meaningless on their own (referred to by Motora as "facts") begin to generate meaning between one another. The inherent dynamism of consciousness, as well as the fact that there is always "something more" to encourage us to find connections between these different moments, is precisely what we need to look at when discussing the generation of meaning. Presumably, as these connections between experiences become more intricate, so too do the concepts we are able to master and utilize.[24] Hence, even if we are not directly perceiving something in front of us, we are still able to abstract certain connections we have seen so far and handle them on a conceptual level (e.g., we can report to our friend that our mother has stolen back her roses, even when the roses are no longer in front of us). This does not mean that we exit the realm of "direct" experience, but it also does not presuppose that we forced conceptual content or meanings onto consciousness from an exterior position. In this way, Motora manages to explain the generation of meaning in experience *without* assuming there is a pre-given subject looking at things from an "external" viewpoint.

Overlap with Nishida and Remaining Problems

Now that we have seen the core ideas involved in Motora's explanation of how meaning is generated in direct experience, we can see how his work relates to Nishida's early philosophy. Some connections will be obvious, such as Nishida's long documented fascination with psychologists like Wundt and James. Others, such as Nishida and Motora both insisting that meaning can only be generated by relations between different moments in experience, will likely already be visible with relation to the previous chapter. However, for the sake of clarifying what Nishida is trying to say, I would like to offer a brief comparison between his work and that of Motora and show some crucial differences between them. As we shall see, it is precisely these differences that clue us in to Nishida's core enterprise in *Inquiry*.

Before getting ahead of ourselves, though, we ought to highlight precisely what these similarities are. To be certain, we have seen in the previous section that Motora avoids the ontological problem of generating meaning in direct experience by showing how meaning is born over the course of the stream of consciousness. That is, Motora does not presuppose that individual moments are meaningful on their own, nor does he assume that there is a subject providing meaning from without. This general view matches perfectly with the quotations we have seen from Nishida in the previous chapter. Consider the example of the bell we analyzed before: As we have already seen, the judgment "this is a bell" in Nishida's work merely "indicate[s] the relation between present consciousness and other consciousnesses" (IG: 9). In other words, the judgment "this is a bell" is possible only when the sound that I am hearing in this moment is put into connection with the moments that have come before (my previous experiences of having heard a bell) or my expectations of what will come after (my decision to hurry up and get to school before class starts). This recognition does not come from somewhere outside of experience, but rather comes from recognizing that experiences connect and feed into one another. For Nishida as well, consciousness is a dynamic stream, whose changes bring us to find new elements and "meaning" consists of our capacity to identify and abstract these elements even when they are not directly in front of us.

An additional source of similarity between the two is a shared skepticism toward oversimplified distinctions between direct and indirect experience. For reasons similar to Motora, and partially owing to James, Nishida also refuses to admit an absolute distinction between inference or judgment and direct experience, noting that "the activity of thinking [itself] constitutes a kind of pure experience" (IG: 13). While Nishida at times describes meaning and judgments as states of disunity in which the "state of pure experience thus breaks apart and crumbles away" (IG: 9), seeming to set himself up for a strong distinction between meaningful states of reflective judgment and pure experience which stands prior to this, he is quick to follow this up by stating that such distinctions are actually only a matter of degree (IG: 9). Again citing James, Nishida argues that even the experience of relations must in the end be disclosed within pure experience and, thus, real (IG: 13). The upshot of all of this is that we do not have two distinct realms between what is given directly and what is given indirectly; in the end, all experiences belong to the same dynamic stream of consciousness that we refer to as pure experience.

As an aside, one may say that this vision of pure experience ultimately containing thoughts, judgments, and meanings could work for Motora but not Nishida. After all, the explanation given above seems to contradict the fact that Nishida implies that we separate ourselves from the domain of pure experience when reflecting on what has occurred previously and make judgments that abstract one element from the concrete whole of experience.[25] For Nishida, there seems to be a definitive difference between the state of consciousness prior to judging that a flower is blue or a cookie is delicious and the state of experience in which we are reflectively aware of such things. Moreover, in Nishida's case, pure experience is associated with cases of skillful performance; musicians, rock-climbers, and artists all achieve pure experience and "overcome" the kind of reflective consciousness that thematically judges "this flower" to be "blue" or the cookie to be "wonderful." However, even in these "paradigmatic" cases of pure experience, it seems that Nishida, in the end, avoids any absolute distinction between judgment and pure experience, for the simple fact that such judgments do not necessarily require us to presuppose any distinction between subject and object in all cases. As Nishida explains, judgments that have been made regularly no longer require reflection:

> When a judgment has been gradually refined and its unity has become strict, the judgment assumes the form of a pure experience. For example, as one matures in an art, that which at first was conscious becomes unconscious. Taking this a step farther, we are led to the conclusion that pure experience and the meanings or judgments it generates manifest two sides of the same consciousness.
>
> (IG: 10)

When certain elements of pure experience appear unfamiliar to us at first, such as when we come across an unknown object, there is a relative "gap" between subject and object in some sense (e.g., when we hear an unfamiliar sound and wonder what it was). The same holds when an object we desire is out of grasp (e.g., when the sugar cookie on the table is distractingly tantalizing us in our hunger). For Nishida, judgment or selective action take place as a way for us to close this gap between these two different aspects in pure experience (e.g., judging the sound to be a bell or eating the cookie both serve to regain unity between subject and object and allow us to lead our lives in peace). In either case, though, once an action or a judgment becomes regular enough to be conducted without needing to separate from what is happening "in real time," then these trains of thought and judgments can be made without any need for a gap in pure experience. The student can hear the bell, recognize it as a sign that class will start soon, and enter into a dead sprint for the classroom without any need to stop and think about what is going on. The meaning of the bell is, in a sense, experienced "directly," without forcing us to leave the present moment. To touch upon an earlier point, it is likely this process of mastery that allows us to account for both pure experience's dynamism and its descriptions as a pristine state of things "as they are."

So far, there seem to be no major differences between Motora and Nishida. In either case, we start with the intuitive distinction between direct and indirect experience and massage it until we see that the actual difference is between individual moments which are mute in and of themselves and experiences that have generated meaning by being put into relation with other moments. Hence, for neither Nishida nor Motora does the generation of meaning presuppose the existence of any kind of trans-experiential Subject or Soul, making judgments about the content of experience. To the contrary, both authors seem to collapse such distinctions between the inside and outside or subjective and objective elements of experience. We also see in the work of these thinkers a genuine debt to psychologists like James and Wundt, who showed how it is possible to base discussions about meaning, judgment, and truth on a psychological analysis on the nature of concrete experience. And yet, despite this proximity, there are two key points that separate the two which deserve close analysis, both of which will be explored over the remainder of the section.

The first point of contention lies in a disagreement about the nature of judgment, truth, and the formation of concepts. As we have seen, Motora relies heavily on concepts developing through *association* in his psychology, assuming that concepts form merely through the identification of similar perceptual elements between experiences. This is a point on which Nishida's more Hegelian tendencies distance him from Motora:

> The notions of pure experience and thinking derive from two different views of what is fundamentally one and the same fact. [...] From the perspective of concrete thinking, the universality of a concept is not what we usually say it is—that is, an abstraction of similar natures from something concrete. Rather, it is the unifying force of concrete facts. Hegel likewise writes that the universal is the soul of the concrete.
>
> (IG: 17)

Nishida follows this up in the next paragraph by making the following noteworthy claims about pure experience and thinking:

> Because pure experience is a systematic development, the unifying force that functions at its foundation is the universality of concepts; the development of experience corresponds to the advance of thinking; and the facts of pure experience are the self-actualization of the universal. Even in the case of sensations and associations of ideas, a concealed unifying activity operates in the background.
>
> (IG: 17)

Concepts, for Nishida, do not seem to form purely through the classical empiricist appeal to similarity or the physicalist's appeal to neurological processes causing our brain to make one connection or another. Both count as ideas that Nishida deemed bound for failure, given that any such associations would require some kind of "unifying force" to put them together in the first place. Hence, although it may be possible to approach Nishida's position from the perspective of psychology, the above-quoted explanations clearly separate him from Motora's account of meaning (despite the long-standing belief that Nishida himself fell into psychologism in *Inquiry*).[26]

The second point relates to another issue we brought up at the beginning of the chapter. Again, as Lotman has pointed out, even if Motora seems able to explain how meaning forms temporarily over the stream of consciousness, he does not seem able to explain how pure experience, i.e., the one true reality on Nishida's view, could ever be meaningful in and of itself. For Motora, questions about whether the entirety of reality itself was meaningful were not necessarily relevant to his procedure as a psychologist attempting to explore the nature of experience. Or, rather, looking only at experience and meaning "from the inside" seemed to run contrary to his project of reconciling interior and exterior views.[27] However, Nishida does not only want to explain how individual subjects come to *think* that their experiences are meaningful, but rather show that the meanings and values we experience are actually being generated within the stream of consciousness. If whatever meaning we happen to feel can all be written off as a psychophysiological phenomenon, then presumably any religious impulses we feel or desire to help someone naturally in a state of pure experience could also be described as little more than a "trick of the mind." A skeptic could say that these psychological states need not be related at all to any ontological claims, particularly about things like religion or morality, but are rather indicative of whatever psychological function causes us to feel that something is meaningful. If Nishida is to overcome such a view and show that there is a value to achieving a state of pure experience, he will presumably need to make a strong ontological claim showing *how pure experience itself* can be meaningful without taking an external standpoint.

In the end, the divergence between Nishida and Motora seems to come from the fundamental difference in motive between the two authors. As we have explained already, Nishida's goal was to explain only what could be derived from direct experience, i.e., to explain concrete reality while recognizing that there is no "external" perspective that we could take while discussing it. This seems slightly different than Motora's aims of reconciling our ability to introspect on experience with our ability to investigate it from an "objective" or "scientific" perspective. As a result, to say we develop conceptions of length or distance

Nishida's Solution: Concrete Universals and Pure Experience

In the previous section, we have introduced two seemingly unrelated difficulties to Nishida's philosophy via comparison with Motora Yūjirō. The first is that Motora's view of conceptual content and judgment seems to lead to conclusions that Nishida is hesitant to accept in *Inquiry*. Indeed, while his early work has often been accused of psychologism, it seems clear that Nishida at least wanted to avoid the same path as his psychologist predecessor. The second is that the scheme endorsed up to this point seems to render reality itself as meaningless; a mere fact appearing to our consciousness with nothing to give it meaning. With all of that said, however, fleshing out certain ideas regarding the universal in Nishida's philosophy that we saw in the last chapter can help us solve both problems at once. Hence, we will start with the first problem and work our way back to the second.

As we have seen, Nishida is not satisfied with psychologistic explanations of how association occurs within our consciousness. Yet how, for instance, can I identify "red" from concrete objects and establish it as a universal conceptual category on a Nishidian view? On the one hand, it seems safe to assume that some kind of vulgar Platonism wherein universal categories exist above or beyond what we can concretely experience would run afoul of Nishida's methodology, insofar as it would suppose something outside of pure experience. On the other hand, however, as we mentioned before, a nominalist viewpoint would also struggle, since we would need to establish some kind of criteria for how we become able to apply the proper names to particular things (and, again, Nishida is not interested in any kind of physicalistic account of the psychological mechanisms that cause us to associate things). Luckily for Nishida, however, there is an alternative:

> We ordinarily think we know the universal through thinking and the individual through experience. But apart from the individual there is no universal. That which is truly universal is the concealed power behind the actualization of

the individual; the universal is located within the individual as the power that causes the individual to develop. [...] The true universal at the base of the unity that is found in the activity of thinking therefore must be the concealed power that takes as its content the individual actuality. The universal and the individual differ only in that one is implicit and the other explicit; the individual is that which is determined by the universal.

(IG: 17–18)

Universals are, on this view, "seeds" that give shape to the individual. Universals contain the *blueprint* in the background of individual elements of pure experience, but (as an example) the particular shade of red that the roses before me take can only manifest itself as pure experience progresses. I did not have a conception of redness from birth, nor did I merely make it up out of thin air. Rather, the red-ness found in different elements that come together within my stream of consciousness serve as instantiations of this seed reaching its potential.

When we referred to "patterns" in the previous chapter, it is precisely this universal (expressed here as a "seed") that we were discussing. Put more bluntly, Nishida's alternative to transcendent, ahistorical universals and mere nominalism is to make an ontological claim about the reality of different patterns built into experience. While this tendency is certainly stronger in the middle of his career, even in *Inquiry* one could realistically take a view that universals like "blue" or "round" are *real* patterns that manifest themselves as they are given time to develop over time at different moments. Again, the core point is this: the red-ness of a flower is not merely something that I "subjectively" created, nor is it "objectively" determined by something that goes beyond experience. Red-ness is a pattern that is *implicit* in our experience until it has been drawn out over the course of our conscious lives. For this reason, when we deem the ball "red" it is not a mere fiction or product of our psychology: It is the result of reality's own developmental process.

Now, one may wonder how Nishida could possibly justify any claims about the ontology of patterns without betraying the philosophical methodology we highlighted in the previous chapter. After all, how could one establish that such patterns exist without exiting the scope of what is made available to us in direct experience? While this may indeed be difficult to do in a satisfying way with the information that is available in *Inquiry* alone, the basic elements needed to understand his ideas are present. First, using red as an example, let us see how we can assign meanings to different colors in *Inquiry*:

> In the establishment of reality, then, both a unity at the base of reality and mutual opposition or contradiction are necessary. [...] Red things come into being in opposition to things that are not red, and things that function are established in opposition to things that function reciprocally. When these contradictions disappear, reality disappears as well.
>
> (IG: 56)[28]

While the ontological claim about reality and contradictions could make this passage seem more difficult to understand than it actually is, the idea is intelligible once we have put it in conjunction with what we have seen so far. Experiential elements, like red-ness, exist as patterns by virtue of distinguishing themselves with other elements, like green-ness. As such, this pattern or seed of "red" does not "just exist," but rather establishes itself through differentiation with its position relative to other colors over the course of our experience. In short, as time goes by and change naturally occurs within experience, distinctions between red and green (and blue/orange, purple/yellow, black/white, etc.) will inevitably make themselves clear not through the external act of a cognitive subject, but by contrasting with one another and, in doing so, allowing themselves to be identified as patterns to be made explicit in judgment.

One may object to this example of color by saying that Nishida assumes too much and takes "red" for granted when colors themselves may be social constructs (and, moreover, there are languages and societies that do not even recognize such categories as "red" or "green").[29] However, to do so would be to miss a more fundamental point. Nishida is not making any detailed claims about how we establish detailed categories for different colors, but instead highlighting the fundamental fact that certain colors will always establish themselves through contrast with other colors (and presumably make themselves known explicitly). No matter where we draw the line as to what precisely is "red" or "pink," or whether we decide that these shades of red-ish tones are actually hues of entirely different colors, this does not change the more fundamental fact that what we typically refer to as red will *never* be next to any green-ish shades on any color wheel. No amount of color mixing with red will ever result in a reddish green or greenish red. These two shades of colors will *always* be complementary to one another, no matter what kind of linguistic framework we borrow. So long as this fundamental fact holds up, then red can establish itself and make itself known over the course of our experience by contrasting itself with green.

There are plenty of counterpoints that deserve to be explored and plenty of cases that do not work so easily for Nishida (some of which we will touch upon in the conclusion). Alternatively, I think we could clarify this view by comparing it to contemporary authors in the philosophy of neuroscience.[30] What is more important, though, is how this conception of the concrete universal, that which develops meaning through distinguishing itself through differentiation, does not only apply to particular concepts like "red" or "triangle." Rather, Nishida insists throughout *Inquiry* that concepts can only be made sense of because, at the foundation of pure experience, there must be some *unifying force* that puts different individual moments into relation with one another:

> According to empiricism, all of our consciousness develops through the activity of external objects. But if there is no internal a priori character to respond to the functions of external things, then no phenomena of consciousness can arise. This is like a seed: no matter how it is nurtured from without, it cannot become a plant unless it has the power of growth within itself. It is also true of course that no plant grows if there is only a seed. […] The activity of true reality is the self-development of a peerless entity; distinctions between the internal and the external and the active and the passive are formulated by thinking in order to explain that development.
>
> (IG: 53)

In the end, for Nishida, pure experience—the one true reality—is the *ultimate* unifier or concrete universal insofar as it is precisely what presents itself in different ways in each and every conscious moment. It is the "seed" that grows through manifesting itself in our individual experiences. These moments, the individual experiences that make up the entirety of our conscious lives, are precisely what helps us make judgments about, and draw out the meaning of, the world we live in and they all derive from the same universal function. Crucially, in the same way that distinctions between "red" and "green" are not fictions we create psychologically or properties of external objects, the meaning of pure experience itself and the judgments we make about it are not just a mirage. They are part of the process in which the "great system of consciousness develops and actualizes itself" (IG: 16) by resolving the conflicts and contradictions (e.g., distinctions between red and green, etc.) that arise within lived experience. Hence, in the same way that red and green make themselves known over the course of our experiences, so too do the structures of pure experience make themselves known by manifesting in each individual moment.

To draw on an idea that will be fleshed out in Chapter 4, a simple way of making sense of this idea would be to think of pure experience as being similar to a *mathematical function* or *series* of sorts. There is an internal logic to experience that makes itself known as it dictates how different entries into the "series" appear. Depending on the "values" put into the series of experiences that have come before, the shape that our present experience takes may certainly differ. However, this does not mean that the internal logic at play has necessarily changed. Insofar as the universal elements of pure experience establish their own meaning through their development in our stream of consciousness, we may conclude that this "function" (i.e., pure experience) is, in and of itself, meaningful somehow. Or, better yet, we may conclude that meanings and values lay dormant in this function and only make themselves known through its development. Again, this claim may seem odd, but the fact that pure experience has some sense of meaning or value baked into it is crucial for not only the methodological reasons discussed at the previous chapter (insofar as it helps guarantee that the judgments we make about pure experience can be "true" or "false"), but also in as much as it indicates that the experiences we enjoy on a daily basis are truly meaningful. In other words, those times that we spend gazing at flowers without thinking too much about them are not the disappearance or the erasure of meaning, nor are they themselves a vapid waste of time. Rather, these pure experiences (in the sense of a state of consciousness in which we have no thematic sense of ourselves as subjects in opposition to the world around us) are our chance to feel a deeper connection to the very structures of reality that produce such meanings and, as we shall discuss soon, profound ethical and religious values.

Even after this explanation, there are still plenty of questions left. One may still wonder—putting the methodological questions discussed in the previous chapter aside—how we can so easily make connections between the ontological claims Nishida is making and the remarks I have just made regarding ethical and religious values. As I just mentioned, more precise answers to questions regarding ethics and religion will come up multiple times over the course of the second half of this book. For now, however, we will walk away with the following conclusion. Pure experience is, in the end, not only the psychological realm in which we discover meanings and relations between different moments, but also in and of itself the ultimate concrete universal that continues to make itself known to us and elaborate its intricacies over the course of our lives. Those moments of pure experience in which we find ourselves in the "zone" during a sports match, giving the performance of our lives during a violin recital, or even staring at flowers blankly might not be experiences free from meaning, as we worried they might be at the beginning of this chapter. Rather, it seems possible to think that such experiences are the zenith of meaningfulness; a direct experience of the ultimate universal that makes meaning possible in the first place.

Tying Things Together and Facing Unresolved Issues: Takahashi Satomi's Critique and the Development of Nishida's Views on Facts and Meaning

Keeping what we have seen so far in mind, we can finally see how Nishida tried to avoid the possibility that the achievement of pure experience is little more than a reminder that reality (and our lives within said reality) is entirely meaningless without losing sight of his methodological principles. Much of what Nishida had to say in this regard appears to be convincing in at least some sense. Despite the constant assertions that his philosophy in *Inquiry* was, in the end, psychologistic, Nishida managed to make a sharp distinction between himself and psychologists like Motora. Moreover, to reiterate a crucial point, Nishida seems to avoid reaching the conclusion that pure experience is, in and of itself, meaningless. Instead, he shows it to be the activity that generates meaning in otherwise mute experiences. However, we have still yet to ask a crucial question: does Nishida's theory actually work? To wrap this chapter up, apply everything we have learned so far, and understand the deep-seated issues that Nishida was attempting to solve over the course of his career, we will revisit Takahashi Satomi's early and influential critique that Nishida was unable to distinguish between the facts of experience and their meaning, and that this somehow renders his philosophical project unintelligible.

Now, before getting into the tough details, a bit more context is in order. Written in 1912 directly after the book, Takahashi Satomi wrote the first critical review of *Inquiry*. Takahashi praises the work throughout his writing and shows a deep understanding of pure experience. His critique was nevertheless wide-ranging, covering all the core problems that faced the first and second sections (e.g., the ontological and epistemological elements) of *Inquiry*. While there are many different points that Takahashi brings up throughout the review, the root of his issues seems to start from the following core problem. As Takahashi points out, Nishida puts himself between a rock and a hard place by taking pure experience as both a "direct" state of experience, in which there is no discrimination between subject and object, and the one true mode of reality, which would include all types of experience.[31] Either pure experience is one particular state of consciousness that stands in contrast to "impure" experience, thus rendering Nishida's claim that it is the sole reality implausible, or we would have to explain how judgments about this one true reality can be formed without stepping outside of pure experience. Having come this far, we can surmise that Nishida rejected the first alternative and attempted to explain the generation of judgments and meanings (both about the content of pure experience and the entirety of pure experience itself) through a developmental process of self-differentiation (a point Takahashi himself seems to have grasped).[32]

Yet, as Takahashi reasons, if this is indeed the case, and "pure" and "impure" experiences are part of a larger, dynamic activity, then we are still left with a substantial issue. Takahashi starts with the familiar claim that Nishida is unable to explain epistemic fallibility and mistaken judgments and finds a more fundamental problem:

> From the standpoint of Mr. Nishida's theory of pure experience, epistemic mistakes will likely be a problem of meaning. Yet, he takes meaning and judgments to arise from the discrimination already present in experience. Otherwise, he takes meaning as the vector of development by differentiation [分化発展] and finds that which develops by differentiation to necessarily to be the act of an even greater unity. As such, it appears that he becomes unable to explain fallibility. [Yet], meaning does not necessarily need to occur through [the act of] an even greater unity, but rather must truly be that which refers to facts. Just as we can look up to the stars with our eyes here on our heads as well as looking up to the stars in the sky, we must [both] stand within the facts of pure experience and be able to transcend pure experience.
>
> (Takahashi 1912/2001: 319)[33]

The claim that Nishida is not actually able to explain mistaken judgments is noteworthy. If there is no difference between the facts of experience and the assertions we make about them, after all, the kind of discorrespondence necessary for a false judgment to occur can never take place. Yet, although Nishida might be able to avoid this particular critique concerning fallibility,[34] Takahashi is aiming for a more fundamental issue. Less worrisome than the issue of fallibility is its root cause. In other words, insofar as Nishida seems incapable of distinguishing meaning from facts. Indeed, as was mentioned in the quotation, Nishida's attempt to explain meaning as arising over the course of a greater unifying process does not work as *meaning implies the need to be able to transcend what is merely given in direct experience*, lest we be stuck in a situation in which the facts of experience merely mean themselves.

One may ask here why we need to make this distinction or what we mean by meaning transcending pure experience. Could we not just say that facts mean themselves and leave well enough alone? While it might be enticing to ignore this difficult line of questioning, doing so could cause us to overlook some crucial problems for Nishida's early philosophy. We have already seen

Takahashi reference the issue of fallibility, but this is not the only potential problem for Nishida. For example, in hallucinations, there *should* be a clear distinction between facts and meaning. Hence, we ought to be able to make a distinction between *thinking* that I am seeing a dancing elephant and there *being* an elephant in the room. However, if there is no distinction between my judgment that there is a pink elephant dancing a graceful waltz before me and the actual fact of the matter, then we are left to question what, if anything, separates veridical experience from hallucinatory experience (and why we would say the former is precisely veridical while the other would be, by definition, false). Moreover, as we can tell from this hallucinatory case, if we follow Nishida's scheme, we would not even be able to make a distinction between being and nothing (i.e., we could not even differentiate between merely thinking a pink elephant and its existence in our own new case) (Takahashi 1912/2001: 316–17).[35]

Now, perhaps there are ways for Nishida to explain hallucinations without going beyond pure experience (indeed, my assumption would be that Nishida would appeal to what others are experiencing as a way of broadening the system and searching out contradictions),[36] but there is more still to worry about for Nishida. For instance, when I say that 3+3=6, I have apparently gone beyond the realm of what is given in direct experience and seem to have started to speak purely in terms of meanings.[37] After all, these mathematical truths seem to be issues related to universal propositions that are, from the perspective of commonsense at least, not graspable in direct experience. Moreover, Takahashi raises the interesting point that saying 3 and 3 makes sense requires us to speak in terms of a potential outcome that has not yet made itself present to us in direct experience. In other words, we can ask how Nishida would be able to explain the fact that I am talking about a "6" not apparent in my present experience is not clear. All of these ideas go far beyond what I can deal with here, but the point stands: without a clear cut between facts and meanings, Nishida seems primed to run into various basic questions regarding mathematics and logic.

Perhaps more crucially, though, this inability to explain the difference between facts and meanings also seems to preclude Nishida from ever actually giving an account of pure experience as a philosophical concept in the first place. Consider that there is likely no end to the different directions in which pure experience could potentially proceed or develop. Insofar as this is the case, it would—at first blush, at least—not be possible to ever give an account of pure experience in general because pure experience as a whole will never make itself available as an object of cognition. Thus, any observations we make now could easily be contradicted in the next moment. In this sense, we would only have beliefs that have been contradicted and beliefs that have-yet-to-be contradicted, and never any universally valid or true beliefs.[38] Again, if the facts of experience can only mean themselves, then it seems difficult to explain how we could meaningfully discuss the whole of reality when we only have a limited set of particular facts set before us. The end result, according to Takahashi, is an extreme skepticism, wherein the further pure experience develops, the less we know about it. Speaking metaphorically, we could agree that just as "the area tangential to any circle will get larger as the inside of a circle grows, so too will the progress of knowledge generally increase the doubts we have" (Takahashi 1912/2001: 329; See also Wargo 2005: 54–7).

So, in the end, does Nishida's early philosophy fall prey to this line of critique? While I believe that a generous reading of *Inquiry* could potentially help Nishida avoid any of these individual cases, I also think that in some sense the answer must be yes. The reading of *Inquiry* I have proposed neither affords us with any way to sharply distinguish between fact and meaning, nor does it offer any definitive answers to Takahashi's examples. However, Nishida's ultimate response to Takahashi is as unique as it is crucial for our understanding of his project. After Nishida summarizes Takahashi's critique of his ideas on pure experience, he responds:

> If what I have said above is correct, then his [Takahashi's] critique is that [my theory of pure experience] cannot explain the origins of meaning and, thus, pure experience, as the facts that stands in opposition to [meaning], becomes meaningless, insofar as anything can be thought of as meaning or as fact. Yet, as I see it, meaning and facts should not stand independently of or in opposition to one another. In truly direct pure experience, we have fact-*soku*-meaning, meaning-*soku*-fact.
>
> (NKZ 1: 241–2)

The idea that Nishida is heading toward an account of fact-*soku*-meaning in *Inquiry* may not look impressive on its own and appears to be a non-answer to any of the questions we provided above. Yet, the usage of the term *soku*—a term that expresses the necessary interpenetration of two irreducible concepts—is something we should not overlook. As we have discussed before, Nishida outlines the ways that patterns make themselves present to us as experience develops by distinguishing themselves from their opposition. In this sense, what is given in any direct experience is ontologically laden with the *seeds* that will manifest in universal concepts later as experience progresses. However, this does not mean that the immediate facts are necessarily the same thing as the meanings that we derive from them. The two *interpenetrate* with one another, shape one another, and, ultimately, we aim to reach a state in which the two coincide, wherein we know experience precisely as it is and find the meanings that have remained latent within it. As we shall discuss in Chapter 4, Nishida regularly discusses universal "principles" that are common throughout each experience and make experiences commensurate to one another, made possible precisely because the meanings we find in pure experience are ultimately generated by the same universal activity.

Now, while there are still plenty of questions one could ask Nishida at this point, I believe this notion of facts-*soku*-meaning is enough for us to fully grasp Nishida's ultimate intention. This is true insofar as I believe it could likely offer a route toward explaining how abstract concepts like "nothingness" or mathematical statements like "3+3=6" could be explained within the framework of pure experience, granted that both notions like "nothingness" and "the number 2" would be grounded in the structures of experience.[39] But more crucially, it gives us a guide for understanding what it means to say that we find meaning in pre-subjective pure experience. For, as we have hinted at throughout this chapter, Nishida's epistemology opens the door to a dialectic in which meaning develops consistently over the course of our personal lives, but in very specific moments, aligns perfectly with the facts of experience precisely as they are. Nishida thus offers a way to explain how the unity of subject and object can give us an experience of a deeper meaning that stands at the core of experience. That is, in pre-subjective pure experience, we find ourselves in lock-step with the developmental march of the ultimate universal force that makes meaning possible in the first place, finding no difference between its activity and our own.

In the next two chapters, we will follow up these contemplations by examining Nishida's views on ethics and religion outgoing from pure experience. Much like how *Inquiry* was written itself, it is possible to read these chapters independently of what we have discussed here with regard to Nishida, Motora, and their respective attempts to create a radical vision of the relationship between meaning and direct experience. Yet, despite this fact, readers are encouraged to recognize that the considerations in the coming two chapters are likely made possible precisely by Nishida's vision of pure experience itself as a concrete universal; as a world that contains the "seeds" of any and all meanings and values, waiting to be fleshed out as experience goes by.

3

Individualism and Pure Experience

Interpreting the Early Nishida's Ethics with Reference to the Theory of Self-Realization

Introduction

Among the various points touched upon in the previous two chapters, perhaps the most intriguing is how crucial the existential aspect of pure experience is for ascertaining a correct understanding of Nishida's philosophical project. To briefly summarize one of the key points we have found in the first half of this investigation, the philosophy of pure experience was not a merely academic project or disinterested analysis of reality. To the contrary, for Nishida, philosophy was only valuable insofar as it entailed a thorough, radical reappraisal of the nature of one's very life as a self and place within the universe. An honest exercise in the philosophy of pure experience is thus not separable from the life of the individual conducting the investigation.

To put the matter differently, the philosophy of pure experience relates fundamentally to the concrete life of the self and its *development*. From the standpoint of pure experience, there was no pre-given and individuated subjectivity or otherwise the "possessor" of experience that we could call self. Such a conception of selfhood would assume a pre-given distinction between the subject of experience and the world this subject would see, which, as we have noted in the previous chapters, is entirely unforgivable according to Nishida's radical empiricist worldview. Instead, for Nishida, what is referred

---

Sections "Early Meiji Individualism: Fukuzawa Yukichi and Independence" and "Moral Idealism and Self-Realization in the Late Meiji Period" of this chapter borrow heavily from the following previously published article: Stone, Richard (2018). "Independence and Self-Realization: The Historical Background of the Early Nishida's Individualism." *European Journal of Japanese Philosophy*, vol. 3: pp. 31–56.

to as the self is instead the unifying force of pure experience. In other words, it is the primal activity that binds otherwise "mute" experiences into a coherent and meaningful system. As the dynamic activity of constant change in pure experience continues, subject and object are inevitably torn asunder. At this point, it is the activity known as "self" that seeks to restore their unity through either reflective judgment (i.e., unifying gaps between subject and object by identifying the nature of an unknown object that has forced an act of reflection) or the will (i.e., unifying gaps between subject and object by consuming or taking in the desired entity). Perhaps most importantly, though, is that this constant process of obtaining new knowledge through reflection and realizing one's volition through action was the key to the cultivation of the individual person and their respective skills (including their speech, conduct, etc.). Looked at in this way, Nishida's theory is not an abstract description of the universe in a vague sense but is instead a description of how the self—in its most concrete state—can be developed, cultivated, and ultimately achieve a good life. In other words, Nishida's ethics is a theory that emphasizes *self-realization* above all else.[1]

Even outgoing only from this exceedingly brief description, it is not surprising to see that Nishida's articulation of self-realization throughout the third part of *An Inquiry into the Good*—the part dedicated specifically to ethics—constitutes a major aspect of this book. While the title alone can quickly show us that ethics were of central concern to Nishida, of particular import is that this titular Good consisted precisely in a glorified account of the Good of the self. From a historical perspective, it is furthermore worth noting that Nishida's attempt to describe the life of self and the cultivation of the individual person in *Inquiry* had a noticeable impact on many early-twentieth-century Japanese youths. As we shall discuss in greater detail at the end of this chapter, future thinkers like Nishitani Keiji (西谷啓治, 1900–1990) and Kurata Hyakuzō (倉田百三, 1891–1943) were quickly enchanted with the way that Nishida approached such issues and saw within his philosophy a path to tackling their own actual problems. In addition to both these existential and practical concerns of his younger readers, one can also find in Nishida's early philosophy the seeds of the Kyoto School's multifaceted attempt to deal with matters concerning the nature of the individual.[2]

Yet, despite this apparent historical significance associated with Nishida's early ethics, it has often been dismissed as the weakest and least original aspect of his concept of pure experience. Indeed, one commentator has described Nishida's ethics as a mere summary of what thinkers like T. H. Green (1836–82) and Onishi Hajime (1864–1900, 大西祝) have said, claiming also that it has little to do with his overarching theory of pure experience.³ Putting aside the question of how fair this particular assertion is, we ought to recognize that there are important connections between Nishida's early moral philosophy and many of his important contemporary ethicists at the end of the nineteenth century. More specifically, Nishida's philosophy has often been associated with "the theory of self-realization (自己実現説)" for good reason. In other words, Nishida's ethical arguments, and many of the premises they make on self-realization is achieved within a communal setting, share core similarities with the popular Meiji position that started with the importation of T. H. Green's ethics into Japan and continued developing throughout the late nineteenth and early twentieth centuries.⁴

Here, we face a similar (albeit slightly less perplexing) question to those of the previous chapters. Namely, why is it that Nishida has been hailed as an important source of development for the Japanese individualist tradition even though it is—possibly—little more than a mild tweak on one popular theory among his contemporaries? Additionally, as an extension of this main question, it seems to me also necessary to clarify the nature of this position so as to identify the extent to which Nishida can be identified with this tradition and, moreover, contextualize the importance of the "tweaks" he provided to one dominant line within Japanese thought. Hence, my concern in this chapter is twofold. My first concern in this chapter is to highlight what problems Nishida was facing in the mid-to-late Meiji era and what influences shaped his theory. In other words, my aim is to sketch the debates in the background of *Inquiry* to become better informed of both the goals of Nishida's ethical agenda, as well as the parameters within which he tackled problems concerning the individual (insofar as there was a certain atmosphere that conditioned the way that any author of the time would address these problems). To achieve this goal, we shall sketch the genealogical line leading up to Nishida's ethics in *Inquiry* in the first two sections. Upon finishing this sketch of the framework that Nishida wrote in, we will move on to see if (and how) Nishida renovated these debates in the third section before revisiting the impact it had on young readers like Nishitani and Kurata in the conclusion. As we will see over the course of this chapter, Nishida's basic claims—that an individual achieves self-realization by joining with a more universal ideal—is notably similar to many of his predecessors. Yet, at the same time, I believe that Nishida's structural rigor concerning the nature of the self and pure experience opened the door for a level of detail not previously provided by any other Meiji authors was a noticeable difference between the two sides. Keeping this two-pronged enterprise in mind, we shall look over Nishida's texts for signs of possible new or unique developments in the greater scheme of modern Japanese ethics.

Early Meiji Individualism: Fukuzawa Yukichi and Independence

To begin, we should recognize that public discourse regarding what we could call "individualism" (in the narrow sense of the word) was quite limited in Japan before the Meiji period. Indeed, if one were to refer to individualism as a position that argues for the necessity of recognizing (1) equality among individuals, (2) independence and autonomy of these individuals, and (3) the innate importance of individuals, then it would be rather difficult to find something quite the same in pre-Meiji Japanese intellectual discourse. To be more specific, as authors like Nakamura Hajime (1964: 333–5) claim, the Japanese emphasis on the individual's embedding in various vertical relationships acted as a barrier to recognizing inherent equality amongst individuals. By that same token, George Sansom (1984: 59–76) notes that pre-Meiji Japanese ethics lacked what he calls a "liberal tradition," insofar as there were seemingly no systematic efforts to fight for equal tolerance amongst individuals with different preferences. Indeed, as one can see in the analyses of Douglas R. Howland (2001: 94–121), even the linguistic framework for discussing concepts like individuals (個人), rights (権利), and freedom or liberty (自由) developed only in the middle of the nineteenth century and did not settle until the mid-Meiji. Obviously, exceptions to these blanket statements exist, even if we do not have time to give them the space they deserve.[5] Moreover, we should not dismiss the possibility that individuality may have been conceived of in a way different in pre-Perry Japan than it was in the European or American traditions.[6] With that said, however, there is truth to the idea Meiji discussions of individualism added new ideas to the Japanese intellectual canon.

At any rate, the earliest Meiji motive to tackle the problems of individual autonomy and equality in the framework mentioned above was largely practical. After Matthew Perry opened the ports of Japan to the Americans in 1854 (which was soon followed by an onslaught of unfair treaties with the dominant Western powers of the day), plans to reconstruct Japan as a modern and centralized nation-state capable of surviving in the nineteenth century hit the ground running.[7] After the establishment of the Meiji government and the restoration of the emperor in 1868, these efforts took on an even greater importance. This is evidenced by the creation of mass railways and postal service, changes in tax policies and other large-scale reforms. It was in this context that theorists began to debate what was to be expected of each individual in a modern nation-state, with great help from the newly imported Western literature. In addition to the legal and economic queries concerning the limits of individual autonomy in a country shifting to a capitalist economy, closely related questions of what it meant to have a population of educated, self-sufficient, and morally sound individuals took center stage for early Meiji intellectuals.

It was in this context that the so-called enlightenment thinkers of the Meiji era, represented by groups like the Meiji Six (明六社, named to reflect the fact that the group formed in the sixth year of the Meiji period) publishing group made important new strides in the field of Japanese ethical thought. The group included figures as diverse as the man responsible for the term *Tetsugaku*, Nishi Amane, later minister of education, Mori Arinori (森有礼, 1847–89), or noted Confucian scholar—and later proponent of a unified sense of Japanese morality—Nishimura Shigeki (西村茂樹, 1828–1902). In general, members introduced and commented on moral and practical issues facing Japanese society in the nineteenth century and frequently taking hints from British or French positivist philosophers while doing so. This project included a large scale of issues, ranging from those as broad as equality between men and women to questions as specific as which form of writing (be it alphabetic Japanese or English) could best encourage public literacy. While the group was represented by both more progressive and traditional members alike, one trend among their writings was that Western learning, if practiced effectively, could help improve Japanese social policies and, thus, foster the kind of moral and responsible individuals one would expect of a modern nation-state (Shikano 1999: 40–7).

Out of all these early Meiji enlightenment authors, the most radical, and hence noteworthy, scholar is none other than Fukuzawa Yukichi (福澤諭吉, 1835–1901). Fukuzawa was a leader in Western studies, having first achieved fame with his *Conditions in the West*, published in several volumes from 1866 to 1870. Fukuzawa adopted a radically individualist view of how the Japanese nation should proceed in the new era. The preamble to *An Encouragement of Learning* effectively demonstrates Fukuzawa's thought:

> Heaven, it is said, does not create one person above or below another. This signifies that when we are born from heaven we are all equal and there is no innate distinction between high and low [...] Nevertheless, as we broadly survey the human scene, there are the wise and the stupid, the rich and the poor, the noble and lowly, whose conditions seem to differ as greatly as the clouds and the mud. Why is this? The reason is clear. In the *Jitsugo-kyō* we read that if a man does not learn he will be ignorant, and such an ignorant man is stupid. Therefore the difference between the wise and the stupid is traceable to the degree of learning.
>
> (Fukuzawa 1872/2013: 3)

What followed was an illustration of the pragmatic consequences of this truth, articulated both in *An Encouragement of Learning* (1872) and the later *An Outline of a Theory of Civilization* (1875). For Fukuzawa, the individualism present in Western liberal authors like J. S. Mill (1806–73) offered far more utility to the preservation of the Japanese state than did any efforts to cling to outdated and impractical customs. If anything, Fukuzawa attempted to show that Japanese politics up to this point had given far too much authority to a small group of persons at the top, who in turn deprived individuals of the autonomy which they needed to become self-sufficient. At the very least, individuals needed to be *independent*. This entailed, if nothing else, becoming responsible for oneself and being ready to defend one's nation (Fukuzawa 1872/2013: 19–27; 59–67). Yet, this was not possible in an environment in which individuals remained uneducated and restrained due to class-based inequality. For Fukuzawa, it was thus time to put an end to Japan's history of stifling individual thought and interests. Instead, it was time to allow individuals the right to pursue their various interests as equals while encouraging their education and cultivation.

Keep in mind that, insofar as the very problem that many early Meiji thinkers sought to solve was that of dealing with newly encroaching Western powers, individualism was not discussed as merely a moral problem. What we could refer to as individualism during this period was almost always discussed insofar as it was a necessity for Japan to become a modern state. Fukuzawa himself proclaimed that "the only duty of the Japanese people at present is to preserve Japan's national polity" (Fukuzawa 1875/2009: 36). Put differently, to maintain an independent and free Japanese state, it was necessary to encourage and educate independent and self-sufficient individuals. Individuals had to be able to act freely and responsibly and needed to be able to take up arms at a moment's notice—a feat not possible if individuals are entrenched in vertical relationships that prohibit them from taking self-responsibility. Thus, Fukuzawa's main goal was to demonstrate that the independence of the nation hinged upon the independence of individuals, in both the sense of protecting the country from external threats and the sense of maintaining public morals domestically. Fukuzawa's individualism was, seen this way, motivated largely by its relationship to the realization of a stronger Japanese state.[8]

In opposition to this pragmatic argument, opponents of Fukuzawa largely focused on two related points when assessing his position. The first point was whether such an inherently "Western" outlook could possibly be applied to Japan at all. Even the earliest comparative sociological research in Japan made it a strong point to emphasize the underlying notion that there was a key difference between the West—which took individuals to be the most basic unit of society—and Japan—which was centered on hierarchical family structures (Nagai 1954: 62). Moreover, many disenfranchised writers and artists expressed their frustration at those like Fukuzawa for their unseemly and un-Japanese preference for everything Western (Brecher 2012: 808–10). As we have seen, Fukuzawa himself seemed to be unimpressed with those clinging to the ways of the past and did not hide the fact that he found such efforts counterproductive. The second point was if individualism could coincide with the new government's project of centralization. While Fukuzawa was, above all else, interested in the independence of the nation, he was openly critical of government invasion into the lives of individuals and claimed that it was counterproductive to their independence. However, conservative writers for the entirety of the Meiji period often emphasized terms like "loyalty" to stress that the needs of the state came first (Paramore 2009: 141–2). Needless to say, the Meiji government itself also seemed to be wary of giving up too much control over to individuals, and thus viewed liberal or individualist enlightenment writings with suspicion.[9]

Although this introduction is far too brief to provide any new knowledge concerning the problem of individualism during the early enlightenment years of the Meiji period, I believe it is still possible to say that we have at least seen the basic questions and positions that were present at the start of the era. For our purposes, we must merely recognize that Fukuzawa outlined the way in which the new Japanese state could benefit from the emphasis of individual empowerment while using Western liberal sources as a guide while his opposition questioned whether such sources were detrimental to Japan's situation. Crucially, this back and forth created the general framework for how to debate the topic of individualism. Was individualism beneficial to the state of Japan as a means of self-strengthening? Or was it destructive to national unity and Japanese culture? Was an emphasis on the individual key to survival in the nineteenth century or a betrayal of the state? The shape of this debate itself influenced Meiji debates throughout the era, well beyond just Fukuzawa and the other early enlightenment thinkers. While we do not have time to discuss the various movements which spawned from Fukuzawa's work, we ought to note that the general framework of emphasizing individual cultivation for national independence remained highly influential throughout the era.

Moral Idealism and Self-Realization in the Late Meiji Period

To be certain, major changes did occur between the importation of enlightenment philosophies in the late 1860s and early 1870s and the shift toward the mid-to-late Meiji era. As the Meiji government began to stabilize from the 1880s onward, the intellectual demands of the Japanese population began to change as well. More specifically, as Japanese domestic policy began to settle and it became clear that Japan would finally have a constitution of her own, there was a sense that Japan had finally become a "nation among civilized nations (文明国の一国)." (Gluck 1985: 21) As a result, a wave of national pride swept over the country. At the same time, this awareness that Japan was getting ready to sit at the same table as the imperial powers of the day also brought about a growing conviction that the Japanese needed to organize their collective psyche. Early Meiji liberalism was thus gradually replaced with notions of national morality (国民道徳). In other words, calls for an increase in scope for individual autonomy were often substituted with reminders that morality would crumble unless all Japanese had a common rubric for evaluating one another's actions.[10] The infamous "Imperial Rescript on Education", which announced that the pillars of the Japanese Empire were people's loyalty to the emperor and filial piety (忠孝), was implemented in 1890, and numerous discussions on education in the late Meiji period affirmed that these two virtues were the ground of all morality.[11] However, despite this emphasis on conformity, Fukuzawa's words still buzzed in the background of the era, reminding authors that if Japan were to be truly modern, she needed sufficiently modernized individuals. This left a puzzle: how could the need for independent, and patriotic individuals be reconciled with the need for national unity?

It is on this note that the position which had a more direct influence on Nishida's ethics entered the stage: the theory of self-realization.[12] Starting with Nakajima Rikizō's (中島力造, 1858–1918) introduction of Thomas Hill Green's philosophy[13] into Japan (beginning in 1892), advocates of self-realization would utilize Green's claim that self-realization necessarily benefits the "common good" as a means to champion individual moral cultivation without sacrificing the needs of society or the state. In this sense, we can agree with Hirai Atsuko's claim that proponents of the theory of self-realization were something of spiritual successors to Fukuzawa Yukichi, trying to find space for the individual self in a society dominated by conformity (Hirai 1979: 116). Looking at how this notion of self-realization developed, as well as how it was interpreted, will give us a better look at Nishida's intellectual environment. This will also show us the shape of the argument used by some authors to justify increasing attention to individual cultivation as the Meiji period progressed.

So, what are the basic tenets of the theory of self-realization? As the name may suggest, Meiji ethicists formed various ideas about the value of self-development based on Green's claim that the goal of humanity is the *realization* of each individual self's character and moral capacities in such a way that they furthermore contribute to the realization of other persons, i.e., contribute to the *common good*. While a full-fledged explanation of Green's theory (or a detailed treatment of how Meiji authors may have misunderstood, betrayed, or ignored certain aspects of his work) is not possible within the confines of this book, we should try to highlight the main ideas of his concept of self-realization before we discuss its reception in Japan. Now, the first point that we ought to account for is what Green means by self-realization. Green attempted to justify his theory of self-realization by claiming that the very possibility of moral consciousness entails that there exists an *a priori* determined ideal form of humanity, to which all individuals aspire (Green 1883/1997: 179–81). The act of realizing one's own capacities and aiming to achieve a better state is, for Green, equivalent to moving closer to a more accurate reproduction of this ideal human form.

> Through certain *media*, and under certain consequent limitations, but with the constant characteristic of self-consciousness and self-objectification, the one divine mind gradually reproduces itself in the human soul. In virtue of this principle in him man has definite capabilities, the realisation of which, since in it alone he can satisfy himself, forms his true good. They are not realised, however, in any life that can be observed, in any life that has been, or is, or (as it would seem) that can be lived by man as we know him; and for this reason we cannot say with any adequacy what the capabilities are. Yet, because the essence of man's spiritual endowment is the consciousness of having it, the idea of his having such capabilities, and of a possible better state of himself consisting in their further realisation, is a moving influence in him.
> (Green 1883/1997: 189)

In order to paraphrase Green's thick-writing, we should start by noting that the divine mind referenced above (otherwise referred to as the eternal consciousness or "God")[14] is itself precisely the *a priori* determined ideal human form alluded to above. Although as Green points out, no one has ever truly achieved such an ideal form or fully realized all of their capacities as a human being, we can (at the least) imagine ourselves to be in a preferable state to the one we are in at the moment. Given that we know this potential state to be better than our current one, we can understand that it is leading us closer to how we ought to be, i.e., toward our ideal state of being. This consciousness thus drives us to continue to pursue this ideal and aim to fully realize all our capacities or, in other words, to come closer to reproducing an idealized state of humanity within ourselves.

Now, although the pursuit of one's ideal form is driven by one's internal desire for self-improvement, it is not a merely individual task. As the individual reaches higher levels of self-realization, his or her desire to give back to society will strengthen thus that consciousness of one's ideal form "must at least keep the man to the path in which human progress has so far been made. It must keep him loyal in the spirit to established morality, industrious in some work of recognised utility" (Green 1883/1997: 184). The individual's contribution to society, moreover, is not one-sided. For Green, the *a priori* determined ideal is only recognizable to the individual as it is reflected in the society in which he or she lives (Green 1883/1997: 192). As humanity continues to progress, the greater social and ethical goals available manifest themselves to the individual and, hence, mediate his or her own quest for self-realization. In this sense, because society helped to form the individual into what it is—or otherwise helps the individual realize what it ought to be—self-realization is not possible outside of a social context. Hence, we can find a feedback loop in which humanity's progress helps individuals pursue their own self-realization, which in turn contributes to the common good of society (Green 1883/1997: 198–202).

Thus, we find in Green's philosophy a powerful tool for writers facing a tension between the increasing need for individual autonomy and the possibility that such a notion of autonomy may be detrimental to society as a whole, or otherwise that it would end in a form of selfishness that no longer has anything to do with the good of society. Indeed, the fact that Green offered a coherent way to affirm the individual self while emphasizing the necessity of a common good for its realization made him a popular philosopher in various corners of Japan. Possibly because of this, however, interest in Green's ideas on self-realization did not necessarily end at strict interpretations of his work. Rather, after the initial importation of Green in the early 1890s, several competing or original versions of the theory of self-realization began to spread throughout the Meiji intellectual landscape. One pattern which was particularly common in late-nineteenth- and early-twentieth-century Japan was to produce simplified versions of Green's thought in conjunction with the prevalent nationalist education policies. To be more specific, many nationalist writers started to emphasize the need for adjustments to Green's formula in order to make it more suitable to the local environment. Due to the general distrust toward religion (and Christianity in particular) in late Meiji Japan,[15] it was preferable for many authors to replace Green's notion of an eternal consciousness (and the Christian undertones it entails) with the loyalty and filial relations stipulated in the "Rescript" (Hirai 1979: 118). In this way, some writers essentially came to equate individual self-realization with being a good member of the Japanese state. This was furthermore compounded by a seeming neglect for Green's more robust discussions of the political consequences of his own thought, which provided a more nuanced picture of the dynamic between the individual's pursuit of self-realization and society. While Green himself took seriously the problem of what kind of rights, public property, and social resistance were necessary for an individual to attempt to more fully realize the capacities needed for moral progress in texts such as "Different Senses of 'Freedom' as Applied to Will and the Moral Progress of Man" and "Lectures on the Principles of Political Obligation," many Meiji authors were content to accept the simple formula that the self-realization of the individual benefited the common good.[16] Or, rather, we could even say that few authors actually attempted to critically assess what was entailed by the common good, presuming it to mean something along the line of contributing to national strength or order (which was not the case in Green's work).[17] Because this formulation was so easy to understand, these nationalist readings would spread so far as to be circulated among lower-level educators (village scholars, to borrow Hirai's terminology), and thus flood late Meiji Japanese moral education with a watered-down version of Green's moral theory in which the individual's self-realization was to be found by becoming an upstanding member of one's family and country.[18] The end result was something akin to a misreading of Fukuzawa's early ideas: More cultivated individuals helped the state, so helping the state was the fastest way to individual self-realization as well.

While these nationalist reiterations of Green may have left the most significant mark on Japanese history out of any form of the theory of self-realization, it is likely that the interpretations which used this concept of self-realization to criticize late Meiji education policies are of more interest to us. Although there is some debate concerning the extent of his connection to Green's philosophy in particular, it seems to me that Onishi Hajime's theories on moral idealism and self-realization can serve an important role in outlining the discursive framework in the background of Nishida's early philosophy.[19] Onishi's basic philosophical position, outlined in his masterwork *The Origin of Conscience* (良心起源論), seems to show this point well.[20] In contrast with the early Meiji positivist or evolutionarily inspired views and contemporary attempts to equate self-realization with one's role in the state, Onishi emphasized the fact that our conscience (i.e., moral consciousness as consciousness of duty or sense of right and wrong) could not be reduced to loyalty to one's nation, Darwinian or Spencerian theories of evolutionary developments in human civilization, rational self-interest, or any other "naturalistic" or "external" forces compelling individuals to act in one way or another.[21] Onishi instead argued that if we are to explain the fact that we have a conscience in the first place, we have no choice but to make a metaphysical supposition that there exists an ideal form of humanity and that we are teleologically inclined to pursue it (OHS I: 147–54). The upshot of this view in Onishi's educational policy was thus that encouraging only conformity to national standards or contribution to the nation-state was not enough to develop a strong sense of morality. To the contrary, individuals had to be left to pursue their own ideals for themselves.

The clearest application of these principles came in Onishi's essays on religious tolerance in education. As a direct response to those like Inoue Tetsujirō, who claimed that the Christian faith was dangerous to a unified Japanese national morality and should thus be left out of educational spheres—replaced instead with the values of loyalty and filial piety embodied by the "Rescript," Onishi counterattacked by claiming that loyalty to the state could never suffice as the basis for self-realization when educating young individuals (OHS II: 219–32). Indeed, evidently keeping in mind those who view self-realization as taking place through fulfilling one's role in the state, Onishi counters below:

> I do not think that any kind of nationalism that looks only at the state has any kind of solid ground [to stand on]. That such a nationalism will be far too narrow [in scope] is an essential block [that nationalism cannot overcome]. I do not think that this kind of nationalism could be enough to give people robust ideals or great hope.
>
> (Onishi 1921: 340)

For Onishi, if education were to be meaningful, it had to reach the level at which the individual could have the space needed to explore philosophical or religious problems. Just as we have stated above, there needed to be something more for these ideals to be met than what could be offered only by practical concerns. As Onishi stated elsewhere, education rested on our ability to create an "image" or "mirror" of what kind of person we wish to become through realizing our faculties (OHS II: 77–8). Thus, on Onishi's view, education needed to allow the individual to come into contact with the deeper questions of life and what precisely it means to be a human, and not merely urge on their development as Japanese citizens (OHS II: 71–9; 331–8). In this regard, as Onishi stated throughout his short career, any view that looks only at the state is bound to be self-defeating, granted that it could never allow for individuals to think about these questions for themselves and, thus, never develop a strong sense of right and wrong.

In this aspect of looking for something that goes beyond the state, we can find a new feature of Meiji considerations on the problem of the individual that (as we shall see soon) was highly important for Nishida. Now, scholars like Onishi who pursued a form of self-realization that went beyond loyalty to the state still justified the individual's position by operating within the framework of self-realization benefiting society as a whole. Moreover, if looked at on a surface level, it may even appear as though Onishi does not differ substantially from his opponents aside from the fact that he believes that allowing space for philosophical or existential questions is more conducive to educating well-cultivated citizens (with the only substantial differences between the two sides being that Onishi does not find Christianity to be harmful to this goal and that he finds current nationalist strands of education to be too narrow to achieve this goal). Although we will not defend Onishi or any other Meiji advocates of self-realization[22] from such criticism here, we should note that merely improving statist educational theories was at least not Onishi's goal. For scholars of Nishida, it is important to note that authors like Onishi attempted to see self-realization as something which has a value in itself that cannot be reduced to its usefulness to Japanese society.

Perhaps the most important difference we should keep in mind is that thinkers like Onishi were more willing to accept the religious or spiritual aspects of moral idealism as a *ground* for the correlation between individual self-realization and society. Although Onishi claimed specifically in *The Origin of Conscience* that his philosophy of moral ideals and conscience do not require one to assume the existence of God,[23] he did leave open a path for a religious ground of society based on a larger human spirit (to which each individual is connected).[24] Even without relying on a specific theology, Onishi seems to imply that self-realization is important insofar as it implies a meeting point between the life of the concrete individual and the moral ideal that we must assume to exist in order to explain the very possibility of moral consciousness.

Now, to be certain, Onishi was not alone in utilizing a sort of macro-personality as a means to reconcile the relationship between individual self-realization and the benefit for society (to the contrary, he seems to have been much more careful not to align his ethics with any specific conception of God than many of the authors we will discuss in this and the next chapter). Indeed, while Onishi was cautious in discussing any possible theological aspects of self-realization, we shall see in the next chapter, many philosophers of the time embraced this notion of a macro-personal human spirit much more actively. Although there are plenty of philosophers to choose from, perhaps the best example of utilizing a macro-personality to unify individual self-realization and society comes from Onishi's disciple, Tsunashima Ryōsen (綱島梁川, 1873–1907). Tsunashima argued that having a religious consciousness of being one with this greater human spirit was a *necessary* component of self-realization. In his earlier years, Tsunashima seems closer to Green, even utilizing the term "eternal consciousness" to assert his understanding of God as a macro-consciousness, which he then affirms as the basis for the coincidence of individual self-realization and society. In his later years, Tsunashima developed a unique (and more radical) position based on "seeing God" to become conscious of oneself as a part of this macro-personality. To be more specific, Tsunashima argued in favor of a mystic consciousness of seeing oneself as one of God's children, which in turn allowed one to simultaneously achieve his or her own individual self-realization, while also directly witnessing something more universally human.[25] Although the terminology changed between his early and later years, the critical point we should remember is that the grounds for self-realization and its importance did not come from the state. Although it was beneficial to the state, it was in meeting with this more universal human spirit that grounded both the social value of self-realization and its worth for the individual.[26]

When we look at the way Meiji authors utilized this concept of self-realization on a superficial level, we find that the most basic framework in which debates concerning individualism took place had not changed from the early enlightenment years of the Meiji period. Insofar as all proponents of the theory of self-realization believed that the pursuit of individual cultivation was necessary for the benefit of society, their work can be considered as a revamped attempt to solve the same problem as their early Meiji counterparts, but this time by using new ideas on moral ideals to bridge gaps between individual freedoms and communal needs. However, we must also recognize that there were now new layers to these debates which would have allowed asking the deeper question of what it might *mean* for the individual to achieve self-realization. In addition to an emphasis on how stronger individuals would be necessary for a stronger society, there was furthermore a burgeoning sense that individuals required something *beyond* the state. Specifically, in cases like Onishi and Tsunashima, there were debates on whether the quasi-religious, existential aspects of individuality were necessary for self-realization (and thus necessary for a stronger society). As we shall confirm in the next section, it was in the context of just such a movement that Nishida himself attempted to carve out space for his unique ideas on self-cultivation.

Self-Realization and Contributions to Individualism in *An Inquiry into the Good*

Now, it is finally time for us to return to Nishida to see how these debates shaped his work and how he may have contributed to their development. It should not surprise anyone that the Meiji-born Nishida demonstrated an affinity for individualism from a young age, even if his early work mostly avoided concrete political issues.[27] Despite his early philosophical writings being markedly unpolitical in nature, Nishida greatly valued the importance of individuality and even seemed to harbor a great deal of respect for Fukuzawa Yukichi (see Yusa 2002: 64; Goto-Jones 2005: 52). What's more, Nishida was one of the students who took Nakajima Rikizō's earliest classes on Green and initially intended to write a manuscript interpreting Green's philosophy upon graduation (before eventually becoming disillusioned with his work).[28] References to Green can still be found plentifully in his work published before *Inquiry*. Finally, his respect for authors such as Ōnishi and Tsunashima could be found throughout his diary and letters. Keeping all of this in mind, Nishida's biographical interest in these topics as well as exposure to these topics is borderline undeniable. The question posed here, then, is not whether Nishida can be connected to this genealogical strand. Instead, our goal in this section is to evaluate how this framework shapes Nishida's text and what new twists he provided in *Inquiry* to find possible contributions his early work may have made to ethics in Japan. My response to this question is simple: Nishida's capacity to tie his ethical arguments together with his philosophy of pure experience offered both a philosophical backbone for his work and a window into the aesthetic or existential aspects of the life of the individual.

Before going too far ahead of ourselves, however, it would be beneficial to take a step back and give a brief, schematic presentation of Nishida's theory of self-realization before discussing what makes it important to Japanese intellectual history. While the following list is not an extensive interpretation of his early ethics, we should note the following points when discussing Nishida's notion of self-realization:

1. Nishida's theory of self-realization is complementary to his ontological and epistemological discussions of pure experience. As such, Nishida does not assume a pre-given individual person who then achieves the realization of their self. Although we may typically try to define individual things and persons in spatiotemporal terms (i.e., as being spatially distinct from other individual persons and things), Nishida denies this understanding of the individual person as a spatially discrete body among other individual bodies on the grounds that time and space are secondary to pure experience and, thus, should not be taken for granted (IG: 19). Instead, Nishida asserts that the individual forms through the development of pure experience. In other words, the individual is not given, it is made.
2. What does it mean for the individual to be developed or made? Insofar as I can tell, Nishida is referring to the process in which meaning is generated in pure experience. That is, when we come across conflicting information and need to make a judgment or find ourselves lacking the object of our desire or need, we reflect in ways that make the implicit relations between experiences explicit or otherwise perform an act to bring us closer to what is lacking in experience. These connections manifest themselves as the knowledge available to us and the actions and habits we can perform. It is likely for this reason that Nishida claims the individual to be one "system" in pure experience. The results of this system manifest themselves as the habits, speech patterns, and behavior of the individual who has amassed these experiences.[29] Given this fact, the act of developing the individual can be considered to have an ethical value in and of itself as the path toward the "perfect development" of the self and its faculties.
3. Note that the self-realization is not one ethical value among many but is rather taken as the good itself. Although Nishida's systematic dismantling of the other alternatives is too long for us to delve into here, the upshot of his analysis is that there is no other possible basis for ethics than what is given in pure experience.[30] As one might expect of Nishida's brand of radical empiricism, any theories of ethics that assume moral laws from without are doomed to failure, given that we could never ground any moral forces that completely transcend our experience. Following Nishida's methodology, we cannot admit any moral laws that we cannot have an experience of. Moreover, as we have discussed extensively in previous

chapters, any values and meanings that arise in our lives can only be the product of the self-development of pure experience itself and, as such, could only be discovered through an analysis of it.

4. Hence, as far as Nishida is concerned, reclaiming a state of consciousness in which there is no gap between subject and object has a supreme ethical value. In the developmental process mentioned above, there is a gap between how things ought to be (unified) and how things are (disjointed). As an example, if I am hungry, there is a gap between how I am (unfed) and how I would ideally be if I reunite with the object of my desire (e.g., a sandwich). For a more interesting example, consider a basketball player who must still think about her jump shot and remains focused on how her form ought to be in comparison with the actual act of shooting. Here, the player has experienced a gap between how things *are* and how things *ought* to be. However, a more skilled player, or a player who has entered the colloquial "zone," has no such distinction. In other words, there is no distinction between how they *are* shooting and how they *should* be shooting the ball. In this way, the disruption of consciousness provides a sort of distinction between *is* and *ought*. This distinction is then rectified in the achievement of pre-reflective pure experience. Put differently, the formations of the ideals that we strive for and the development of the self are based in the movement of pure experience as a disjunction between how things ought to be before their eventual reclamation of this state in the reunification of subject and object.

5. Keeping the points made above in mind, one may be tempted to accuse Nishida of selfishness, in that he seems to overly value the self, its faculties, and the completion of the gaps that halt its development over the needs of society, deliberation, the law, or other external forces that would typically keep us from doing as we please. However, as far as Nishida is concerned, this is a false dichotomy, given that the movement of pure experience does not limit itself to only one individual person. Indeed, as we have discussed before, one of the basic principles of pure experience is that it does not presuppose that experiences be held by the individual, but rather takes the individual to be formed within experience. Because of this observation, Nishida chooses not to limit the developmental movement of pure experience solely to the individual person. Instead, the development of pure experience occurs at the societal, national, and even cosmic level. In other words, the development of pure experience (the self) can only occur at a "trans-individual" level. The development of pure experience is

simultaneously the realization of the individual self and the realization of a trans-individual personal consciousness understood in its ultimate form by Nishida as "God." This concept of a trans-individual consciousness as God thus offers a connection between the Good of the individual and the Good of the community, thus providing a ground for Nishida's ethics to avoid charges of mere selfishness.

Looking over this abbreviated explanation, we can easily see that there are more than a few similarities between Nishida and the position described in the previous section. Perhaps Nishida's metaphysical assertions relating to the nature of the individual as something that cannot be merely spatially, temporally, or legally defined add new wrinkles to the equation. Yet, on at least a superficial level, the theoretical connections between Nishida and his predecessors bring them to roughly the same theoretical destination. First, we can see that in either case, the realization of the self requires the pursuit of the self's completion of its ideal form. At the same time, though, this is not possible as a solitary or selfish assertion of how one wants to behave independently from the state or the rest of society. To the contrary, the realization of the individual person and the ideal they pursue in either case is taken as the key to a strong society—as Nishida mentions, any society that fails to raise the individual is anything but a healthy one (IG: 137–8). Additionally, such claims are grounded by its relation to some notion of a larger, trans-individual self or personality.

I would also reckon that some of the weaker points of Nishida's ethics find their roots in Meiji period moral idealism as well. For instance, as we shall discuss in greater detail in the next chapter, attempting to illustrate a personality in terms of a "greater" unity seems difficult to permit from a methodological standpoint and may not even be an accurate reflection of what Nishida was "actually" trying to say. Additionally, our previous allusion to the fact that Green's very serious and concrete discussions of what legal and property rights an individual requires to be able to pursue the ideal form of their self were lost on his early Japanese interpreters proves to be true in Nishida's case as well. Hence, although one could certainly try to make a political theory out of Nishida's theory of pure experience, such a view would not come directly from the text itself. Or, perhaps better, the lack of concrete political discussions most likely makes it possible to deliver just about any political message through Nishida's early philosophy.[31]

With that said—putting Green himself aside—I do not think that any of Nishida's predecessors were able to introduce any comparable level of systematic *grounding* for their claims that Nishida had made about self-realization.[32]

Although it may be easy to look at the relation between Nishida's ethics and his ontology as coincidental or secondary (as we mentioned in the introduction of this chapter), I do not believe this to be the case. To the contrary, as we briefly outlined at the outset of this book, the argument for self-realization Nishida makes hinges upon the structures in which pure experience develops through the process of disruption and unification. The following quotation is rather long, but I believe it provides a window into the connection between pure experience and ethics.

> As discussed earlier, the development and completion of a thing is the fundamental mode of the establishment of all reality, and spirit, nature, and the universe come to exist by this mode. The good, conceived of as the development and completion of the self, amounts to our obeying the laws of the reality called the self. That is, to unite with the true reality of the self is the highest good. The laws of morality thus come to be included in the laws of reality, and we are able to explain the good in terms of the true nature of the reality called the self. Internal demands, which are the basis of value judgments, and the unifying power of reality are one, not two.
>
> (IG: 126)

While there is quite a bit to unpack here, I will be brief and only point out a few things that are necessary for being able to decipher Nishida's ethics and their contribution to the development of individualism in Japan. The first—and most important—point is that the connection between the developmental process of pure experience and ethics is not negligible. This is the case insofar as the movement of pure experience, i.e., the development of the self, is the only possible source of any grounds for non-abstract ethical values. In this way, Nishida's ethics find their foundation in the development of reality/the self and thus have a logical basis to support them.

Regarding our initial question of how Nishida contributed to the advancement of ethical thought in Japan, we can start first by pointing out how this logical formulation provides more suitable technical solutions to questions left unanswered by the popular discourse on the topic. The first of which is why the fulfilment of demands or ideals leads to positive or praiseworthy development in moral character. Here, we must remember Nishida believes that the development of pure experience is not arbitrary. Upon claiming that his own ethics can be considered a form of energetism, Nishida makes the following claim:

> Assuming that our consciousness is constituted by a synthesis of various faculties and constructed such that one faculty controls the others, then in energetism to

follow reason and on that basis control other faculties is the good. Originally, however, our consciousness is one activity, and a single, unique power always functions at its base. This power manifests itself in such momentary activities of consciousness as perception and impulse; in conscious activities like thinking, imagining, and willing, it assumes a more profound form. To follow reason means to follow this profound unifying power.

(IG: 130)

This quotation explains something Nishida states clearly throughout *Inquiry*—reason is none other than one aspect of pure experience's quest for unity. In other words, by seeking unity, pure experience seeks to put the different elements present in experience into a harmony (as opposed to leaving them in disjointed chaos). By extension of this, Nishida can argue that pure experience is rational by nature. Again, Nishida can make such claims in virtue of the fact that entailed in pure experience's tendency toward unity is an implied tendency toward harmony. Although conflict and contradiction are produced naturally throughout the dynamic changes that occur throughout our lives, pure experience always functions in such a manner that it integrates more information into a system where they can coexist with one another by means of attempting to reconcile these contradictions.

The second point that we ought to consider in more detail here is that this dynamic pursuit is—in and of itself—the process that gives birth to the ideals that we strive for and, in this sense, allows Nishida to attempt to provide a philosophical foundation for his moral idealism. Given that the state in which the gaps between subject and object (i.e., the conflicts and contradictions in experience) have been resolved is equivalent to reason, we summarily understand that such a state could be equivalent to the "ideal" state of experience.

Consciousness is not an assemblage of sequential actions but a single unified system. [...] Granting this, what is the order that is distinct in each of the various activities of our spirit? At lower levels, our spirit, like the spirit of animals, is simply an instinctual activity—that is, because it functions impulsively in response to objects before us, it is moved entirely by physical desire. But no matter how simple, phenomena of consciousness necessarily possess ideational demands; however instinctual the activity of consciousness might be, the activity of ideas is hidden behind it.

(IG: 128–9)

Putting these two points together, then, can help provide a foundation for Nishida's ethics of self-realization. As Nishida himself mentioned when stating that the laws of morality are one with the laws of reality, *self-realization is integrated into the very structure of pure experience as the pursuit of a more rational, ideal harmony*. The reunification of subject and object is—thus—capable of serving as the logical basis for a theory of self-realization. Conversely, prolonged gaps between subject and object and the discord they present run contrary to this harmony and are thus understood as evil by Nishida in his early philosophy.[33] It is here—in the logical grounding of self-realization in the structure of reality— that Nishida likely made his most substantial contribution to ethics in Japan.

To be clear, I do not think that this is the only notable feature of Nishida's ethics in comparison to his predecessors. Perhaps just as interesting as the logical foundation for his ethical ideas in the structure of reality is the aesthetic streak in Nishida's early philosophy. By this I mean that Nishida tends to romanticize ethics, valuing a beautifully led life over one of reflective contemplation or deliberation. Consider the following claims:

> Although they resemble each other, pleasure and happiness are different. We can achieve happiness through satisfaction, and satisfaction arises in the realization of demands for ideals. "Eating course food, drinking water, and bending one's elbow to make a pillow—pleasure also resides therein," said Confucius.
>
> (IG: 124)

> From this perspective, the concept of good approaches that of beauty. Beauty is felt when things are realized like ideals are realized, which means for things to display their original nature. Just as flowers are most beautiful when they manifest their original nature, humans attain the pinnacle of beauty when they express their original nature. In this regard the good is beauty. No matter how valueless conduct might appear when seen in light of the great demands of human nature, when it is truly natural conduct emerging from the innate talents of the person, it evokes a sense of beauty.
>
> (IG: 125)

Quotations like these hint at one overriding and—in some respects— problematic tendency in *Inquiry* to glorify non-reflective skillful performances for their ethical or religious value over acts based on careful deliberation. This claim can make sense, given that repeatedly performing an activity until it can be executed without deliberation can be considered a sign that one has maximized their potential (insofar as there is no gap between how things *ought* to be versus how they *are*). Additionally, as Nishida explains using the old concept of sincerity (至誠) or phrases like the most solemn demands of the self, this state reduces any conflicts between what one *wants* and what *needs to be done* (IG: 133–4). Yet I do not believe that it is controversial to say that this line of thinking leads Nishida to some difficult questions. For instance, we could easily come up with activities in which mastering one's full potential leads to a skillful or elegant performance that is not morally "good" in any usual sense.[34] In this context, the conflagration of skillful performance and ethical values leads Nishida to a potentially "trans-ethical" dimension of thought, wherein such aesthetic pursuits (for lack of a better term) triumph over our usual concern with social norms. Hence, although Nishida provides a logical formulation for how self-realization occurs, he does open himself to potential critiques. It is not without reason that Green himself insists that self-realization can only be achieved by reflection, insofar as it is necessary for thinking about all of one's self, others, and society.[35] Hence, without any fleshed out discussion of what happens when conflicts between (long-term, well-practiced) desires and laws/rules/norms based in discursive language, one is left with the impression that Nishida's ethics are restricted to dealing with the level of our lives that has nothing to do with political issues.

With all of that said, my goal in pointing this out is *not* to disparage Nishida's ethics. To the contrary, I think that pairing this aesthetic inclination with the aforementioned logical formulation is the most fascinating aspect of his early moral philosophy. This is particularly poignant when we look at Nishida in comparison to the burgeoning tendencies in the work of those like Onishi to move away from looking at the individual as merely one constituent of a nation-state. Nishida's theory of pure experience is interesting precisely in virtue of its inseparability from the life of the individual, not as a member of the state or as a moral agent or as the bearer of rights, but as a lived individual facing *inescapable existential qualms*. More precisely, Nishida's ethics provide a logical formulation for how we can understand the development of each individual in its most concrete way of being.

As was also partially alluded to at the end of the last two chapters, Nishida was not the only one with a renewed interest in the "internal life" of the individual. Takeuchi's (1970) association of Nishida's philosophy with late Meiji romantic literature is useful, given that we find romantic authors of the same generation expressing a similar interest in leading a beautiful life.[36] Yet, Nishida did not only account for this concrete aspect of our self-realization or aesthetic fulfilment. Instead, he provided a full-fledged account of its centrality to our lives and offered a path to logicizing post-Russo-Japanese War interest in the life of the individual. Keeping this in mind, I would like to hint at the role this mysterious combination may have played in Japanese intellectual history by looking at two important examples of authors who were inspired by Nishida's capacity to complete the separation of the individual's inner-life and its political life: Nishitani Keiji and Kurata Hyakuzō.

Concluding Remarks—Self-Realization in *An Inquiry into the Good* and the Troubled Young Men of the Taishō Period

As we have seen in this chapter, Nishida's early ethics can be better understood if considered within the framework of Meiji individualism. Starting from the earliest Meiji individualists, the need to juggle conflicting goals was immediately apparent. At once, self-sufficient, and responsible individuals (as well as the rights and freedoms needed to ensure their existence) were perceived of as a necessity for becoming a "modern" country. Simultaneously, though, the need to create a centralized nation-state with common beliefs was equally apparent. One popular response to this conundrum was the theory of self-realization, which emphasized that the actualization of individual goods was only possible insofar as it contributed to the common good. Nishida, who received his education in philosophy during the height of these efforts, likely inherited many of the same concerns when attempting to formulate his own individualism. At the same time, we have shown here two developments Nishida provided to this line of thought in early modern Japanese ethics: a systematic foundation for his ethical claims and an interest in the existential or aesthetic aspects of the self.

Considering that we have made significant efforts to highlight the technical contributions that Nishida's work offered, I would like to once again emphasize that these two aspects of Nishida's philosophy were not separate from each other. The notion that Nishida's *Inquiry* has been counted among the triumvirate of important titles for soul-searching young men in the Taisho (1912–26) period is a widely accepted claim. Indeed, alongside titles such as Abe Jirō's (阿部次朗, 1883–1959) *Santarō's Diary* and Kurata Hyakuzō's *Departing with Love and Knowledge*, *Inquiry* was a favorite among young men seeking to make sense of their lives in a turbulent time that featured an influx of Western literature and an upturn of students leaving their homes to study in larger schools. This was not by accident. To the contrary, Nishida's more rigorous philosophical assessments of the life and good of the individual seem to be what ensured his position in the collective psyche of young Japanese men. Among these young men who were influenced by Nishida's work we find the aforementioned Kurata and Nishitani Keiji, both of whom provide excellent examples for highlighting what it was about Nishida's individualist streak that made him so popular. To close this chapter, I would like to take a short look at both of their relationships to Nishida's putative individualism.

First, in Kurata's case, Nishida's *phenomenological* formulation of how the self is able to pursue its desires without merely prioritizing itself over the good of others proved to be the decisive reason for his interest in Nishida. Indeed, as Kurata himself describes, before meeting Nishida, a mixture of familial tensions bred a solipsist epistemology, focused entirely on the certainty of his interiority in contrast with the dubitable nature of other minds. According to his recollection, this created a vicious circle in which Kurata used his solipsist worldview to justify a crude rational egoism, devoid of any friendship or compassion for others. Even amidst the turmoil that this caused in his personal life, though, Kurata found in Nishida's philosophy a savior of sorts:

> I never doubted the notion that the individual consciousness of my [own] self was the most fundamental and absolute reality. I believed that, first, my self existed and only after that could various experiences take place after this. Yet, this epistemology was utterly mistaken. All of my turmoil, anguish, and the pathologies borne from them were contained in this mistake. The most primitive state of reality was not individual consciousness. That is one independent and complete natural phenomena. It is a unitary *Sein* with no such consciousness of self or other. It is the only reality. It is the only background. It is the spontaneous self-development of a singular experience. It is neither subjective nor objective, but is rather one absolute. Individual consciousness is not only something which is developed outgoing from the most primitive state of reality, its existence presupposes other selves to stand opposed to it as a necessary condition. For there is no subject that exists on its own without an object.
>
> (Kurata 1912/2020: 272)

As Kurata tells the story, it was this realization that helped him overcome his existential dread. Recognizing that individuated subjectivity is actually a secondary state to the life of the individual was what reminded him of the virtues of pursuing a greater unity beyond reflective consciousness: namely, love. This realization was so moving to Kurata that, according to him, his first meeting with Nishida's epistemology caused tears to come to his eyes (Kurata 1912/2020: 271). Putting aside for the moment the matter of whether this is an appropriate reading of *Inquiry*, Kurata's assessment shows an interesting facet of Nishida's contribution to early modern Japanese thought. The epistemological foundation for Nishida's ethics and his denial of the primacy of individuated consciousness gave weight to claims of love and unity between humans in ways that appeared otherwise arbitrary to the young writer.

Perhaps a more refined statement of the same feelings can be found in Nishitani's writings on Nishida. As a high-school student struggling with interpersonal relations during the same era as Kurata, Nishitani describes a slip into nihilism. While those around him fawned over the work of Abe Jirō and his exploration of the interiority, Nishitani seemed to feel the opposite: the more he reflected upon an interiority cut off from the rest of the world, the more he felt isolated and prone to further nihilistic tendencies. Once again, it was Nishida's epistemological foundations for his emphasis on the individual that proved appealing for the young Nishitani. Asserting Natsume Sōseki (夏目漱石, 1867–1916) to be similar, we find that the logical framework of Nishida's thought appealed to Nishitani.

> The pursuit of the self we see in thinkers like Soseki and Nishida differed from that of the generation that followed them. Theirs was a quest for the self that began from itself as center and reached outwards instead of simply turning further inwards in search of itself. For them, the more one probes the interior of the self, the more one fails to understand the self. It is something like a road that begins wide but branches off in all directions the further one advances on it and finally ends up in a swamp or disappears into underbrush.
>
> (Nishitani 1991: 8)

Contrary to the popular tendency of his time to contemplate the life of the individual self from a purely inward perspective, Nishida and Sōseki offered a differing framework. Nishida in particular gave a thorough structural account of what this entails and why it ought to be accepted. The philosophical underpinnings of *Inquiry* thus gave a voice to what Nishitani describes in his synopsis as an experience similar to coming out into a great clearing, free of any obstructions or hidden paths that obstruct our self-understanding. Once again, we find that the epistemological basis for Nishida's claims about individuality proves to be the decisive factor in spreading his thought in the Taisho period.

Naturally, these are only two examples. Yet, both point to a common conclusion about Nishida's place in the history of Japanese individualism: the simultaneous shift toward the concrete, existential, or aesthetic aspects of individuality and the schematic foundation of his theory of self-realization through pure experience worked in tandem to provide a fresh take on the life of the individual in the modern Japanese canon. To clarify, this new take was very much a response to the preexisting framework for discussing the realization of the individual person starting with early Meiji authors like Fukuzawa and, in this sense, keeping this background in mind can lead to a more fulfilling reading of his early ethics. Still, as we can see in the testimonies of those like Nishitani and Kurata, it was precisely the continuity with preexisting Meiji intellectual concerns that made Nishida's "original" contribution to discussions of the life of the individual self in modern Japan all the more compelling.

4

Revisiting the "True" Self in *An Inquiry into the Good*

As Seen from the Perspective of Meiji Organicism

Introduction

Once again, the conclusion to the previous chapter brings us back to possibly the most pressing issue at stake in *An Inquiry into the Good*: the life of the self. Indeed, there seems to be an intuitive appeal to the concept of the "true" self in Nishida's early work. The notion that thematic consciousness of one's self as an individuated subjectivity is a secondary state of being in contrast with our greater or true self is one of the most intriguing aspects of Nishida's early philosophy and an important reason for his prominence in twentieth-century Japanese thought. Although many early-twentieth-century writers and philosophers in Japan stressed the importance of the "interiority" regarding selfhood, Nishida set himself apart by instead seeking a "greater" sense of self. As was the case for Nishitani in the conclusion of the last chapter, we can see that Nishida offered an escape from the claustrophobia of being "stuck in one's own head" with a carefully weaved philosophical argument. To say that Nishida's notion of a true self was a crucial aspect of earning his reputation as modern Japan's first philosopher would not be an overstatement.

Beyond the fact that Nishida's theory of selfhood was an important factor in setting the tone for his popularity in twentieth-century Japan, though, this concept of a true self played an important ontological, epistemological, ethical, and religious role in Nishida's philosophy. Of course, even if we understand the importance of Nishida's theory of selfhood, the pressing question of what this true self amounts to still remains unanswered.[1] In response to this question, it is important to note something mentioned by Nishitani himself that should likely be obvious to readers at this point: part of the reason for Nishida's popularity in the early twentieth century was thanks to his background with philosophy in late-nineteenth-century Japan.[2] Indeed, as we have seen to a certain extent in the previous chapter, the concept that individual selves were somehow only a small part of something greater was not uncommon. Insofar as many Meiji authors argued that individuals were connected to their community via a macro-personality, we can borrow Inoue Katsuhito's (2016) terminology in noting similarities between Nishida's work and the "organic" view of selfhood and personality in late-nineteenth-century Japan. As we shall discuss in greater detail as we proceed in this chapter, this position was largely defined by a tendency to look at individual persons as part of a "living totality" that "unifies the various parts with their various functions" (cited in Inoue 2016: 17). In other words, this organic position took individuals to be "cells" of something larger than themselves. If we connect Nishida to this tradition, then our previous question can be answered easily: the true self would be this trans-individual, living totality in contrast with our usual, smaller selves. Additionally, for reasons that will become apparent as we proceed, such an argument could easily help one grasp the relation between Nishida's theory of selfhood and the religious import that he places upon it. Hence, given both Nishida's familiarity with late-nineteenth-century philosophy in Japan as well as his own tendencies to contrast the "small" self with our "true" self, it is not unreasonable to think that an investigation into the relation between Nishida and Meiji organic philosophy could be an important hint for understanding his conception of self.

Keeping this in mind, we will strive to achieve the two following goals. First, we will attempt to clarify the nature of this organic view of selfhood, as well as its religious consequences. Second, we will use this as a springboard to assess whether Nishida's notion of the true self (as well as the intrinsically related notions of personality and God) ought to be understood within the continuity of this organic worldview. To accomplish this task, we will proceed in the following order. First, we will start by introducing the circumstances in which the concept of personality developed in the Japanese philosophical world. Specifically, we will highlight the fact that this understanding of the self was spread significantly throughout the Meiji period in a large variety of authors, due in part to the popularity of the previously mentioned philosophy of T. H. Green. In the second section, we shall see how this notion of a trans-individual consciousness or self connected to what has been deemed as the organic strand of philosophy present in mid-to-late Meiji philosophy. To better understand this trend, we will look at how the relationship between a living and personal conception of reality and the individual persons that compose it as this theory was taken up by the most extreme proponent of this view, Miyake Setsurei (三宅雪嶺, 1860–1945). In doing so, we shall see Miyake's argument in favor of taking the universe as a greater consciousness, of which our individual selves are a part of and analogous to. With this background knowledge in place, we will finally be able to look at how this tradition related to Nishida's own concept of self in *Inquiry*. As I shall contend, while the vital aspect of reality was an important contribution from such organic philosophy, it is not entirely necessary to read Nishida's theory of self as being a mere statement of the relation between part (individual self) and whole (true self). Indeed, although it is almost beyond doubt that Nishida did endorse a greater unity with reality as a whole to some extent in his early philosophy, this schema of "big self" and "little self" carries with it a variety of aporias and runs contrary to Nishida's own methodology. In response to this fact, we shall unfold an alternative reading of the interrelated terms of self and God in Nishida that seems to me more in line with the methodology and spirit of *Inquiry*. Finally, in the conclusion, we will discuss how tendencies among his contemporary philosophers may have led Nishida to express certain ideas in ill-fitting ways and reference how these issues may have pushed him to develop as a philosopher. However, though this conclusion will mark an important step away from those like Miyake, we will see that there are still undeniable influences from his predecessors on his work that remained within him as he continued evolving as a philosopher.

Organic Philosophy in the Late Meiji Period: Self-Realization and the Virtue of Losing One's Self

Over the course of the previous chapter, we came across one of the more striking trends in Meiji ethical discourse: the notion that the individual and her community are connected by a trans-individual personal consciousness. In many cases, in no small part thanks to the prevalence of a very specific interpretation of the work of T. H. Green, this macro-personality was equated with the ideal form of our being; an ultimate endpoint for human consciousness. Regardless of the nature of this macro-personality (whether it be understood as "God," "the universe," "Japan," or anything else), the goal of the individual was to pursue their ideal form by attempting to achieve this ideal by unifying with this personality.

Given that we have already talked about the philosophy of T. H. Green in the mid-to-late Meiji period in significant detail in the previous chapter, we will forego any further in-depth analysis of this notion of self-realization. However, in lieu of that, I would like to point attention to the quasi-mystical formulation here between a bigger "person" or "self" and the individuals that compose it. Indeed, by the end of the Meiji period, it had already become apparent to observers that this formula for moral idealism had been co-opted with specific movements in the Japanese case. The writer Tomonaga Sanjūrō (朝永三十郎, 1871–1951) describes the philosophy of personalism popular among his contemporaries as follows:

> A philosophy centered on the Buddhist notion of no-self continues to exercise a broad and deep control over people's minds, while customs focusing on the universal retains its strength among people as a vestigial influence from the feudal era.
>
> (Cited in Inoue 2016: 16)

This was soon followed by the prediction below:

> Personal idealism will be trans-personalized or non-personalized as it enters our country.
>
> (Inoue 2016: 16)

Tomonaga's observations bring us to two important points. First, it has been often pointed out that—with some admitted exceptions—personalism in Japan shied away from emphasizing the importance of the individual proper.[3] Second, regardless of whether or not "customs focusing on the universal" can be so univocally applied to Japanese thought, there certainly was a tendency to link this unity between individual self and a greater macro-personal consciousness with the notion of losing or forgetting the self in traditional Japanese religious texts.

Here I would argue that this second point about the importance of losing oneself (and thus finding a greater self) applies to almost every important late Meiji metaphysician to some degree. Importantly, though, this trend manifested itself in the work of various authors with a surprisingly wide array of justifications. Kiyozawa Manshi, for instance, seems to describe in *Spiritual Activism* how the logic of co-dependent arising could act as the basis for a worldview in which introspection helps us realize that individual (part) and absolute spirit (whole) are immediately one with each other.[4] Tsunashima Ryōsen, on the other hand, provided a more phenomenological description of the three "visions" he had of God that stood at the basis of his religious philosophy.[5] Certainly, there were technical differences in how to describe this "greater self," with one pertinent example being that—while most major authors declared this macro-consciousness to be personal in some degree—critics like Inoue Tetsujirō split hairs over whether or not the "greater" self of the universe could be conceived of in this matter. However, even in cases like this, we see that such arguments appear to be more a matter of vocabulary than genuine differences in content.[6]

In the case of any of these authors, though, we see that at the center of this trend lies a distinct mereological claim: individual persons all serve to comprise one part of a greater, living whole (be it the national consciousness, humanity in general, or reality itself). Although it would be a stretch to imply that all the authors mentioned above shared the same view, it is not without reason that Inoue Katsuhito has included authors like Kiyozawa and Tsunashima as representatives of the movement we referred to as the philosophy of organism in the introduction. The rationale behind the name is simple: if the universe/nation/humanity consisted of a living macro-consciousness that is composed of to our smaller selves, then the two can be thought of in the same terms as an organism and the cells that compose it. Although not all authors employed this comparison, it appears to be an apt metaphor for many popular Meiji ideas. What is more—as we shall get into later—it is undoubtedly present in Nishida's philosophy. Given all of this, a more in-depth look into this line of thinking is in order. To do so, in the next section we will cover the thinker who most literally and extensively argued in favor of an organic worldview: Miyake Setsurei.

The Philosophy of the Organism in the Late Meiji Period— Focusing on the Philosophical Worldview of Miyake Setsurei

Miyake Setsurei (born Miyake Yūjirō) is perhaps better known as a journalist than a philosopher. In particular, his central position as a journalist with the (very briefly mentioned in Chapter 1) *Seikyōsha* publishing group is likely his most noteworthy contribution to Japanese intellectual history. In line with the overall goals of this publishing group, Miyake was most well recognized for his efforts to search for a Japanese essence that should not be uncritically abandoned in favor of Western habits.[7] Yet, even if he is not frequently mentioned as a philosopher in current times, we would do well to remember that he was among the first to expressly state his desire to articulate his own personal philosophical worldview. His effort to do so in *The Cosmos* (宇宙, 1909),[8] even earned him a particular reference from Takahashi Satomi as a "runner-up" of sorts in the race to become modern Japan's first original philosopher. In this section, we will look at this highly praised philosophy as a thoroughgoing example of organic philosophy, thus that we have a concrete example with which to compare Nishida as this chapter proceeds.

Now, even before *The Cosmos*, Miyake had already introduced the basic principles of his thought in an earlier essay, "A Brief Introduction to my Worldview" (1892). In this article, Miyake starts with two parallel processes between the individual's mind and body and the universe. These intuitions likely lie at the core of his philosophy, so we will review them here:

1. First, the dreaming (or delusional) mind is taken as the most direct form of consciousness and relates only to itself, cut off from the rest of the world and—hence—does not need to be logically consistent or do away with contradictions. It is a world of ideas only. The awakened (or otherwise enlightened) mind conflicts with this in a relative sense, insofar as it recognizes itself to only exist in relation to the objects about which it thinks and perceives. However, even if we say as much, the awakened mind as well consists of ideas. Moreover, although it appears to be relatively more consistent, we are often faced with contradictory information when we are awake as well. Thus, the two are analogous with one another.
2. Second, our corporeal body similarly appears as if it were an independent and distinct physical entity. And, insofar as it can move and act on its own, we can agree with this notion. Yet, at the same time, something similar could be said of the universe, which is similarly a moving and changing entity of which our body is a mere part. While it may be common to think of the universe as a lifeless entity, Miyake believes this to be a mistake, instead claiming that there is a "force" pervading throughout the universe, in which its parts (planets, stars, etc.) consistently change and develop, just as the cells grow in our own body. Once again, body and cosmos prove to be two analogous entities.
3. However, in both the "death" of the mind and the "destruction" of the body, all these relative distinctions are reduced to naught. Death is presented by Miyake as a lack of consciousness of discrimination and non-discrimination; as a state of freedom and release from the tensions that occur between mind and world, body and cosmos, or even mind and matter. The True, The Good, and The Beautiful were all to be found, for Miyake, in the slip into unconsciousness and the annihilation of such distinctions between small and great.

The worldview being presented by Miyake in this initial article is actually not too different from the dialectic presented by Inoue Enryō in the first chapter. There is an individual mind and body, which can at once be distinguished as individual while also being *analogous* to the whole in which it belongs (the universe).[9] Hence, the individual body and mind of our self is at once a *distinct* individual entity while also remaining part of a greater, *indiscriminate* whole (the "mind" and "body" of the universe, in this case). Yet, amidst these two contradictory directions, we see that "death" presents a quasi-mystical experience of doing away with this tension and bringing out a deeper unity between them (which is likely comparable to Inoue's middle path). This release from the distinction between the individual as an independent entity and as a part of something larger brings us freedom in its truest sense, as well as a view of what is True, Good, and Beautiful. While the lack of a rigorous defense of his ideas and methodology earned his early work criticism, these intuitions can ultimately be taken as the backbone of Miyake's organic worldview in *The Cosmos*.[10]

To start, a brief look at *The Cosmos* shows a defense of the two immediate assumptions about the universe needed for Miyake's worldview to work. The first is that the cosmos itself is active (and that this cosmic activity is orderly). In other words, Miyake's conception of the cosmos houses a vital power (compared by Miyake himself to Schopenhauer's will) that permeates throughout all of existence and causes the constant change and activity we see in the universe ranging from the degradation of atoms to the birth and destruction of planets. However, in contrast with Schopenhauer's blind will, Miyake's vital force is "rational" and "orderly."[11] Given that "it would be quite difficult to interpret the almost infinite amount of stars in infinite space all moving in a strict and orderly fashion as being meaningless" (Miyake 1909: 105), Miyake surmises that the cosmos is not something that merely houses entirely disparate parts moving independently of each other, but rather has an internal order to it. This seemingly indubitable orderliness of the cosmos was proof enough for Miyake of two things. First, it shows that we need to rid ourselves of the notion of a purely material, inorganic universe, which moves without any purpose or rationale. We can say this given that we would be hard-pressed to explain why its components avoid devolving into chaos without any underlying purpose behind them otherwise (Miyake 1909: 103). Second, the fact that these components were not capable of living outside of their relation to other components and the universe as a whole can motivate us to accept the fact that we as individuals are "cells" living within this orderly whole.

The second premise that Miyake acts on is that the universe is a determinate whole that can be compared with other organisms. While Miyake does accept the notion that the universe is an infinite expanse and constantly changing, he rejects Herbert Spencer's split between the knowable and unknowable aspects of the universe. Instead, Miyake argues that the structural similarities between the individual selves and the universe as organisms makes it possible for us to study this infinite expanse of space in the same way we would any other organism:

> That which we call the natural sciences is still far from being able to investigate the great organism known as the Cosmos. Yet, although at our current level of knowledge we are still not able to know the Cosmos, in the future we should proceed in a direction similar to how physiology and anatomy investigate the human body; we must research the formation and structure of this great organism. [...] The Cosmos itself is a great organism, a great living creature, and thus should be researched through cosmological physiology, cosmological anatomical studies, cosmological organ studies, and cosmological evolutionary studies.
>
> (Miyake 1909: 107–8)

As one can glean from this quotation, for Miyake, studying the structure of the universe by looking at its constituent parts is no different than studying the anatomy of animals by dissecting them and looking at their organs; although one may not be observing the organism in its entirety, taking a sample of cells can clarify the general functions of the organism (Miyake 1909: 105). Now, Miyake was not shortsighted enough to believe that his contemporary scientists were capable of this feat in his time or that using Earth alone as a representative of the entire universe would be good science, but on principle "cosmic-biology" was theoretically possible for structural reasons.

This claim about the relation between part and whole is our basis for a more refined version of the worldview proposed in the beginning of this section. Yet, in *The Cosmos*, Miyake also clarifies that this analogy does not work *only* between self and universe. The universe can not only be looked at in terms of a macro-organism analogous to our human bodies. It can also be broken up and looked at in terms of different levels. Our human bodies are composed of by various cells, certainly, but these bodies cannot exist independently. Rather, our individual selves are what come together to form a nation, and their cooperation is necessary for the state to function properly.[12] Similarly, one nation cannot exist in a vacuum, but can only truly find its purpose when it plays its role in the development of world history. This goes on, from the Earth playing its part as one planet in our solar system to the Milky Way being one cog in the cosmic order of our universe. Our individual selves, then, do not exist on their own. To the contrary, they are part of an "infinite continuity" that gradually increases in levels of consciousness leading up to the personal consciousness of the universe.

Crucially, in Miyake's case, this continuity from individual to cosmic consciousness is given a paramount ethical (in the broadest sense of the term possible) value insofar as it calls for the various individuals within the universe to preserve the order of things and to realize their own good life in the process. As we established in the previous paragraph, each level of reality feeds into the next and helps continuously greater levels of activity flourish. Yet, in reaching a greater level of unity with the universe, individuals are able to in turn flourish themselves. For instance, actively contributing to the healthy development of the whole for humans in their current form (this whole would typically be the state) is taken as the key to creating strong, independent, and healthy individual selves. In other words, serving their purpose within a greater society is the purpose and the Good of the individual self. Moreover, our connection to the universe is the only standard for which science and philosophy can judge the Truth of any statements they make, and scientific progress can only be made by continually learning more about its great expanses. Additionally, not only are its components (flowers, trees, mountains, etc.) stunning, but the Beauty of the vast expanse of space itself is likely a source of aesthetic captivation for those of us with the cognitive capacity to understand it. Keeping all this mind, Miyake declares that the individual self is not only born from the larger activity of the universe, but that its capacity to actualize any ethical, epistemological, or aesthetic needs is dependent upon its connection to said larger activity. Here is where we return to what in his earlier work seemed an insufficiently justified implication: the notion that "[t]he cosmos as an organism should be taken as the True, as the Beautiful, and as the Good" (Miyake 1909: 617–18).

If there seems to be a mystical component smuggled into Miyake's thought, then this is not at all by accident. To be more specific, Miyake discusses the mystical notion of forgetting one's smaller self (小我) to gain the greater self (大我) as the "subjective component" of organic philosophy (Miyake 1909: 109). While perhaps unsurprising, this quasi-mystical aspect between the various needs of the individual and the universe it lives in can clue us in to broader religious trends and conceptions of what we (up to this point in human history) have referred to as God. Although Miyake is critical of what is usually entailed by the term "religion," he does seem to wax poetic about the possibility of becoming able to join with the universe in its entirety someday.[13] Instead of insisting upon a notion of God as a creator or an abstract entity, Miyake highlights a dream for the future in which all conscious organisms[14] achieve total harmony with the greater consciousness of the universe:

> [J]ust as consciousness surpasses unconsciousness, [there will be] a macro-consciousness that surpasses [individual] consciousness. This macro-consciousness will connect the consciousness of the human species on this planet and that of equivalent beings on other planets. In this way, the supermen (超人) of this planet and the supermen of other planets will become able to clearly know the relation between the slightest movements of the self and the great activity of the cosmos.
>
> (Miyake 1909: 295)[15]

Hence, in Miyake's vision for the future, the smaller, partial consciousnesses of individual "supermen" will be entirely in tune with the greater consciousness of the universe, thus to the point that they will be able to understand even the smallest changes occurring within this greater self. There will thus be a total harmony in the infinite continuity leading from subatomic particles and the great organism we understand as the cosmos. As we will mention again later on, it is worth noting that in *The Cosmos* Miyake does not stress the annihilation of the relation between self and universe in the same way he did in his 1892 article, instead preferring to emphasize the unity between the two. Still, the point remains clear: our individual self is none other than one cell in a larger, common organism (i.e., the cosmos) as it constantly changes and develops itself and constantly seeks to find a greater degree of unity with this universal consciousness. This, I believe, is the most explicit and thoroughgoing example of one trend that—as we established previously—lurked in the background of a great deal of different Meiji thinkers.

Self and Religion in Nishida's *An Inquiry into the Good*— The Organic Interpretation

In the previous section, we looked through Miyake Setsurei's philosophy as an example of an organic view of the universe as a lived and conscious entity, of which our smaller individual selves are but one part. Following this theory, by means of abandoning our individual selves and joining with the infinitely great universe, we can come into contact with a greater, more profound sense of life, epitomized by Miyake in our meeting with the Good, the True, and the Beautiful. Such a view of self, person, and religion has often been—for good reason—attributed to Nishida's early philosophy. Indeed, there is plenty of textual evidence available in *Inquiry* to support this notion. Direct comparisons could be made outgoing solely from the fact that Nishida also compares individual person to cells in an organism in several passages (albeit possibly only in a metaphorical context).[16] But even if we choose to overlook these passages as mere metaphors, it is not difficult to see the influence of those like Miyake in the background of *Inquiry*. In this sense, reading Nishida in line with these organic principles is likely the easiest way to form a coherent reading of his early philosophy. However, I believe that a careful inspection of Nishida's early philosophy can hint at the possibility that he was not—or at least should not have been—an organic philosopher (or that we will at least find substantial methodological inconsistencies if we follow an organic reading). In this section, we will clarify the nature of these issues and explain how Nishida's conflagration of his philosophy of pure experience with the organic philosophy espoused by his contemporaries jeopardizes his philosophical endeavor.

Before highlighting these inconsistencies, however, I think that we should first start by looking at what this organic reading of Nishida entails. One immediately recognizable similarity can be found in Nishida's denial of any atomistic or primitively given individual self. Such an abstract distinction between the internal mental subject and the external world was not tenable on Nishida's view. Seemingly tied up with this fact, though, is the assertion that the individual person is a "small" or inauthentic self:

> Pure experience can, as discussed earlier, transcend the individual person. Although it may sound strange, experience knows time, space, and the individual person and so it is beyond them. It is not that there is experience because there is an individual, but that there is an individual because there is experience. *The individual's experience is simply a small, distinctive sphere of limited experience within true experience.*
>
> (IG: 19)[17]

This quotation seems to provide a clear image of pure experience as being "greater" than our typical "small" individual consciousness. Additionally, frequent references to the notion that we can find our "true" self by letting go of this "smaller" domain of experience serve to provide more explicit evidence that pure experience can be conceived of as a macro-consciousness, or the "whole" of experience of which we individuals are but a "part."

Equally important to this organic reading of Nishida is the central theme that the true self is not just a metaphysical supposition, but that the union with a universal consciousness (or otherwise, with the consciousness of the universe) carries with it a supreme ethical value. Similar to Miyake, Nishida argues that the various ethical goods of the individual were found in seeking a greater unity with the universe:

> Our true self is the ultimate reality of the universe, and if we know the true self we not only unite with the good of humankind in general but also fuse with the essence of the universe and unite with the will of God—and in this religion and morality are culminated.
>
> (IG: 145)

> The most profound religion is thus established upon the unity of God and humans, and the true meaning of religion is found in grasping the significance of this unity, *in breaking beyond one's own consciousness and experiencing the lofty universal spirit that functions at the base of consciousness.*
>
> (IG: 156)[18]

To continue with our metaphor of an organism and its cells from previous sections, the individual finds their true self by shedding off the barriers separating her from the rest of the universe as it is constituted by other personal consciousnesses. In doing so, she loses the delusions of existing as a separate and distinct entity, artificially cut off from reality. This allows her to awaken to the true nature of herself as something which is fundamentally one with the universe. It is in this harmony with the universe that the individual discovers a Good not otherwise accessible to ordinary consciousness.

Keeping the previous paragraph in mind, we can easily surmise that Nishida's notion of God could be understood as the universe itself. To summarize, we see that the universe itself appears to be a greater and lived conscious being (self) that embraces all individual consciousnesses. As Nishida states:

> Because our infinite spirit is never fundamentally satisfied by the unity constituted by an individual self, it inevitably seeks a larger unity, a great self that envelops both oneself and others. [...] God, the unity of the universe, is the base of this unifying activity, the foundation of our love, the source of our joy.
>
> (IG: 82–3)

> From natural phenomena to the historical development of humankind, there is nothing that does not assume the form of great thought and great will. The universe is an expression of God's personality.
>
> (IG: 161)

Read within the context of the previous section, these seemingly obtuse quotations become almost immediately intelligible. God, as the universe itself, gives birth to (yet is not separable from) all of the individual selves that constitute it. It is in this sense of embracing all living individual persons that we can view reality itself as an organism of sorts and is likely the reason that Nishida almost seems to endorse such an organicist worldview in the previously cited passages of *Inquiry*.

The above-presented reading of Nishida's early philosophy of self as being structurally similar to those like the aforementioned Miyake Setsurei is thus easy enough to follow. For clarity's sake, I will state that there are differences we have not touched upon. Nishida's more explicit references to religion contrast with Miyake's tendency to avoid referring to mystical experiences in religious terms. Additionally, there is an implicit anthropocentric streak running throughout Nishida's philosophy that is (at least superficially) antithetical to Miyake's interest in nonhuman lifeforms. However, at its core, the ample number of passages in Nishida's early work describing the "true self" as a consciousness of the universe—and supplementary implication that the consciousness of the individual is a "small" part of this greater self—provide sufficient textual support for adopting such an organic reading. Insofar as this is the case, it is likely possible to shift our conclusion from the previous section concerning Miyake's philosophy and apply it directly to Nishida's notions of self and God. Following this line of thought, pure experience is a living consciousness and any conception that we may have of our true self is nothing more than the activity of this "organism." This is, without doubt, one possible way of interpreting Nishida's theory of selfhood in *Inquiry* and has likely served to encourage a great deal of scholarship on his work.

Given the frequency of these passages throughout the text, it appears almost obvious that Nishida viewed his own philosophy as compatible with the kind of organic worldview espoused by those like Miyake. Yet, as I mentioned at the outset of this section, looking at pure experience in these terms may not be the foothold we need to get a fruitful vision of Nishida's conception of self in his early philosophy. If nothing else, even if it may be the easiest reading, such a view of self and God (i.e., the universe) may not be the most profitable way to read *Inquiry*. First, I do not see how such a mereological claim could possibly be reconciled with Nishida's methodological principles. To reiterate a crucial point, pure experience should not allow for empirically unverifiable or dogmatic assumptions. If the assumption that consciousness is individuated is considered empirically unverifiable, then why would the assumption that consciousness belongs to the universe be any more aligned with empirical reflections than the notion that it is inherently individuated? Miyake is able to make these claims about—for lack of a better term—small and great self based on his claim that individual and cosmos are somehow analogous to one another. However, any argument in favor of this analogy seems absent from Nishida's perspective.[19] Thus, we are left with the question: how could one ever ground claims about unity between the individual (part) and a universal human consciousness (whole) without taking an external perspective to see their relationship? This is a question that I see no hope for answering within the confines of Nishida's methodology in *Inquiry*. This raises several troubling possibilities. Did Nishida not take his own methodological claims seriously? Otherwise, did he employ them only when convenient for continuing his own argument (i.e., to deny a mind-independent world and pre-individuated conscious subject)? Or were his ethical/religious notions developed under separate rules from his ontological/epistemological theories? In this case, how do the two sets of theories relate to one another?

This understanding of our true self as being found in a unity with a greater self, i.e., with the universe, brings with it an additional theoretical risk that Nishida himself tried to avoid: the issue that we will call here the "double unity" problem. That is, if we look at the individual as a smaller unity (i.e., the unity of the individual's memories, perceptions, thoughts, etc.) and reality itself as a larger unity (i.e., the universal human consciousness we have referred to), then we run into the question of how one relates to the other and how the individual self emerges from the larger self.[20] Putting the fact that Nishida insisted that there are no two such unities to be found in pure experience aside, I am not confident that a satisfactory manner of accounting for such a dual unity is even desirable. The easiest way to account for these two selves, I suppose, would be to take Nishida to be endorsing the notion that the universe's consciousness gives birth to the individual consciousness, as Miyake had. Yet, doing so would likely bring Nishida uncomfortably close to the emanative approach that Tanabe Hajime (田辺元, 1885–1962) would later accuse Nishida of in 1930.[21] Moreover, it was precisely this reading of Nishida as advocating a smaller self appearing from, and desiring to return to, a larger self that led postwar Marxist historians to accuse him of advocating an Idealism that subjugates individual freedom to the needs of a larger national spirit.[22] Even if we assume that these political critiques miss their mark (whether it be because they are too abstract or too eager to draw certain conclusions), this dual-self reading still leaves us with an empirically unfounded access to the whole of the universe and Tanabe's questions of whether Nishida merely attempted to sneak religious quietism into what should be a critical philosophical project.

All things considered, I believe that these two issues prove themselves to be substantial problems when looking for a convincing reading of the notions of self and God presented in *Inquiry*. However easy it may be to understand these terms in the context of organic views of reality, a pseudo-mystic reading of Nishida's early philosophy is not likely to provide any substantial philosophical insights for modern debates on selfhood, at the very least. Naturally, as we have highlighted in this section, there is ample textual evidence to connect Nishida with those like Miyake and their distinction of a larger self in comparison with the smaller individual person, and I do not think that this is accidental on Nishida's part. Even accepting this, though, I think there is an alternative reading of Nishida's concept of the self that is hidden within *Inquiry* and it that can be gained by tweaking this easy reading so as to avoid problematic mereological claims about our small-self (part) and big-self (whole). Keeping this in mind, in the next two sections, I will highlight some passages that seem to me to point to another *possible* interpretation of Nishida before assessing how it became entangled with the reading we have outlined here.

An Alternative Reading—Interpreting Nishida's Concept of Self as a Function of Experience

Our first order of business in presenting this alternative reading is to accept the following disclaimer: a non-organic reading of Nishida's philosophy does not entail a denial of the quotations we have already looked at (for the most part, at least). My contention is that a more careful look at some of the keywords in the quotes given above (specifically, "universal" and "base") will be enough to point us toward another reading of *Inquiry* that can also abate the potential issues that arise in an organic reading of his philosophy and the questions of a second self it presents. To be clear, I do not believe that my reading requires any leap of faith or introduction of elements that were not present already in *Inquiry* to begin with. To the contrary, I believe that everything I will say here is completely consistent with what we have seen in the first three chapters. Still, we do need to recognize that Nishida himself appears to be sympathetic toward the organic view that we have attributed to his predecessors like Miyake Setsurei, and that the non-organic reading here is closer to a distillation of an alternative view of the self in Nishida's earliest philosophy than it is a revelation of what Nishida "actually meant" to say.

Now, the first and most important task for achieving this goal is to take Nishida's use of the words great or true self in unity to contrast with our limited, individuated self-consciousness as either a metaphor or a conflagration of ideas in the background of his thought with more worthwhile intuitions unique to Nishida. While it is certainly the case that Nishida asserts that there is a greater self in many passages (particularly those related to religion), his actual arguments on selfhood do not require us to introduce the entirety of the cosmos or any other secondary self:

> That consciousness must be someone's consciousness simply means that consciousness must have a unity. The idea that there must be a possessor of consciousness above and beyond this unity is an arbitrary assumption. The activity of this unity—apperception—is a matter of similar ideas and feelings constituting a central hub and as such unifying consciousness.
>
> (IG: 44)

What Nishida has done in this passage is provide a simple and effective argument against the typical assumption that we need to be aware of our own awareness (or, more poignantly, that there needs to be "someone" who is in possession of the experiences being had). As Nishida correctly argues, such an assumption is both empirically unfounded and entirely unnecessary to explain the concept of self. Yet, as we have mentioned in passing at the end of the previous section, to argue that there is a macro-self from which all of our individual selves arise would fall prey to the same line of critique. The lack of an individual owner of experience does not mean that we need to replace our typical notions of self with a "bigger" one. All we need, to use Nishida's phrase, is a "hub" capable of uniting our conscious experiences into a system and—in the process—establish the necessary context needed to identify myself as the subject of the current experience. In this sense, to assume that the denial of a pre-formed individual self entails the espousal of a greater self-qua-universe is to fundamentally miss the point of Nishida's critical assessment of selfhood. In other words, this hub does not need to be declared as either great, small, diachronically enduring, or momentary; it need only serve as the basis for tying experiences together and contextualizing our current situation.[23]

Yet, if all Nishida has done here is show that consciousness is not individuated, how can we understand his argument that our self is universal? As we have seen in the previous section, Nishida refers largely to God as the unifying power at the base of our individual consciousness and equates this unifying power with a universal human spirit. While one may naturally be inclined to read this as an endorsement that there is a larger, macro-consciousness from which our individual selves are born, we should remember that Nishida's usage of the term universal is very specific. Nishida explains:

> We ordinarily think we know the universal through thinking and the individual through experience. But apart from the individual there is no universal. That which is truly universal is the concealed power behind the actualization of the individual; the universal is located within the individual as the power that causes the individual to develop. […] The true universal at the base of the unity that is found in the activity of thinking therefore must be the concealed power that takes as its content the individual actuality. The universal and the individual differ only in that one is implicit and the other explicit; the individual is that which is determined by the universal.
>
> (IG: 17–18)

As we mentioned before, the universal is *not* merely an abstract category that exists beyond experience. Instead, the universal itself is described as a "concealed power" that is inseparable from—and can only be actualized through—its concrete realization in individual instantiations. In short, the universal exists as a pattern of sorts, which can only manifest when given concrete shape through the determinations of the individual over the course of our experiences.

Looking at the notion of self in Nishida's early philosophy while keeping these points in mind opens the door for what I believe to be a more fulfilling interpretation of his work. Conceived of in this way, what lies at the base of consciousness is not an abstract world-soul that contains all the individual selves throughout the world. On this reading, the "universal" aspect of the self would likely be something closer to the *structural framework* of experience itself; it is the universal features in experience that allows for the hub between individual experiences to form. Otherwise, to borrow a useful metaphor for this, I think that one could look at Nishida's conception of the self here as a universal "function" (in the mathematical sense) for experience that, once the values for each "variable" have been properly inserted, can manifest itself into particular experiences. In other words, the self (as we have established at the beginning of the preceding chapter) refers to various activities in pure experience that serve to unite the gaps that open up between subject and object (namely, thought and will) and—in this process—organize the stream of our conscious experiences into a meaning-laden system (insofar as it is, after all, this "function" which gives structure to content and allows for comparisons with other experiences). Along this reading, I believe that the *individual person* would best be understood as the product of this function—i.e., the product of a systematically unified system of meanings and experiences and—thus—does not "emerge" from pure experience or change in form.[24] All we need to admit is that the aggregation of past experiences gathered in a particular stream gives shape and context to present consciousness. This view can help us to better understand the claim made in Chapter 3 that the behavior, tendencies, and speech-patterns of an individual person reflect the knowledge they gain and the habits they form over the course of the development of pure experience.[25]

If this interpretation is valid, then I believe it is possible to distill a view of selfhood in *Inquiry* that cannot be reduced to an account of small-unity and big-unity. To the contrary, Nishida's true self is a mere hub that helps tie together experiences that happen to enter the same stream. This hub need not belong to one diachronically persistent individual or the entirety of the cosmos or anyone at all. In other words, for Nishida, there is a hub which brings experiences together, and only then does it become possible to contextualize an experience as being "mine" (quite literally, we see "that it is not that there is experience because there is a self," but instead that even identifying the notion of a self presupposes context has formed in the stream of consciousness thus that one is able to distinguish "her" experience from "your" experience). We may note here that being able to identify oneself as *one* individual with a specific perspective does not change the structure of the self or imply that it has emerged from a larger range of experience. Instead, it merely means that—even though distinctions between subject/object or self/other are not inherently given in direct experience—the stream of consciousness has picked up enough information in past experiences to make such distinctions. Looked at in this way, instead of solely arguing for a union with a greater self, there seems to be a significant attempt in Nishida's work to follow William James in rigorously advancing what those like David Hume (1711–76) had already argued for as personal identity in the eighteenth century.[26]

Hence, by focusing stringently on how experiences within a stream of consciousness can coincide with one another to give form to an individual person (expressed through their actions, speech, etc.), Nishida, on our reading, can offer a coherent view of selfhood in his philosophy without betraying his methodology or taking a standpoint external to the sole reality of pure experience. Yet, although this view is successful in leading us away from the methodological issues that come with the organic view of self in Nishida's work, it also brings us back to square one for this particular chapter: why is Nishida able to (or at least, why does he claim to be able to) talk about the "trans-individual" aspects of pure experience? Additionally, why does he seem to allow for "trans-individual" conceptions of personality such as God or the state? Do such statements not force us to recognize a "mystical" element of Nishida's philosophy? If not, on what grounds is Nishida able to talk about the relation between individual humans and God as the basis for religious experience?

Regarding the first question, we can answer doubts concerning what Nishida means when he refers to the trans-individual elements of pure experience by recognizing that a system of conscious experiences need not be limited to the individual insofar as the same universal structures (discussed in the previous paragraph) are functioning at their base. Nishida explicitly states this to be the case in the following passages:

> I have outlined the activity of consciousness as established within a certain sphere by virtue of a unity. Yet many people do not believe that such a unity exists outside that particular sphere—for instance, some think that yesterday's and today's consciousnesses are totally independent and cannot be regarded as one consciousness. From the standpoint of direct experience, however, this distinction is relative, not ultimate. [...] If we draw fine distinctions between the successive ideas, we can think of them as separate consciousnesses; but if we view them not as separate, individual realities but as one activity of consciousness, then we can regard yesterday's and today's consciousnesses as a single activity of consciousness.
>
> (IG: 60)

> In the same way that an individual's consciousness constitutes a single reality in which yesterday's and today's consciousnesses are united, consciousness that spans a lifetime can likewise be regarded as singular. Taking this farther, we see that this is not limited to the scope of just one individual, for a person can likewise link his or her own consciousness with that of another and regard them as a single consciousness. Just as a principle is the same no matter who thinks about it, at the base of our consciousness there is something universal. By means of it we are able to communicate with and understand one another.
>
> (IG: 62)

Both of these quotations hint at what I believe to be the most viable way to read Nishida's early philosophy. As Nishida argues, the systematization of *our lived and perspectival conscious experiences* certainly seems to start with the individual's present consciousness, but it by no means stops there. The fact that past bodily sensations, perceptions, and feelings provide meaning to our present consciousness and help shape us as a person can be gleaned even from the example of the bell mentioned in Chapter 1. Yet, beyond only this relation to our experiences as "individuals," the lessons we learn after being scolded by our parents, the new information we gain from talking to other people, and the cringe we feel when we see another person in pain are all equally likely to provide meaning to our experiences and shape us as a person. The reason this is possible in either the case of past experiences or experiences of other minds is because all experiences share the same structures (referred to by Nishida as principles) and, thus, can be integrated into the same system.[27] This explanation that experiences are all commensurate in virtue of the fact that they share the same principles, then, gives Nishida a coherent path to explaining both (1) how different individuals are able to aggregate knowledge beyond what is immediately designated to them as being strictly one's own experience (without leaving one's own perspective!) as well as (2) how communities and societies could seem to have common-knowledge (a quasi-"personality" that stands in virtue of the fact that it is largely shared with other inhabitants).

In either of these two cases, our explanation does *not* presuppose that Nishida needed to introduce a macro-consciousness from which we all emerge. Rather, all we see is merely that Nishida's notion of personality does not need to restrict itself to the individual person because the organization of conscious experiences does not require that experiences be had by the "same" subject of experience to be integrated into a system. Now, one could profitably employ purely metaphorical discussions of a trans-individual organism that gathers a variety of experiences into a unified system. But, given that there is no need to suppose any particular entity in possession of said system, such talk would indeed be nothing more than a metaphor. Thus, despite Nishida's own tendencies to utilize such language, we can see that references to finding a "greater" or "true" self may actually be detrimental to unearthing the more novel view of selfhood in *Inquiry*. Instead, a more fruitful reading can be found by focusing on Nishida's claim that pure experience tends, by nature, to integrate differing experiences together to form increasingly more comprehensive systematic networks between them.

Yet, what of the third question? This non-organic reading of Nishida's claims that pure experience goes beyond the individual should be able to help us respond to the first and second questions we have posed regarding the matter of how we can understand his religious philosophy without resorting to the mystical tendencies that appear to be present throughout the book. However, it is without doubt that uniting with a communal human consciousness or the universe itself offers a clear view of religious purpose while explaining how individual experiences share universal structures likely does not. Additionally, Nishida's frequent references to the union of man and God signal that he did—to at least some degree—intend to express something similar to early Meiji authors' focus on the great and small self. Still, although addressing the religious aspect of his thought is possibly the hardest aspect of Nishida's early philosophy to rewrite in a non-organic fashion, it is possible to explain religious consciousness in *Inquiry* without smuggling in a second self. To the contrary, I believe that it may be the aspect of his theory of selfhood that would benefit the most from doing so. Hence, in the next section, we will attempt to sketch a reading of Nishida's early religious philosophy that does not require a smaller and greater self.

An Alternative Reading—Re-considering Nishida's Notion of Religious Consciousness

Now, to revisit the problem at hand, we have seen in the section "Self and Religion in Nishida's *An Inquiry into the Good*—The Organic Interpretation" that many of Nishida's explanations of religious consciousness mention unity between oneself and the universe itself, i.e., God. These claims—in addition to tendencies to talk about a "greater" or "true" self that we humans aspire to join with—substantiate a popular view that Nishida's theory of religion is the story of the individual joining with a greater world spirit that goes beyond their smaller self. This view can furthermore help us situate Nishida in the context of popular trends in Meiji philosophy, as we have seen that many of his predecessors (like Miyake Setsurei) seem to espouse this view. And yet, the problems this presented for Nishida's philosophy—both in terms of internal consistency and methodological foundation—pushed us toward an alternative reading of his philosophy, which shows that a careful look of how Nishida used the term "universal" suggests not a greater self of which we are all but one part, but rather underlying structures of experience that make individual perspectives commensurate and capable of being organized into the same network of meanings. While this reading of self and individual person in *Inquiry* can help us avoid justifying a second self—or other secondary questions, such as how this greater self could be verified within the confines of Nishida's methodology or where our "small" self emerges from—it does bring with it the question: what do we make of Nishida's insistence on the union between self and his notion of a personal God? How could our proposed alternative possibly point us in the direction of any inkling of religious experience?

As was the case in the previous section as well, an alternative reading of religious consciousness in *Inquiry* requires that we look back over the basic terms causing problems. First, we need to re-address what exactly is being *asked* of religion in Nishida's worldview:

> The religious demand concerns the self as a whole, the life of the self. It is a demand in which the self, while perceiving its relativity and finitude, yearns to attain eternal, true life by uniting with an absolutely infinite power. Paul expressed it when he wrote, 'It is no longer I who live, but Christ who lives in me.' [...] True religion seeks the transformation of the self and the reformation of life.
>
> (IG: 149)

Two points jump out in this quotation: (1) the fact that religion is a matter of transforming the life of the self and (2) the juxtaposition between the relative and limited individual and the infinite, greater life of God. Putting these two features together provides intuitive evidence for returning to what we have referred to as the organic reading of Nishida. Indeed, the "death" of the individual self is simultaneously posed as its "rebirth" in a greater consciousness. Our challenge is describing this act of rebirth without recourse to an account of a second self.

The first point that we should consider is that, once again, a more careful reading of Nishida leads us away from any kind of mysterious union between a smaller self and "God" as a bigger self. Certainly, Nishida does emphasize the union between man and God, insisting that the true self is found in God. Yet, a careful reading of many of these passages leads to a key point about Nishida's conception of religious consciousness: when Nishida refers to God, he does so as the unifying *power* or *activity* at the base of consciousness, and not as an *entity* that can be measured in terms of size or in terms of part and whole. Reading Nishida in this way while keeping in mind the discussion of "principles" in the previous section can likely help us make sense of otherwise awkward passages like the following:

> Construed in terms of the self-awareness in God's personality, each of the unities in the phenomena of the universe are none other than God's self-awareness. For example, the fact that the sum of the angles of a triangle is equal to the sum of two right angles is necessarily regarded in the same way by each person in each era. This, too, is one instance of the self-awareness of God.
>
> (IG: 162)

What does this mean? It means—as Nishida himself specifies—that God is not a greater spirit or the totality of the cosmos or really anything at all (IG: 82). What Nishida refers to as God is, as far as I can tell, none other than the possibility for the "function" described in the previous section to exist in any experience, in any era, in any place. God is thus none other than the universal principles or patterns underlying experiences that ensure they can remain unified and commensurate with one another in an orderly system (presumably in opposition to random and unintelligible chaos). Hence, when Nishida argues that the true self is found in the act of becoming aware of one's unity with God, he is arguing for something far more down-to-Earth than becoming one with the totality of the universe: becoming aware of the "true" self is becoming aware of the activity found in any experience.

In this sense, once again, the notion that religious consciousness in *Inquiry* is dependent on a "greater" or "true" self could be something closer to a by-product of his connection to his predecessors than an accurate representation of his theory of the self. The notion of the union between humans and God refers to joining with an activity, not an entity. At this point, one may be tempted to introduce a "bigger" activity which we join in religious experiences. Still, this would once again raise the same questions we faced during the section "Self and Religion in Nishida's *An Inquiry into the Good*—The Organic Interpretation" of how these two unifying activities relate to one another. Additionally, if the unifying activity we are referring to here is "merely" the experiential structures that make it possible for the sum of angles of any triangle to be 180 degrees (as it was presented in the quotation above), then any talk of a second self would raise the question of whether the inauthentic experiences of a smaller self are ever lacking in such structures. While it certainly may be possible to distinguish this interpretation of a "true self" from a *misidentification* of it with an abstract notion of an individuated subject-as-substance, this would indicate an epistemological error on the philosopher's part and not the existence of a greater activity that contrasts with a smaller self-consciousness.

Yet, the question remains: how can we possibly discuss Nishida's early religious philosophy without slipping back into the same bad habits? My belief is that joining with the activity of pure experience itself does not require the introduction of any greater entity (such as the universe), but it does entail a form of *harmony* in pure experience that is not dissimilar to what Miyake described (and is consistent with what we have described in the previous chapters). Indeed, as we have seen throughout our investigation, the basic form of pure experience is activity, constantly seeking to fill the gaps that open up as pure experience changes. In this sense, it is likely that the default mode of our daily life is actually a rather hectic activity, filled with constant attempts to quell the discomforts and conflicts in our lives (whether they be something as small as picking up a banana to deal with our hunger or something as grand as mediating a debate between two contradicting opponents). It is almost certainly for this reason that Nishida explicitly equates the subject and object divide with suffering, and the religious demand with the reclamation of unity:

> As consciousness differentiates and develops, subject and object oppose each other and the self and other things go against each other. In this process, life brings us demands and anguish; we are separated from God, and the Garden is forever closed to Adam's descendants. But no matter how far consciousness differentiates and develops, it cannot separate from the unity seen in the union of subject and object; in our knowledge and volition, we are always seeking this unity.
>
> (IG: 151)

As Nishida explains, the constant demand upon us to reclaim unity and work through these contradictions causes discomfort and suffering once we have left the metaphorical paradise of conflict-free consciousness. Extrapolating a bit from this conclusion and considering it alongside what we have seen thus far, I believe that religious consciousness can be better looked at as a rare state of peace amidst this constant dynamism. While Nishida gives plenty of examples throughout the book, the common thread running through the states in which one "achieves" pure experience (mountain climbers, painters, and appreciators of fine music, just to name a few) is that there is a lack of resistance internal to the progression of their experiences. The mountain climber no longer needs to think about which foothold to choose next, the violinist does not need to focus her attention on getting her timing right, and one listening to fine music can relax as the melodies flow into his ears. These moments, in which the dynamism of pure experience is carried out without any internal discord, then, are not only a brief respite from the constant conflict and contradiction found in our day-to-day lives, are an unobstructed window into the endless activity that allows for all of our meaningful experiences to take place: precisely the self in its purest, unaltered form.

As a final suggestion for reading the early Nishida profitably, I would like to argue that we ought to depart from Nishida's tendency to discuss a greater unity and instead view his theory of religion in a more negative sense. That is, I believe that the best way to look at Nishida's religious theory is to consider more seriously the *death* of the individual. To be a bit more specific, I believe that Nishida's conception of religious consciousness is best read as a total *negation* of the conflicts and contradictions that accompany pure experience in our day-to-day lives.[28] While the early Nishida preferred to discuss such conflicts in positive terms of overcoming divisions between subject and object and achieving further unity (i.e., achieving a state in which we come to know reality precisely as it is, and there is no distinction between the facts of pure experience and their meaning), I feel here that Nishida could stand to learn from Miyake's early philosophy: the "death" of the individual is not merely an overcoming of individual consciousness—it is better conceived of as an annihilation of the very categories of unity and disunity. It is—paradoxically—a respite from our typical tendency to endlessly reunify the gaps that appear in our experience and, instead, merely enjoy their flow as they pass us by. It is the achievement of a rare sense of calm and peace among the utter dynamism of the world we live in, the constant disruptive activity it features, and our usual tendency to try to achieve unity once again amidst this hectic flow.

Conclusion—Separating from Meiji Philosophy and the Refinement of Nishida's Theory of Selfhood

Over the course of this chapter, we have shown the path to a non-mystical, methodologically sound interpretation of *Inquiry*. By paying careful attention to how Nishida uses key terms (universal, in particular), it is possible to avoid getting caught up in a relation between a "small" self and a "big" self without losing anything of note. Even his religious philosophy, which appears most vulnerable to being understood in terms of "small" and "great" selves, can be profitably re-read instead as a release from the constant oppositions and conflicts that haunt all living beings. In this sense, we ought to acknowledge that distinguishing Nishida's theory of selfhood from popular theories at the time may not only lead to a more profitable reading of *Inquiry*, but could also provide a more accurate reconstruction of what he was trying to describe in his philosophy of pure experience.

Particularly, the fact that Nishida (as we will mention briefly in the conclusion of this work) later decried the mystical tendencies of his early philosophy as missing his intended point is not without some merit. I say this insofar as this fact points us to an as-of-yet underappreciated aspect of Nishida's relation to his philosophical predecessors: the importance that his attempts to distance himself from such preexisting frameworks had on his capacity to refine his philosophical arguments. Indeed, it was only in his very next text, *Intuition and Reflection in Self-Awareness*, that Nishida would give up both the terms pure experience and frequent references to a "true" or "greater" self in favor of more technical descriptions of the structures of self-awareness. This would culminate, as we shall discuss in the conclusion in greater detail, in altogether rethinking the structure of the self in *From the Actor to the Seer* as that which "mirrors the self within itself." Included in this shift is an acrobatic attempt to describe the self as something that is neither an individuated substance nor a "piece" of the universe, but instead that which can be seen as the reflection of the reflections of the various events that happen in the world. As I see it, this was not a wholesale abandonment of his notion of self in *Inquiry*, but instead a removal of the obstructive elements that had mixed into his worldview. Nishida's philosophical growth occurred at least partially thanks to his capacity to shed unnecessary influence from his Meiji predecessors and their use of the language of "small" and "great" selves.

Still, it is without question that Nishida also resorts to explanations of pure experience in terms that are immediately comparable to Miyake's work. Even writing off most of these discussions as a poor choice of explaining the concept that we seek to integrate further information into our systems beyond merely what is immediately perceived by individual subjects, there are still instances in which Nishida describes the individual and God in terms of part and whole.[29] Beyond this, it is clear enough from the passages that we have already mentioned that Nishida himself seemed to consider pure experience as an organism in some capacity. If a reader dissatisfied with my reading of Nishida were so inclined, I have no doubt that they could find sufficient textual support to argue that (for better or worse) Nishida genuinely believed we find our true self by breaking through our usual subjectivity and experiencing the activity of the universe in its entirety, beyond any individuated perspective.[30] Insofar as this is the case, it is not so easy to entirely separate Nishida from his predecessors in the Meiji era.

Additionally, it is not necessarily the case that his organic predecessors' influence was a destructive force in all cases. While there are important differences between himself and Miyake Setsurei, the fact that reality itself is somehow alive and orderly was a crucial insight that would manifest itself in various ways throughout Nishida's career. Nishida's early understanding of/inclination toward Schopenhauer was largely influenced by those like Miyake, who had a similar tendency to stress the primacy of the will without falling into the same pessimism that Schopenhauer had. As is well known, these tendencies were amplified by the appearance of an absolute will at the base of reality in his next work, *Intuition and Reflection in Self-Awareness*. Yet, even as the more immediate relations receded into the background after Nishida moved past this text, his pursuit of a living conception of reality persisted. His later philosophy was indeed defined by Nishida himself as an attempt to come to grips with the concrete historical world in which we are born into, labor within, and eventually perish from. Hence, although the mereological claims about small and big selves that were espoused by those we have inserted into the organic tradition may not be present in Nishida's own philosophy, this does not mean that the organic tradition had no influence on him whatsoever, nor does it mean that it was a bad influence that poisoned his good ideas. For this reason, although we seem to have a crucial distinction between Nishida and the representative of one chief trend in Meiji philosophy, it is still not so easy to absolutize this difference between them or use it to simply justify the notion that Nishida was modern Japan's first philosopher. Considering what to make of this vague oscillation between a continuous line of influence in Meiji thought and a hard mark that separates Nishida and his predecessor will be our final task in the concluding chapter of this investigation.

Conclusion

Continuities and Discontinuities with the Meiji Era—Nishida Kitarō as a Turning Point

Introduction

With the end of the previous chapter, we have now completed a tour of the key facets of *An Inquiry into the Good* in relation to key thinkers and intellectual trends in the Meiji era. We started this investigation with a simple, seemingly ignorable question: How can Nishida both be the "starting point" of modern Japanese philosophy and part of the critical continuity of Meiji thought? Over the course of the past four chapters, we have established clearly that *Inquiry* did not exist in a bubble. Nishida's ontology, psychology, ethics, and religion all have deep-rooted connections to movements in the Meiji era. In this sense, we can likely see a point I have been repeating since the introduction of this book: treating Nishida as a genius who popped up out of nowhere—or otherwise downplaying his connection to his predecessors in the Meiji era—does not only Nishida's predecessors, but also his readers and, ultimately, Nishida himself a great disservice.

And yet, it would be slightly mistaken to come away from this exercise thinking that Nishida is not original or that his reputation as the starting point of Japanese philosophy is completely worthless. In any of these chapters, there seems to be some new transformation taking place within Japanese philosophy that is observable in *Inquiry*. This is not to say that Nishida was talking about something completely different or that he merely tacked on additional points that his predecessors had not considered. Rather, we have seen that Nishida seemed to be the product of a process of *methodological refinement*. By taking the intuitions and ideas that started with his Meiji-era forerunners as far as they could go while upholding strict principles in the philosophy of pure experience,

Nishida was able to point us toward something more than what we had seen before him. Put differently, Nishida was able to establish new ideas by setting up strict methodological limitations and taking a critical attitude toward his own thought. More importantly, though, this attempt to critically ground his own theories can also serve as a guide for his readers toward paths they could take to build on and think for themselves in new ways.

In this final chapter, we shall briefly reflect on what it means to say that Nishida is the "starting point" of modern Japanese philosophy while keeping in mind both what we have seen so far and how Nishida's work developed as his career went on. The general idea expressed here will be consistent with everything we have seen so far going back to the introduction. If we mean to say that Nishida appeared out of nowhere and that his philosophy somehow bucked the "translational" or "syncretic" trends of the Meiji philosophy before him, then claiming *Inquiry* as the origin of modern Japanese philosophical thought is a misrepresentation of the facts. However, if we instead mean to say that Nishida's early philosophy was a turning point in a gradual process of methodological refinement in which budding ideas were given the rigorous and critical attention they needed to grow, then we can appropriately understand Nishida's place in the Japanese canon (and better detail how many important lines of thought in modern Japanese philosophy were able to grow from his contributions). Explaining what this means and how Nishida's career took off after *Inquiry* shall thus be our goal here.

Continuity, Themes, and Meiji Influence in Nishida's Work

In this section, we will briefly revisit and summarize the core themes that came up and thus make explicit what strands of Meiji thought influenced Nishida's project. There are, as far as I can tell, three main elements of Nishida's thought that resonate strongly with his predecessors in the Meiji era.

Searching for "True Reality" beyond Shallow Monisms/Dualisms

Perhaps the most immediately identifiable conclusion comes from Chapters 1 and 2: Nishida shares with many of his predecessors a desire to account for true reality, and not merely settle for abstract descriptions of particular elements within it. This trend in Meiji thought, as we have mentioned, has been well-documented by previous historians. The most notable movement associated with this trend was precisely the one mentioned in Chapter 1, the notion of "reality-*soku*-phenomena" that stood in the background of Nishida's work. Regardless of whether it be Inoue Enryō, Inoue Tetsujirō, or Nishida himself, there seems to have been a strong intuition that philosophy needed to go past any kind of abstract monism or dualism and account for reality, *precisely as it is*.

There are multiple reasons one could give to explain this development. As we will touch upon again soon, it is not unreasonable to think that calls for the "ultimate" reality were a reaction to the pragmatic and positivistic trends in early Meiji philosophy. Otherwise, as we discussed briefly in Chapter 1, the perceived affinity between the Buddhistic notion of *soku* and Western resources (namely, Hegelian dialectics) could have opened eyes for many scholars in that period. Or, perhaps, one could merely note that this vision of philosophy was just one prominent trend in the nineteenth century on a global level and that, as a result, it is not particularly surprising that Japanese authors also joined in using terms they were familiar with. Regardless of what one thinks of as the cause, however, the general spirit of Nishida's philosophy evidently reflects this burgeoning development. The core themes outlined in Chapters 1 and 2 show this. Starting with a distrust of abstracting individual elements of experience through language and arguing that concrete reality could never be reduced to mind, matter, or a Cartesian dualism between the two were the cornerstones of not only the two Inoue's philosophies, but also of Nishida's early work. Moreover, the question of how to describe this incredibly rich reality without carving the world up into false dichotomies was a task just as present in Buddhist reformers like Inoue Enryō as it was in early psychologists like Motora Yūjirō. Nishida's interest in, and approach to, questions of how to approach ultimate reality thereby show his proximity with many of his Meiji predecessors. Additionally, Nishida's work also seems to reflect his place within a process of methodological refinement among authors looking to describe concrete reality.

Individual Freedoms and the Moral Ideal

A point we have seen thus far is that this interest in true reality was not a mere academic concern for writers like Nishida. There were exceptions to this rule, but the aforementioned pragmatic concerns about how to ensure the independence of the Japanese state and delineate the limits of individual freedom in the new government seem to have done a great deal to help Western philosophical knowledge flow into Japan. At the same time, though, it left many wondering about what it means to be an individual beyond just one's political obligations.

What does it mean to live and to die? How do we reconcile our role in the state with our religious demands to know the nature of our true self and the world we live in? As we have discussed in Chapters 3 and 4 in particular, Nishida was one of many young men who had become engrossed in such questions during this dynamic time.

The crucial point that we find here is that Nishida addressed these problems within a certain genealogical continuity. Nishida learned from authors who had proposed a certain notion of self-realization based partially on the work of T. H. Green and left a certain degree of room for religious interests that could not be reduced to one's role in the state. More specifically, these authors found themselves relying on the notion of a moral ideal—i.e., an ideal formulation of humanity that one finds in their relation to the greater whole to which their individual self belong—in order to both avoid accusations of selfishness and explain how a certain spiritual or religious dimension is a necessary condition for human morality. While there were various competing visions of what this moral ideal was or what kinds of consequences it could bring, Nishida seems to have learned most from those like Onishi Hajime or Tsunashima Ryōsen; authors who believed we needed to admit a certain degree of freedom for people to fully flesh out the spiritual implications of this moral theory for themselves. Nishida's individualistic streak, his refusal to separate the metaphysical and academic from the ethical and religious, and his own thoughts about what kind of "ideals" pursue in our ethical lives all make much more sense in this context.

Part and Whole/Individual Person and State/Self and Reality

Both points seem to come together into one of the odder, yet more important, movements of the Meiji period: the tendency to equate the relation between the individual person and the whole to which they are a part to the cells of an organism. I use this vague notion of "whole to which individuals are a part" because that "whole" seems to have been taken as any number of things. It could be individual and state, individual and the universe, or individual and God. Or, at times, it could have been all three put together at once. At any rate, the idea that losing one's "small" self, as a cell of sorts, and finding something greater, whether we call it reality, God, or whatever else you prefer, was simultaneously one of the most popular trends in the Meiji era and one of the aspects of *Inquiry* that has most enthralled many of Nishida's readers.

Perhaps one point that we could not make explicit enough during the preceding chapters (that deserves more recognition than we can give it here) is that this final trend seems to have been the lynchpin between this search for true reality and the moral idealism so many espoused. After all, how could the notion of a reality that goes beyond the scope of thought or our ability to describe it outside of metaphor possibly coexist with the metaphysical presumption of something like the ideal notion of a human (something which would, presumably, be completely entangled with discursive thought and the capacity for reason and language)? One answer seems to have been the idea of "losing oneself" in this reality. Finding some kind of harmony with everything around you, feeling at one with reality in a way that could not be achieved as a purely reflective subject, and ultimately realize one's capacities to their fullest made sense from both a metaphysical and a moral or religious perspective. It is not surprising, then, that these ideas seemed to have remained in the background of Nishida's early thought.

Though there are other themes that could be identified, I believe these three in particular stand out to me as showing how Nishida's work inherits, and develops, a constellation of ideas that were prominent in Meiji philosophy. Moreover, these were not ideas on the fringes of Nishida's philosophical enterprise. To the contrary, they were central to his development and, as we have seen over the course of this book, understanding the framework that he was working in can help us appreciate the finer points of his philosophical venture. In sum, Nishida's early philosophy was indeed representative of the Meiji period, not just in its willingness to blend East and West into something new, but also insofar as it embodied many of the most important themes in that period.

Development, New Beginnings, and Bridging the Gap

So, as I have stated from start to finish, Nishida's philosophy does seem to have inherited many of its core elements and concerns from the Meiji era. However, we must avoid making a mistake here. While one may be tempted to assume that Nishida's status as a Meiji thinker and the implication that almost all of the main ideas he works with in *Inquiry* have deep connections to previous Meiji philosophers implies that he is somehow unoriginal, I do not think this is the case. Rather, Nishida seems to have used these core ideas as something closer to a foothold or a means in which he could more critically pursue his own thoughts. In this regard, *Inquiry* might be the ending point for certain strands of Meiji philosophy as much as it was the "beginning" of original philosophy in modern Japan. This duality between the end of many Meiji era trends and the beginning of original philosophy seems to converge with one another as the start of Nishida's own project and its various developments. As we saw briefly at the end of the previous chapter, part of what makes Nishida's early philosophy interesting is the way that it attempted to go beyond the current footholds and terminology available to him and find new ways to express ideas in a more logically rigorous way. Hence, although fully exploring all the ways that Nishida's project changed in the years after *Inquiry* would be impossible here, I will shortly address how this philosophy of the Meiji era transformed and branched off in key ways for the development of modern Japanese thought.

More specifically, I would like to focus on the topic of methodology and self as Nishida's philosophy matured leading into the logic of place in his middle period. While this may sound as though I am talking about two different or random things, this is hardly the case. Considerations on the self, i.e., on the person which lives, works, and dies in this world, stood at the crossing point between Nishida's metaphysics and his existential or religious concerns and, thus, held a supremely important role in his philosophical venture. This does not mean that the two overlapped in the way one would expect on a Venn diagram, where they both belong to distinct and independent sets of things that Nishida cared deeply about. Rather, Nishida's insistence that philosophy calls for a total rebirth and a concrete rethinking of the nature of the reality from a concrete perspective makes them intrinsically linked. In this sense, this crossing point between demands for methodological rigor and demands to answer life's big problems seems to stand at the core of every important development we saw between Nishida and his predecessors, insofar as they were two sides of the same coin. Philosophy was not just academic affair, but it had to provide answers to concrete existential problems. It is because of this point that we cannot be satisfied with uncritical or incomplete and unfounded worldviews. In brief, Nishida was left with a question: How can one account for the concrete life of the self as it is lived through in everyday experience, within the realm of thoroughgoing, critical, and, ultimately, reflective, philosophical thought? Put differently, how can we do philosophy without resorting to mere abstractions?

As we have seen throughout particularly Chapters 1, 2, and 4, Nishida did indeed struggle to answer these questions to the best of his ability and it is not clear if he reached a fully coherent answer within the pages of *Inquiry*.[1] We have dealt with these problems by focusing on the strand in Nishida's thought that attempts to handle these problems by taking the self as an "originary activity" that establishes context through putting different moments in experience into relation with one another. Yet—as we can see in the previous chapter—it is not difficult to counter these claims by pointing to passages in which Nishida seems to view the true self as something "greater" than the small self of reflective consciousness or that the true self is found only once we join with the entirety of the universe. This inconsistency raises questions that are not so easy to answer. First, we can ask, is reflection a "break" or "rupture" in pure experience or is it just a different mode of pure experience? Depending on how one answers this question, different methodological problems may arise. Second, we are left with questions about individual consciousness and "who I am" in the end. Am I just one part of the universe? Am I the universe itself? Is my individual self a part of, or subordinate to, a larger overall whole (the state, the universe, etc.)?

Given that these problems lurked in the background of his early thought, it should not come as surprising that his next major work was titled *Intuition and Reflection in Self-Awareness* (1917). As the title of the book suggests, Nishida doubled down on his efforts to reconcile direct experience (intuition) and thought (reflection) by locating them within the overarching experience of the self (self-awareness). Here, Nishida abandoned the notion of pure experience (both in name and as a philosophical tendency to glorify the unity of subject and object). As a replacement, Nishida attempted to show that both meanings and values and our intuition were part of the fundamental mirroring structure of experience known as self-awareness.[2] That is, Nishida tries to reconcile what is given directly in immediate consciousness (i.e., in intuition) with what is found in the act of explicitly contextualizing said experience (i.e., via reflection) by appealing to the inherently reflexive nature of consciousness and thus show that there is no discrepancy between them. Now, at this stage in his career, Nishida attempts to tie this reflexive structure of experience to his notion of an absolute will that holds together the constant splitting of subject and object in reflection away from their initial unity in intuition. Doing so, Nishida seemed to reason, would provide a pervading force throughout consciousness that could tie together individual moments of experience.[3] While I believe all of these themes were already latently present in *Inquiry* and Nishida himself largely dismissed *Intuition and Reflection in Self-Awareness* (and its tendency to talk about uniting with the Absolute Will) as an unfortunate surrender to "the enemy camp of mysticism,"[4] it does signify an important hint for discussing the structures of self and reflection that would be further refined in the work that is typically considered the beginning of his middle period, *From the Actor to the Seer* (1927).

Specifically, we see that instead of trying to distinguish between inauthentic or small reflective self and the true, intuiting self, Nishida more carefully explicates how the fundamental activity referred to initially as pure experience takes place as a "mirroring" function that ties together pre-reflective and reflective consciousness. The brilliant move that Nishida makes to reflect this in his more mature philosophy is to refer to the self as the "place (場所)" in which the various "mirrorings" of our experiences arise. Nishida explains the modifications he has made while hinting at a contrast with his prior position in the essay "On Internal Perception":

> In our self-awareness, before the self knows the self there is no self. Before the self acts, there is no self. [...] Yet, in what kind of realm of objects (対象界) does the content of self-awareness develop? The self reflects itself within itself. The mirror that reflects the content of the self must be the self-itself. The shadow of the self is not reflected upon things. [...] Normally the term self-awareness is merely thought to mean that the knower and the known have become one, but I believe that true self-awareness is knowing yourself within yourself. If one merely talks about the unity of subject and object, then this could be considered something we refer to as pre-reflective intuition. But for self-awareness to be possible, we must add that this happens within oneself. Self-awareness is found when the knowing I, the known I, and the place that the I knows itself are one [with each other].
>
> (NKZ 3: 350)

Here, I believe we see a more careful manner of explaining what Nishida was attempting to say in *Inquiry*. Nishida is not merely arguing for a pre-reflective unity between subject and object as true self-awareness. Instead, Nishida is arguing that the self is the "place" in which various experiences are all tied together and reflect upon one another. It is the overarching unity underlying distinction between subject and object in reflective judgment and the unity between them in bare intuition. Importantly, this self is not an object to be found in the world (as a shadow reflected upon different things) but can rather only know itself as it is found tying together the amalgamation of these various experiences. What we had referred to previously as a hub in Chapter 3 now becomes the "place" or "mirror" upon which experiences are reflected, making itself present only as it finds itself mirroring its own actions in other moments.[5] It is, by the middle period of Nishida's work, "the place of absolute nothingness"; the ultimate event that gives context to all individual moments but itself can never be made an object of further contextualization.[6]

Thus, while the seeds for this more mature insight were likely already present in *Inquiry*, Nishida's attempt to fully flesh out these ideas brought him a great distance from earlier talk of small and great self or mystical unities with the universe. What we must not lose sight of, however, is that these developments did not take place only in terms of the verbiage used to express the insights in play. Rather, what we find in Nishida's movement toward his middle period is a doubling down on *logic* or *methodology*. The notion that reality was the ultimate concrete universal that was constantly articulating itself in particular experiences may have started in *Inquiry*, but it only became stronger by Nishida's middle period. By this point, however, Nishida made painstaking efforts to explain the relationship between universal and particular. While he does refer to them in terms of "part" and "whole," he is very clear that this is not true in the same way it would be for a thing that takes up a certain area of space or a temporal term in a certain sequence of events. Instead, the particular and universal also exist in a relationship of mirroring, wherein universals can only be reflected in their systematically articulated particular instantiations.[7] Somewhat similarly to what we have mentioned when discussing mathematical functions, eventually Nishida clearly avoids any vision of universal and particular in which the two belong to separate realms or one transcends the other. In this sense, Nishida seems to be looking for a more rigorous, logical explanation of explaining the concrete fact of our selfhood beyond abstract notions of a trans-experiential Self, but also appears set on finding the *logical structures* that make our intelligible experiences as selves possible.

I suppose much more could be said about how Nishida's thought developed from the early days of pure experience to his more "logical" philosophy of place, but I think there is a more important point to note here. That is, Nishida's attempt to account for the self in its most concrete state, without resorting to abstract visions of a trans-experiential Subject as the possessor of experience, while also taking seriously the fact that he was writing from the perspective of a philosopher giving critical and logical descriptions of the world, took him from the footholds he was able to grasp onto at the end of the Meiji era, and toward more careful and rigorous accounts of his philosophical vision that do not immediately resemble anything we have talked about thus far. Moreover, these changes to the core logical principles of his philosophical view give him new paths to adjust how he conceives of other issues, such as time, judgment, or—although the space given to thematically discuss ethics, politics, and religion dwindled from the time between *Inquiry* until his final writings—topics of free-will or good and evil.

Perhaps even more importantly, though, these constant adjustments and attempts to more clearly express his philosophical worldview put Nishida into dialogue with other Japanese thinkers who could build off these ideas. Takahashi

Satomi's engagement with *Inquiry* has already come up, but things did not end there. Consider once again Tanabe Hajime's critique against Nishida's logic of place. As we have stated previously, Tanabe accused Nishida of a kind of religious quietism, conflating philosophy and religion by appealing to some kind of hypostatic relation to a greater entity. In contrast, Tanabe claimed, philosophy needed to be dynamic; it needed to constantly reorient itself in accordance with its historical period and previous arguments.[8] In the grand scheme of things, this disagreement may not appear to be incredibly important, but keep in mind what we have just said about Nishida's attempt to rethink our relation to concrete reality as a whole which we ultimately aspire to and find ultimate knowledge in. Looked at from this perspective, we could perhaps understand Tanabe as arguing that Nishida had not yet gone far enough. Accurate or not, Tanabe's efforts seem to have brought Nishida to redouble his efforts to avoid any kind of association between his epistemology and immediate knowledge of final, all-entailing whole.[9] Moreover, Tanabe's efforts to avoid these same perceived mistakes and offer a logic that he found more concrete were likely the most vital point in his philosophical growth as well.

There are many other critical dialogues involving Nishida worth mentioning. Critiques from Tosaka Jun (戸坂潤, 1900–1945), Sōda Kiichiro (左右田喜一郎, 1881–1927), and many others pushed Nishida to consider many complex topics and question his philosophical views. While there are too many examples to cover them all exhaustively, in my view it is this process of growth, entering into dialogue with other philosophers, and providing the footholds needed for far more nuanced and diverse theories to be put forward that makes Nishida's reputation as the starting point of modern Japanese philosophy sensible. Again, this reputation does not mean that Nishida merely dropped his connection to everything that came before him or that he appeared out of nowhere. It means that his philosophy pointed to new avenues for himself and others (both in and outside of Japan). As we have seen many times now, Nishida's search for methodological rigor had already begotten detailed arguments in *Inquiry*, but it did not stop there. Even after the precise content of his philosophy started to be described in different terminology or he chose to engage more with the arguments of Neo-Kantian authors like Hermann Cohen (1842–1912), Paul Natorp (1856–1924), or Emil Lask (1875–1915), Nishida pushed these intuitions further and allowed them to produce more in-depth investigations. So, to summarize an idea I have been repeating ad nauseam, it can be meaningful to say that Nishida is the start of original philosophy in early modern Japan. However, this can only be the case if we contextualize this statement properly by recognizing that this growth was part of a long process searching for methodological rigor and very specifically started from ideas present in Meiji philosophy and continues on into the present day at the hands of his contemporary readers across the globe. In this sense, any attempts to search for an absolute gap between premodern and modern, or truly Japanese and foreign, are likely bound for failure.

Final Thoughts on Nishida and the Meiji Period

So, we have more or less managed to answer the questions that we started this investigation with. In other words, our answer to the question of what makes Nishida the "origin" of modern Japanese philosophy is simple. That is, if we claim that Nishida appeared out of nowhere or that he "actually" stated his own thoughts while his predecessors only repeated what the wise thinkers of yore had said, then we are completely mistaken. None of the thinkers covered in this book intended to merely repeat anyone any more than Nishida intended to merely repeat what they had already pointed out. If, however, we say that Nishida allowed for certain key philosophical trends to rapidly grow through the pursuit of more rigorous methodological considerations—both during and after his writing of *Inquiry*—then we can better understand his important contribution to the advancement of original philosophical contemplations in modern Japan. While this marks the end of our investigation, something ought to be said regarding what can be learned from this exercise. There are, in my estimation, three interrelated points that deserve a bit more consideration.

The first point to address is a practical one. We now know that Nishida's place in history comes on the back of various important Meiji authors, but we have not said much about what new avenues of research are available because of these findings. Should researchers of Nishida also read the texts of Onishi Hajime or Inoue Enryō? Should more attention be given to these thinkers regardless of their connections to Nishida? My point here is not necessarily to imply either of these things (although I would be happy to see any of the thinkers in this book taken more seriously as philosophers). In the end, I think that it is quite enough for us to more clearly understand that Nishida did not appear out of thin air or merely from his ingenious interpretations of classical Zen Buddhism/Western Philosophy, given that discussing him as such prevents potential scholars from seeing the intellectual resources in the background of his thought. This kind of clarification may sound trivial for those who are familiar with Nishida or have had even minor exposure to the sources lurking in the background of his thought, but considering how important even throwaway lines about Nishida's status as the father or origin point of modern Japanese philosophy are for motivating interest in his work among new scholars, I do not think that this conclusion should be written off or ignored. If there were to be any normative claims to be made as a result of our thoughts so far, I believe it would be solely that we ought to be careful with how we introduce Nishida in comparative or introductory contexts and avoid uncritically referencing his unique status without additional clarification.

The second point is theoretical and builds off this notion that we should not present Nishida as appearing out of thin air. While none of the conclusions I have presented here are a direct answer to any tough questions about what constitutes philosophy, I do think that they lend themselves to a particular view of history that could help people interested in pursuing these questions further. That is, throughout this conclusion, I have referred to *Inquiry* as a non-trivial "cut" or "turning point" in Japanese philosophy. In other words, despite the clear historical influences in the background of *Inquiry*, it is undeniable that changes occurred in philosophical research after its publication. While one could invoke the later Nishida's notion of a "continuity of discontinuities" or some altered conception of Thomas Kuhn's (1922–96) paradigm shift to explain what we are seeing here, I do not think we need to go so far. Or, rather, a commonsense recognition that certain events can serve as a turning point for how philosophy is discussed and practiced is perhaps more productive here. Thus, as a theoretical conclusion, I think we can walk away from this exercise saying that these cuts not only exist (and that Nishida is an example), but that they signal a *transformation* instead of something completely independent of what happened before.

Once again, this claim does not signal any kind of metaphysical commitments about the nature of philosophy or historical progress, nor does it answer the kind of disciplinary questions needed to address issues like what makes philosophy "Japanese" or if there "actually" was philosophy in the premodern era. With that said, I do think that this case study would lend itself well to any authors who wish to account for philosophy as a plurivocal concept without falling into unmitigated relativism.[10] Nishida's place as the starting point in modern Japanese philosophy is not an arbitrary claim, insofar as *Inquiry* ushered in many important methodological developments for both Nishida and other influential Japanese authors. However, I see no reason that it needs to be the "only cut" in terms of how philosophy transforms over time. Nishi Amane's coining of the word "philosophy," and its ability to somehow unify Western philosophy as a field of study on Japanese shores, could be a cut in and of itself. Descartes's

Meditations could also be conceived of as a cut when we consider its impact on philosophical methodology in Western modernity. There are, over the course of philosophical progress, a sundry of potential cuts that deserve recognition and signal a change in how philosophy is practiced. Identifying these cuts, recognizing them for what they are, and being able to make sense of what has happened on both sides of them seem to me a non-trivial job for historians of philosophy.

Still, one may wonder if this job of identifying cuts can be meaningful (or if this notion of "cuts" that occur over the course of the history of philosophy does not, in the end, collapse into total relativism). After all, if the idea is that certain events transform how philosophy is discussed and practiced and there are no definitive standards for what counts as a cut, then it seems easy to reach absurd conclusions. Is not everything a "cut" if we want it to be? Is the notion of a "cut" intelligible if it can possibly happen with a degree of regularity? Going in the other direction, can we even discuss philosophy as a unified concept if it has been cut into so many different pieces at so many different times? While one may take these questions as a critique of my position, I view such issues as being necessary for coming to grips with what philosophy is in the first place. I have no definitive answers as to what the precise criteria for a "cut" could be or if we could reunite these cut up strands of thought into a unified conception of philosophy, but I do believe that critically researching these kinds of transformative periods, seeing what changed, and finding some kind of continuity among all of the different visions for how philosophical dialogue can be practiced is a critical job for historians of philosophy.

This leads me to my final, and perhaps simplest, point. In the end, Nishida was a philosopher of the Meiji period and contextualizing him in this way is one pathway for unlocking the most interesting elements of his thought. It might be possible—or, on occasions, necessary—to look at him as just one philosopher, outside of his cultural context. It can also be helpful to look at him in the context of the Japanese intellectual tradition at a much larger scale, especially considering his well-documented connections with Zen Buddhism. But there seem to be some things that can only be identified when we look at Nishida from the perspective of his own contemporary philosophical community. The problems that were debated by those who taught Nishida, the premises that Nishida accepted and denied, or even the contributions he made to those problems that helped fuel his fame as a philosopher become more evident when we look at him in this way. Not in an abstract sense, not as some kind of mythological figure, but as a living philosopher who dealt with the same qualms and concerns as those he learned from and grew up with.

Notes

Introduction

1. The first English to Japanese dictionary was produced by Fukuzawa Yukichi in 1860, relying both on his trip to San Francisco in the late 1850s and a Chinese-English dictionary. Precise details aside, the fact that there was not even an English-Japanese dictionary in the 1850s can likely be taken as a testament to how quickly things changed in Japan during the second half of the nineteenth century.
2. At the point that Nishi Amane and Tsuda Mamichi had gone to Holland in 1862, there were only sparse explanations of Western governance and legal theory widely available to Japanese scholars (such as Katō Hiroyuki's [加藤弘之 1836–1916] *Tonarigusa*, written in 1861). The following two decades, however, saw a linguistic revolution of sorts, with key translations like Nakamura Keiu's rendering of *On Liberty* by J. S. Mill (1806–73) or *Self Help* by Samuel Smiles (1812–1904). Within this flow came a dynamic process of deciding on how to best standardize translations of Western concepts. The complexity of translation, the dynamic process of settling on standardized philosophical terminology, and more precise discussions of what was translated when can all be found in Howland (2001).
3. Nishida, like many other great writers in this period lost his brother, Hyōjirō, during the war with Russia. During the period leading up to *Inquiry*, Nishida also experienced the tragic loss of his second daughter, Yūko, at the unfortunately young age of six years old in 1907 and his daughter Aiko in the same year. The connection between these gut-wrenching experiences and the already philosophically sensitive Nishida's desire to know more about this reality we live in has been explored thoroughly by many scholars, including Fujita Masakatsu (2007: 15–37).
4. Nishida expresses this idea in a 1902 letter to his lifelong friend, D. T. Suzuki (鈴木大拙, 1870–1966) lamenting the state of current Western ethical research. Nishida complains that Western ethicists are "[…] purely intellectual. The arguments are cogent, but there is nothing that reaches the *soul-experience* at the depths of the human heart" (NKZ 19: 63, soul-experience written in English). The idea here is that, less than engaging in empty academic discussion, the philosopher ought to pursue those existential concerns we humans all have. This is a theme we will return to repeatedly over the course of the book.
5. This vision of the history of philosophy in Japan is summarized cleanly by Bret Davis introduction to the Kyoto School in the *Stanford Encyclopedia of Philosophy*,

where he states that "[i]n the Meiji period (1868–1912), when Japan reopened to the rest of the world after more than two centuries of national isolation, a generation of scholars devoted themselves to importing Western academic fields of inquiry, including 'philosophy.' After many years of studying Western philosophy and Eastern classics, alongside a dedicated practice of Zen Buddhism, Nishida was the first major modern Japanese thinker to successfully go beyond learning from the West to construct his own original system of thought. This he began to do in his maiden work, *An Inquiry into the Good*, published in 1911" (Davis 2022).

6   The contemporary word for philosophy was coined much later than one might think. Nishi Amane—one of the most prolific translators in the nineteenth century—settled on the word *Tetsugaku* 哲学 (lit., study of wisdom) over the course of the 1860s. This came among other potential translations from Nishi, including *Kitetsu* 希哲 (lit., pursuit of wisdom), *Kikyū Tetsuchi* 希求哲智 (lit., pursuing wisdom and knowledge), and *Philosophia* フィロソフィア (a phonetic rendering of the term philosophia into Japanese). This linguistic confusion about whether philosophy was a "new" concept seems to have contributed greatly to questions in the Meiji period about what philosophy is or is not, as well as what distinguishes philosophy as *Tetsugaku* from non-philosophical resources. For more on the history of Nishi Amane and the translational process that led up to the word *Tetsugaku*, see Kosaka (2013: 31–45).

7   As an aside, although I am largely taking it for granted here that Nishida does count as an original philosopher, it is worth noting that some surprisingly contemporary Japanese philosophers disagree with the idea that there has been any such thing as original philosophy done in Japan to the present day (see Blocker and Sterling 2001: 1–3).

8   This characterization seems particularly common when introducing Nishida to laypersons. Even the webpage introducing Nishida's *Inquiry* in the NHK's famous book series states that "During the Meiji period, Japan attempted to bring themselves closer to Western nations in a rapid modernization process. Yet, in Japan, where the word *Tetsugaku*, [哲学] had just been translated, there was likely no one who even thought of creating their own original philosophy. In just such an era, there was a person who fought with Zen and other Eastern [systems of] thought and the newest Western philosophical trends to create an original philosophy unique to Japan. [This was] Nishida Kitarō" (NHK 2019). The Shogakukan manga-fication of Nishida's life and times (overviewed by the Nishida Kitarō Museum of Philosophy) also appeals to readers in this way, displaying boldly on its cover that Nishida was "Japan's first philosopher to influence the world" (Miyazoe et al. 2013).

9   Even limiting ourselves to the realm of philosophy, Takano Chōei (高野長英, 1804–50) gave an early and brief account of the great Western philosophers from

the Early Greeks to Christian Wolff (1679–1754) well in advance of Perry's arrival (Takano 1835/1972).

10 The first explicit statement I have found of Nishida's reputation came from Takahashi shortly after the release of *Inquiry*, stating "if I had been asked before the publication of *An Inquiry into the Good* if there was such a thing as an independent philosophical [哲学らしい] book written by one of my countrymen, or which book that might be, I would have experienced some consternation even while giving a vague answer. Yet now that *An Inquiry into the Good* has appeared, I would be able to give a swift and confident response to this question" (Takahashi 1912/2001: 296). These sentiments were echoed by those like Kurata Hyakuzō (Kurata 1912/2016: 50–1), who found Nishida to be refreshing amongst the "dried up" philosophers in Japan. For both, these statements come with the caveat that they were aware of and respected preceding philosophers like Miyake Setsurei and Onishi Hajime (Takahashi 1912/2001: 296–7; Kurata 1912/2016: 27–8). In this regard, a perhaps more crucial moment was the way in which Nishida's reputation spread abroad through his students studying in Germany in the 1920s and 1930s. In response to foreign curiosity as to whether there was such a thing as "Japanese" philosophy, many seemed to identify Nishida without giving reference to any authors who came before him. Now, John C. Maraldo (2017: 104–7) has also outlined how Nishida came to be known as modern Japan's first philosopher, so those who are curious as to how this reputation spread are encouraged to look there.

11 Defining the scope of Japanese philosophy is a tricky topic, but a good starting point for delineating potential definitions would be *The Sourcebook for Japanese Philosophy* (Heisig et al., 2011: 17–21). The editors highlight four principal meanings of Japanese philosophy as: (i) Japanese authors studying an academic discipline that deals with problems that have been grouped together within one (Western) tradition of thought; (ii) classical Japanese thinking that stands prior to European intrusion; (iii) a specific methodology that, although Western in origin, can involve dialogue between Japanese resources and traditional Western philosophical inquiries (e.g., questioning the nature of time by appealing to Dōgen); and (iv) a philosophical tradition that distinguishes itself from Western philosophy by including certain "Japanese" characteristics (e.g., traditional Japanese views on aesthetics). Noticeably, the editors avoid making conclusions about which of these definitions are "right" and which are "wrong," but rather point out that they all have their own strengths and weaknesses. This clear analysis helps us understand that there are many ways to understand Japanese philosophy, but there is no need to absolutize any of them.

12 The simplest conclusion would likely be that refusing Dōgen (or others like him) the status of philosopher is a Eurocentric worldview that keeps non-European or

American voices from disrupting the status quo (e.g., Garfield and van Norden 2016). With that said, one could also respond to this by saying this is not the case, Dōgen himself need not be forced into role of philosopher for his insights to be immensely philosophically valuable and it can have a philosophical value or be put into dialogue with contemporary debates regardless of what we call him. Or, rather, some may think it would be problematic to refer to Dōgen as a philosopher, considering what Robert Bernasconi (2003) has discussed as the "double bind" we face when putting non-Western philosophies into contemporary Western philosophical dialogues. Indeed, by forcing non-Western thinkers into the category of philosophy, we are forcing ourselves to either shift the content of their work to match the standards of said dialogues or otherwise be dismissed by those operating in a different framework. Thus, the potential political implications of distinguishing "pre-modern Japanese thought" from "modern Japanese philosophy" go too deep for us to deal with here.

13 Let it be remembered that even the idea that there was such a thing as *Sakoku* might not be as obvious as we typically think, given that there was never a full and definitive declaration of closure from the Shogunate (Paramore 2009: 75, n. 84).

14 See Wakabayashi (1986) for a thorough description of Aizawa Seishisai's complex relationship with the impending arrival of Western powers.

15 Consider as an example, Sakuma Shōzan (佐久間象山, 1811–64), who very famously defended a conception of maintaining Eastern Morality and Western Technology (東洋の道徳、西洋の芸術). For many mid-nineteenth-century Japanese authors like Shōzan, there would have been no inherent need to adopt Western ways of life beyond the technical or scientific novelties one could then adapt to Japanese society. How this general view changed in the 1870s is something that will come up more specifically in Chapter 3. For more on the life and times of Shōzan, see Sakamoto (2008).

16 Nishi and Tsuda were in Holland at the orders of the Shogunate from between 1862 and 1865, studying under Professor Simon Vissering. Nishi managed translations on philosophical theories and Tsuda managed translations of political or legal theory. See Kosaka (2013: 7–17).

17 IG: xxxiii.

18 More specifically, parts 2 and 3 of *Inquiry* were written first as separate essays in 1906. Parts 1 and 4 were added before the book's publication in 1908 and 1909, respectively. See Yusa (2002: 76–90; 96–102) for more on the timetable leading up to the publication of *Inquiry*.

19 One overlooked achievement of Nishida's already epoch-making career was his ability to stay on the cutting edge of the newest Western philosophical debates of his time. Alongside this eagerness to learn from the new authors of his day came a shift in his philosophical influences over the years. Tracking down the changing

influences in Nishida's career goes far beyond the scope of our work here, but luckily authors like Heisig (2001), Krummel (2015), or Maraldo (2017) have already offered solid schematic overviews of the developments that took place in Nishida's career.

20 See Heisig 2001: 32–6.
21 This is likely what those like Nakae Chōmin were hinting at when he said there was no philosophy in Japan. This does not mean that the Japanese were "barbaric," but rather that the kind of liberal expression of opinions and free discourse needed to engage in philosophy required moral and political progress that was yet to come in the Meiji period. As Davis (2020) explains, this view of philosophy as a Western discipline that was imported into Japan during the Meiji period has (perhaps surprisingly) been the most dominant view among contemporary Japanese scholars, while Western scholars have been more open to referring to Buddhism or Confucianism as philosophy.
22 This seems to me the opinion of those like Inoue Enryō, who—as we shall discuss in Chapter 1—repeatedly attempted to show how Buddhist philosophy and Western philosophy could mutually enlighten one another and ultimately aim for a middle path.
23 The word *Tetsugaku* (哲学) literally combines wisdom (哲) with the character for study or learning (学), a point not lost on some in the Meiji period (e.g., see the dialogue recorded by Inoue in the preface to *An Evening of Philosophical Conversation*, IES 1: 33). Consider also Inoue Tetsujirō's writings on the Wang Yang-Ming Confucian school, wherein he finds in Confucianism a sense of philosophy that is no less interested in fundamental questions than its Western counterpart (Inoue 1900).
24 Admittedly, this vision of Nishida as a Meiji man who developed within the genealogical continuity of "Meiji Idealism" or "Meiji Absolutism" was much more popular among post-war Marxist intellectual historians. Funayama (1959/1965), Miyakawa (1962), and Miyajima (1960) all view Nishida's place in Meiji intellectual history as a defining aspect of his career. Moreover, while this element has tended to be overlooked in recent years, Inoue Katsuhito (2011) has written a book in Japanese about Nishida's philosophy and the Meiji period. While Maraldo (2017) critically addresses Nishida's status as Japan's first philosopher and others have mentioned the connections between Nishida and specific Meiji predecessors, however, this will be the first book-length contribution written in English dedicated to the subject of Nishida's philosophy and the Meiji era.
25 We will leave the logical operator "soku (即)" in English instead of rendering it as "*qua*," "*sive*," or any of the other frequently given—but never quite perfect—translations. This notion of *soku* can have many meanings in everyday Japanese, generally expressing immediateness—examples include "instant death (即死),"

"prompt decision (即決)," or even something as simple as "same day express delivery (即日配達)." In the context of Japanese philosophy, however, this term is used as a logical operator that expresses the interpenetration of two intertwined but simultaneously irreducible objects. In other words, A-*soku*-B implies that A and B are both immediately tied up and dependent upon one another, but also that A cannot be reduced to B nor can B be reduced to A. This odd operator likely has no English equivalent and will require explanation either way, so we will leave it as *soku* to avoid confusion.

Chapter 1

1 "[I]n the beginning I wasn't thinking about studying philosophy. Originally, I was thinking about going into science. However, at that time [when I was in high school] I read a thin pamphlet called *An Evening of Philosophical Conversation* written by a man named Inoue Enryō and found it to be very interesting, and this stimulated me to start moving toward [the study of] philosophy" (NKZ 24: 80).

2 Information concerning Inoue's connection to the *Seikyōsha* movement can be found in Pyle (1969). Analyses of his work on superstitions and ghost stories (his *yōkaigaku*) are available in Josephson (2006) and Miura (2014). His role in reforming Buddhism is discussed from various perspectives in Snodgrass (2003), Okada (2005), and Kopf (2013). Discussions of his complicated relationship with Christianity can be found in Staggs (1983) and Paramore (2009). Finally, a comprehensive introduction to Inoue's life and work in its historical context is available in Schultzer (2019).

3 Pre-Nishida Buddhist philosophy in general has tended to receive such treatment. For example, Kosaka Kunitsugu (1995) specifically cites Inoue Enryō and Kiyozawa Manshi as being such cases of mere "syncretism" between Western philosophy and Buddhist thought. Kosaka Masaaki (1969/1999: 265–6) refers to the work of Inoue Enryō, Inoue Tetsujirō, and Miyake Setsurei as being more of a "metaphor (比喩)" or "sketch (描写)" of their respective systems than an evidence-based "demonstration (論証)."

4 Inoue provided some of the earliest introductions to the history of Western philosophy (and its relationship to Eastern philosophy) in texts such as *An Outline of Philosophy*. Additionally, he discussed what philosophy means in the first place extensively in forums such as his lecture, *A Brief Introduction to Philosophy*.

5 This connection with "causality" may feel underdeveloped here, but more on the topic of science and Buddhism as it relates to Inoue can be found in chapters 4 and 5 of Schulzer (2019).

6   While space constraints stop us from surveying Hara's work, we should note that his classes—which often compared Buddhist thought with German Idealism and may have served as a prototype to the theory of "phenomena-*soku*-reality"—were taken and appreciated by the authors most associated with this tradition. While information on Hara's philosophy is scarce, Inoue Katsuhito (2011) has shed some light on Hara's lectures and how they fit into the genealogical progression leading up to Nishida's philosophy.

7   IES 3: 350; 358–60. More information on Inoue's complicated relation with Christian doctrine can be found in Paramore (2009: 134–41) and Staggs (1983: 265–70).

8   This may seem unfair on Inoue's part, granted that Buddhist doctrine also has its fair share of "unscientific" beliefs. Hence, one may wonder why Buddhism was capable of being a rational or secular religion while Christianity was not. While there is much we could say here, the key difference for Inoue seems to be that while Buddhism concerns our freedom from suffering and desire by becoming enlightened (and thus seeing *this very reality* as it truly is), Christianity at its core requires that we suppose a transcendent, unverifiable personal God as the "standard of truth," which sets us up for a vicious circle. If one has faith in this God, then their statements will be validated by His existence. If not, however, then there are no empirical grounds for questioning the claims made by His believers and, thus, no means of verifying the standards of truth they establish (see IES 3: 67–9; Schulzer 2019: 88–90).

9   Both Snodgrass (2003) and Godart (2004: 111–3) tend to emphasize the practical elements of Enryo's Buddhist philosophy. Even Takemura's (2013) favorable discussion of Inoue's understanding of philosophy adopts the view that, in the end, theoretical philosophy existed for the sake of returning to practical problems.

10 Consider, for instance, in the public lecture "A Brief Review of Philosophy" Inoue seems to argue that philosophy is necessary for understanding the reason or purpose of one's existence. "Even if there is no pleasure (楽) to be gained from it, insofar as we have been born as humans, there is nothing less convenient than living in this world without knowing the purpose of one's life" (IES 2: 53).

11 I have consulted Takemura (2013: 12) while translating this passage.

12 Of course, this does not make it politically innocent either. While it is hard to say precisely how much one informed the other without falling into empty speculation about Inoue's intentions, it is—at the very least—worth nothing that Inoue's arguments about Buddhism's capacity to coexist with the physical sciences is complemented by his claims that mind and matter are both dependent on, while simultaneously being irreducible to, one another.

13 I am using "phenomena-*soku*-reality (現象即実在)" to refer to the broader tendency in Meiji philosophy to provide an ontology that does not presuppose

any "thing-in-itself" or mind-independent world behind conscious phenomena. Funayama Shinichi (1959/1965) in particular claimed Inoue's *An Evening of Philosophical Conversation* to be the first substantial contribution to this movement. While I would largely agree with Funayama here, two points require caution. First, Inoue Enryō himself did not use this term to refer to his own philosophy. The term "phenomena-*soku*-reality" properly belongs to his contemporary, Inoue Tetsujirō. As such, we cannot easily assume Enryō and Tetsujirō are endorsing the same theory. Second, in line with the spirit of this chapter, it is important not to assume that Enryō appeared out of nowhere. Indeed, Enryō, as well as all other authors commonly associated with phenomena-*soku*-reality, took classes from Hara Tanzan at Tokyo University, whose reading of the *Awakening of Faith in the Mahayana* has been understood as a proto-typical version of trends in Meiji philosophy (see Watabe 1998).

14   Here we should take their respective allegiances with a grain of salt. In particular, the "materialism" in this dialogue is, as Shirai Masato has argued, something closer to a dualist position than what we typically refer to as materialism (Shirai 2012: 102).

15   This play on words forms on two levels. *Ryōchū* and *Enyū* both make up half of "Enryō" (both in terms of writing the name out and in terms of his system of thought). Additionally, the characters for Enryō's name mean "completion." Thus, the teacher Enryō-*sensei*, who has gone past one-sided or overly simplified extremes, was able to reach a more complete view of reality.

16   This may be visible in Inoue's response to critics claiming that the seemingly all-knowing teacher being named Enryō is a sign of hubris. According to Inoue, these dialogues are marked by his attempt to describe this middle path without endorsing any of the biased positions of yore. I would thus argue that Inoue's struggle was an *internal* one, in which he allowed these positions to combat one another until there was nothing left but the completed middle path (or, in other words, *Enryō*) (IES 1: 48–9).

17   Inoue explains this view by using modern Western philosophy as an example in *An Introduction to the Vitalization of Buddhism* (1887): "What are the theories that comprise Western philosophy? We could say they are materialism, idealism, or logicism (唯理). [...] In the beginning, Locke advocated empiricism. Then Leibniz advocated naturalism (本然論) before Kant came to synthesize these positions. Those like Hume tended to be biased toward materialism while those like Berkeley tended to be biased toward idealism. This led to [Thomas] Reid syncretizing the two positions with his mind-body dualism. While Fichte took the subject and Schelling the object [as primary], Hegel harmonized their positions. The German school thus became biased toward speculation (空理) while the Scottish school was biased toward common-sense. He who synthesized these two positions was Cousin in France. Spencer feared becoming biased toward either the knowable or

the unknowable and thus tried to make a divide between them. Modern philosophy has thus been unable to escape from these [biased] theories. Hence, [modern philosophers] all run toward one extreme theory, and while they may desire to find a balance (中正を保持せんと欲して), they have been unable to achieve this goal" (IES 3: 361). A more detailed account about how Inoue understood the history of philosophy is available in Godart (2004).

18 Shirai (2012) and Wargo (2005) have likely given the most detailed analyses of the similarities between the two. Here, we will only briefly review their specific similarities in order to focus more on the root of their shared philosophical intuitions.

19 "It is usually thought that subject and object are realities that can exist independently of each other and that phenomena of consciousness arise through their activity, which leads to the idea that there are two realities: mind and matter. This is a total mistake. The notions of subject and object derive from two different ways of looking at a single fact, as does the distinction between mind and matter" (IG: 49).

20 "While I'm sure readers will be impressed with his clever hybrid-theory, I cannot help but personally wonder: has not Enryō-*sensei* [merely] attempted to mix oil and water?" (OHS 2: 27).

21 Even Nitta Yoshihiro, in his attempt to push Inoue's later thought in *A Proposal for a New Philosophy* to its upper limits, concedes that it was "underdeveloped" and that, insofar as it gave no practical account of how reality differentiated itself as such, it stops at being a "contemplative" philosophy of merely looking at material reality or conscious phenomena from different perspectives (Nitta 1988: 97–8).

22 Wargo 2005: 31; note that this critique is also applied to the other major author associated with the broader notion of phenomena-*soku*-reality, Inoue Tetsujirō.

23 Examples of scholars who refer to this possibility: Funayama (1959/1965), Nitta (1989), and Wargo (2005). Maraldo (2017) mentions in passing a difference in critical method between those like Inoue and those like Nishida and Onishi Hajime. As I mention in endnote 26 of this chapter, Itabashi (2004) also makes similar arguments for difference in methodological rigor in his discussions of Inoue Tetsujirō.

24 This is indicated by the oft-cited reminder from Nishida himself at the beginning of *Inquiry*'s new edition in which he states "[t]hat which I called in the present book the world of direct or pure experience I have now come to think of as the world of historical reality. The world of action-intuition—the world of poiesis—is none other than the world of pure experience" (IG: xxxiii).

25 A slightly more thorough summary of this structure could go as follows: pure experience is equivalent to direct experience *before* any distinctions have been made (such as between subject and object or mind and matter). This claim refers

not only to a psychological state of being unaware of such differences, but rather to the ontological fact that such dualities are not pre-formed in our experiences. Yet, as change inevitably occurs within experience, rifts open within this underlying unity. In other words, pure experience is constantly changing, and as these shifts occur, "gaps" will arise in this initial unity. This can be in the form of conflicting or contradictory information arising, thus necessitating an act of reflection, or a lack felt due to metabolic disturbances causing a break between the volitional subject and its object of desire. These gaps provide an opportunity to clarify what has happened in pure experience in reflective judgment, or otherwise, to return to the intellectual intuition showing the inherent unity between subject and object. Hence, although it is not inherent to individual experiences, one becomes able in these cases to abstract a "material" or "spiritual" perspective out of the initial unity of pure experience.

26 One may wonder if this skepticism was not just Inoue Enryō's philosophical disposition, and not indicative of any novel contributions from Nishida. Here we may note that the critiques made above can likely also be extended to another famous proponent of phenomena-*soku*-reality, Inoue Tetsujirō. Following Inoue's definition, we see that his phenomena-*soku*-reality is a worldview in which "phenomena [of consciousness] exist outside of the subject and as such constitute reality" (Inoue 1894/1944: 612). Along these lines, we thus end up with a similar proposition to what Enryō argued for, wherein we deny any absolute distinctions between subject and object or mind and matter to avoid absurd monisms (the world existing solely "in the subjectivist's head" or completely "independent of what the objectivist sees") or unsolvable dualisms. Instead, Tetsujirō argues that true or absolute reality is something akin to what we have called the middle path so far: a dynamic interplay between mind and matter that goes beyond rigid categories like Idealism or Dualism. Yet, as Wargo (2005: 17–27) has deftly shown, when Tetsujirō is pressed to explicate what exactly this notion of reality standing at the core of all our religious, scientific, and philosophical knowledge, he inevitably ends up in the same situation as Enryō, insofar as Tetsujirō ultimately claims that true reality is "not something to be grasped in our cognition" (Inoue 1897/2003: 155), thereby preventing us from ever corroborating any arguments we make for his claims or make positive efforts to describe precisely what his view amounts to. Moreover (in his quest to do away with absolutely any form of dualism), Tetsujirō refuses to admit any trans-experiential standards of truth, insisting that universally valid knowledge only consists of knowledge that has yet to be contradicted so far, thereby leaving no room for him to ground or universalize his own claims about reality (see Inoue 1894/2011: 617). While we do not have time to explore these issues in detail, a much more extensive and charitable reading (that ultimately leads to similar conclusions) can be found in Itabashi (2004: 11–22).

27 "When one directly experiences one's own state of consciousness, there is not yet a subject or an object, and knowing and its object are completely unified. This is the most refined type of experience" (IG: 3–4).
28 See, for instance, Nagai (2018), who raises the issue by comparing Nishida and Wittgenstein.
29 Consider, for instance, Nishida's statement that "True reality, like the true meaning of art, is not something that can be transmitted from one person to another. All we can transmit is an abstract shell. We may think that by means of the same language we understand the same thing, but to some extent the content necessarily differs" (IG: 51–2).
30 This is a point we will discuss in Chapters 2 and 4, but I will say here that the development of meaning in pure experience is not mere nominalism, which does away with any sense of universals beyond names assigned to things that appear similar, nor does it assume any (in Berkeley's understanding) Lockean abstract universals independent of experience. As we shall see, essences and universals can connect "by themselves" by differentiating themselves from other patterns. More details will be offered on this point in the following chapter.
31 One may wonder why Nishida can claim these structures as "universal" while only having the provisional data given to us in the stream of consciousness so far. While this is a valid question, answering it requires us to deal with Nishida's ontology of meaning and so we will put the matter aside until the next chapter.
32 Consider only one example of this conviction that we find in his letters: "Partly because my teaching demands it, I've read almost all the well-known books on ethics; but unless I start out with metaphysics, I don't seem to get a satisfactory answer. Recently, I began my studies on the history of philosophy and epistemology, not because they are needed for a study of ethics, but *because I cannot escape my metaphysical doubt*" (cited in Yusa 2002: 78; emphasis added by author).
33 Consider, for instance, Miyake Setsurei's testimony that, by the end of the nineteenth century, young men in Japanese universities had split into two types. There were, as before, success-oriented young men looking for practical knowledge from Western learning. However, according to Miyake, at the end of the nineteenth century, there were now also "literary" students, whose sole purpose for studying was to find answers to problems related to the "life (人生)" and "suffering (煩悶)" of the individual. For a summary of Miyake's writings on this topic, see Hiraishi (2012: 24–8).

Chapter 2

1 "For Nishida, the true demand of philosophy emerges as a response to the feeling of anguish that accompanies one's reflections on the totality of life. His further

characterization of pure experience as something utterly meaningless can be interpreted as a provisional solution to the problem of philosophical anguish. *This solution, however, threatens to undermine the whole project of philosophy*" (Lotman 2020: 74; emphasis added by the author of this book).

2   One could argue that there are different conceptions of meaning between our use of concepts in language or judgment and the sense of meaningfulness that one finds in religious or deeply moral experiences. Although this distinction is important, it does not solve the problem at hand. Even if we say that pre-subjective experience has some form of religious value, we would have to explain where such value comes from, how we know it is not a mere conceptual construct, and why pure experience does not devolve into a hyper-nihilistic state in which there is no such thing as religion or morality.

3   If this interpretation is appropriate, then Nishida would not be alone in taking direct experience to be too rich for conceptual language. Even in contemporary analytic philosophy, we find analogous ideas. For instance, consider Heck's assertion that "[t]he leaves on the trees outside my window are fluttering back and forth, randomly, as it seems to me, as the wind passes over them.—Yet my experience of these things represents them far more precisely than that, far more distinctively, it would seem, than any characterization I could hope to formulate, for myself, or for others, in terms of the concepts I presently possess. The problem is not a lack of time, but lack of descriptive resources, that is, lack of the appropriate concepts" (Heck 2000: 489–90).

4   I believe Fujita's (2007: 53–7) discussion of pure experience as prior to judgment and language matches this view well. For example, Fujita argues that the word "red" will never fully encapsulate the primal redness that I experience when I first acquaint myself with that red something (and that Nishida is trying to express this point somehow).

5   James, for his part, took pure experience as a "blooming, buzzing confusion" (James 1890/1983: 462) in which different elements of experience create context by coming into relation with one another. This does not mean that James downplayed conceptual content or found pre-reflective, non-conceptual content to be "more real" than reflective consciousness. Instead, it means that consciousness is a dynamic process of contextualization and re-contextualization, wherein exploring what is on the fringes leads us to new discoveries and horizons. (For a much more detailed explanations, see Krueger 2022.)

6   As we shall see in Chapter 4, although it may be easy to overlook this point, any explanations of how our self-consciousness as individuals is possible, that will likely require us to explain how the individual is formed within pure experience *through* the development of meaning, precisely because of this predicament. To do otherwise would be to either presuppose there is a given individual

self-consciousness which stands outside of pure experience or to appeal to some conception of a self that "arises" in pure experience; something which is not forthcoming in *Inquiry*.

7   As Nishida writes in a letter to his lifelong friend, D. T. Suzuki, "Many different philosophical theories have been built upon logic, but I would like to build [my own] upon psychology. I have recently found things like William James' theory [説] of pure experience to be quite interesting. Do you know if he has finished working on his metaphysics yet?" (cited in Stone and Altobrando 2023: 56, n. 1).

8   For more on Motora's role in educational or moral debates, see, for example, Tanabe (2021) or McVeigh (2017: 77–8). Note also that one of Motora's few publications in English attempted to weigh in on how this mishmash of religions taking place in Japan at the time could give a different perspective on the relation between science and religion (Motora 1905A).

9   See Okubo (2018) for the debt that sociology in Japan owes to Motora.

10 Oddly enough, Motora also seemed to be part of Greater Japan Society (大日本協会) and considered himself a "Japanist (日本主義者)." Keeping this in mind, there has been quite a bit of debate about how to reconcile Motora's socialism with his nationalism (see Okubo 2018; Tanabe 2021).

11 For a detailed account of Motora's life as a psychologist and his position in Tokyo Imperial University, see Takasuna (2007).

12 This seems to have been a core intuition of his from a young age. Even during his early years studying in the United States, Motora is said to have performed experiments with a "wire helmet" on his fellow Japanese students to identify the "sleep brain waves (睡眠脳波)" that he believed must cause the phenomena of dreams. Nothing came of the experiment, but the underlying intuition that there was a dynamic energy that could bridge the gap between physical and phenomenal remained present throughout his career (McVeigh 2017: 80).

13 To be clear, this does not include all psychologists. Rather, Motora believed those like Wundt and James would agree with him on the need for both external or objective observation and introspection as a necessary foundation for practicing psychology in the first place. After all, on the one hand, we see that any good psychologist will actively study the mental functions taking place in the brain as a biophysical dynamic. On the other hand, though, these observations can only take place outgoing from our own conscious perceptions of the world or others' behavior, and thus it is inevitable that any debates on conscious must also start from experience (see Motora 1915: 1117–19; 1128–33).

14 This is a question that remains relevant to contemporary debates in the philosophy of psychology and neuroscience. Motora (and for that matter, many of the Western psychologists in his time) seems to face the same doubts that contemporary neurophenomenologists have had to deal with in showing that first-personal

accounts of consciousness are necessary for studying the mind—and thus that merely modeling the mind is not enough. For contemporary examples, see Zahavi and Gallagher (2007) or Gallagher (2012).

15 While we have already covered Nishida's stance in the previous chapter, Motora similarly believes that attempts to absolutize either the subjective, mental elements of experience or the objective, physical elements of experience will end in either absurdity or abstraction and are thus detrimental to psychological studies (see Motora 1915: 890).

16 For a more detailed view of Wundt's presence in nineteenth- and twentieth-century Japan, his ideas on direct experience, and his influence on *Inquiry*, see Mitsuhara (2021).

17 Motora's *Outline of Psychology* as a whole was composed of roughly thirty-eight papers published in the *Philosophy Journal* [哲学雑誌] between 1902 and 1906. All citations to Motora's work will refer to this series of articles unless otherwise specified. Now, as an additional point, we may note that most of Motora's work on complete and incomplete experience was published in the summer of 1906, precisely as Nishida was working on what would become the second and third sections of *Inquiry* (see Lotman 2020: 75).

18 Motora himself claims that "the author [of this book] will follow Professor James in arguing for radical empiricism" (Motora 1915: 315). See Krueger (2022) for an easy-to-follow guide to how meaning forms in James's notion of pure experience.

19 See Motora 1915: 319. Now, it is hard to say precisely what aspects of Mead's work that Motora was familiar with or what he was referencing at this point in 1906. Still, the general notion that present consciousness is not only what is given to us directly, but "the locus of reality" can be found in Mead's thought (e.g., Mead 1932: 1–31).

20 One may wonder how Motora uses the words "meaning" or "indirect experience," considering that there seems to be a sizeable difference between meaning as a word or sign and meaning in a broader sense of something being significant to us. While I cannot get into this point in detail, my understanding is that Motora is using the term as broadly as possible, taking any kind of "meaning" to be a kind of indirect experience, whether it be imaginary, recollective, symbolic, or anything else.

21 Note also for Motora that the process of association occurring through perception is contingent; with exception to certain logical or mathematical laws (which we will not get into here), our association of ideas leading up to the concept of "horse" pertains largely to our psychological functions and historical background, and not due to any kind of universality among the horses themselves. The fact that Motora cites Berkeley's nominalism positively is telling in this regard. See Motora (2015: 369–72).

22 Motora refers frequently to "horses" and "triangles" that appear to us as similar but gives little in the way of *how* we define something as similar enough to constitute a

horse and not another four-legged animal (i.e., the difference between a horse and a donkey). Importantly, this uncertainty is likely one of the key elements that will help us distinguish between Motora and Nishida.

23 Modified translation cited in Lotman (2020: 76); italics added by the author of this book.

24 More specifically, Motora discusses "higher-level concepts (高級なる概念)," which arise from abstracting different elements from preexisting concepts or representations. For instance, Motora discusses nationality (国民). From what I gather of his discussion, although we may not be able to find any notion of "Eastern" or "Western" people in direct experience, comparing our different particular understandings of various nationalities (Japanese, Chinese, American, etc.), we can start to make higher-level categorizations, such as grouping the Chinese and Japanese together as Easterners. Now, given that nationalities like Japanese and Chinese already presuppose a high degree of abstraction (if for no other reason than I am at least assuming an American in Chicago I have never met before belongs to the same group of people as myself, regardless of physical or mental characteristics), I am not sure the example works well for him. With that said, the fundamental idea that we only gain some concepts through comparison between preexisting concepts is easy to follow, so we will leave well enough alone for now (see Motora 1915: 366–9).

25 Consider Nishida's analysis of the judgment, "the horse runs." While this judgment seems to put together different elements, the horse (subject) and its running (predicate), Nishida argues that this judgment actually occurs through the reunification of different elements that had been abstracted from a single state-of-affairs (representation), i.e., a running horse (IG: 11).

26 Nishida himself noted after the fact that *Inquiry* takes the standpoint of consciousness, "which might be thought of as a kind of psychologism." (IG: xxxi) Crucially, however, Nishida follows this up by insisting that, even if many view his early work as psychologistic, his core intentions were "not just psychological" (IG, xxxii; see also Mitsuhara 2018 for a detailed outline of what aspects of *Inquiry* were and were not psychologistic).

27 In the end, Motora seems to insist less on finding the kind of "one true reality" Nishida is after, and more in reconciling "internal" and "external" experiences, where we make observations on our own consciousness from within and the biophysical dynamics that create conscious energy from without. Interestingly, Motora seemed to think that Zen Buddhism could help bridge this gap, insofar as "'Zen' experience suggests us [*sic*] that we have direct experience of energy," hinting at the possibility of finding the bridge between internal and external in the dynamism of everyday life as made clear through meditative practices (see Motora 2015: 21–4; McVeigh 2017: 84–7).

28 See also Wargo (2005: 98–101) for an account of what Nishida is aiming for and how these ideas regarding color manifested themselves during his middle period.
29 Even Nishida's own native language of Japanese famously blurs the lines between what English speakers would refer to as "green" and "blue," referring to both as *Ao* [青] in many situations. With that said, though, while a full-blooded response to this line of questioning is not possible here, a charitable reading of Nishida would recognize that the precise point at which we draw the line between what we call green and what we do not is less important than the fact that we establish certain shades of colors in opposition to each other.
30 This idea of different colors establishing themselves as universal patterns that cannot be reduced to mere names or "subjective" labels but also do not require any trans-experiential or material elements to establish themselves could likely be fleshed out better by tying Nishida's philosophy to Alva Noë's "phenomenal objectivism." The idea is that colors are ultimately "ways things are disposed to change their appearance as color-critical conditions change" (Noë 2004: 143). In other words, colors are not mere sensations, nor are they relational in the sense of how things relate to the subject's mind. To the contrary, they are relations between things and the experiential elements in the environment that change color conditions (lighting, clarity of view, etc.). Crucially, it is the organism's ecological capacity to navigate this environment that allows these relational patterns to establish themselves clearly. In this regard, colors are both objective (i.e., they are not dependent on subjective psychological capacities) and phenomenal (colors are not mere physical properties of things, but ways in which the environment presents itself). These additional explanations of what it means to say that colors establish themselves through the activity of experience as ecological factors seems to me a key piece that can help us fill in some of the blanks missing in the early Nishida's account, insofar as my ability to cognize red occurs through the distinctions between red things and green things *necessarily* takes place as I navigate my environment. Cashing out this comparison in full is not possible now, but interested readers may consult Noë (2004: 141–61).
31 Takahashi goes so far as to refer to this point as the "contradiction lying at the foundation of his [Nishida's] pure experience" (1912/2001: 304).
32 Crucially, Takahashi did not ignore the fact that Nishida took pure experience as a "unifying force." Instead, he seems to have found Nishida unable to answer crucial questions relating to this process of unification, such as what level (段階) pure experience is in this process of development by differentiation, if it is fundamentally different from non-pure experience, and why pure experience is meaningful if the answer to the two prior questions would be that all experience is pure experience.
33 Emphasis added by the author of this book.

34 We will not delve into the matter here, but Takahashi's point seems to be this: if meaning and facts are two sides of the same coin and experiencing is knowing facts precisely as they are, then in the end we have no grounds to say that judgments are different from how things are. From a Nishidian standpoint, we could respond to this by taking a coherentist position of sorts. In other words, the standards of truth are not a "matter of meaning" per se, but rather one of the relations between one moment in this system and another. Thus, to say that I was mistaken when I thought your coat was red can only be made sense of by comparing my initial experience of your coat in poor lighting to a better view later.

35 The pink elephant example was added by the author of this book and does not come from Takahashi himself. Moreover, to go a bit further and potentially deviate from Takahashi's original argument, I think something could also be said regarding the possibility that fictional characters or myths presenting problems for Nishida's philosophy of pure experience. After all, a horse-man hybrid likely does not "exist" in any sense beyond the meanings or imaginations we ascribe to them, but Nishida does not have any immediate means to distinguish between merely fictional concepts like centaurs and factually existing objects.

36 See Takahashi (1912/2001: 321); Nishida may be able to avoid this by taking an intersubjective or pragmatic view of avoiding hallucinations, noting that "[f]or example, a lamp is here before me. If I am the only one who can see it, it might be deemed a subjective hallucination. But when each of us acknowledges it in the same way it becomes an objective fact. The objective, independent world arises from such a universal character" (IG: 54). Because Nishida does not go any further here, it is not clear how well this answer would survive more rigorous scrutiny, but we will leave the matter alone for now.

37 The same came be said for logical laws. After all, our ability to say that "A is not ¬ A" relies on our ability to speak in universal and formal terms, instead of judging each "A" on a case-by-case basis.

38 This criticism may not hit its mark with Nishida, but it would certainly apply to Inoue Tetsujirō, who claims that—insofar as we cannot admit any transempirical standards of truth—universally valid knowledge is actually knowledge that has yet to be contradicted. In Tetsujirō's case, even 2+2=4 only means that all of our empirical testing has yet to contradict the proposition that putting two things together with two more things begets four things. See Inoue (1894/2011: 617; see also endnote 26 in Chapter 1).

39 These questions are taken up in much more detail in Nishida's subsequent work after *Inquiry*, "Thought and Experience (思索と体験)." For an explanation of how Nishida revised his thoughts on facts and meaning leading up to the publication of his second major book, *Intuition and Reflection in Self-Awareness*, see Mitsuhara (2015).

Chapter 3

1. "In our consciousness, an internal unity always functions at the base of thinking, imagination, will, perception, feeling, and impulse; and all phenomena of consciousness are the development and completion of this unity. The deepest power unifying this whole is our so-called self, and the will is that which most completely expresses this power. Thus the development and completion of the will is none other than the development and completion of the self, and the good is the development and completion—the self-realization—of the self. The highest good, in other words, is for our spirit to develop its various abilities and to achieve a perfect development" (IG: 125).
2. An introduction to the more formal and logical aspects of Nishida's struggle to deal with the individual after *Inquiry* can be found in Altobrando (2016).
3. Hirayama (1997: 91) also mentions Aristotle (384–322 BCE) and another nineteenth-century philosopher, Harold Høffding (1843–1931), though he focuses most on Onishi. Nishida himself took an ambivalent stance on the relation between pure experience and his ethics, stating that "I wrote part III with the aim of expounding the good on the basis of the ideas presented in part II, but one can regard it as an independent ethic" (IG: xxx).
4. Hirai (1979) in particular seems to value Green's influence on Nishida's thought to extreme levels. Takeuchi (1970) also stresses the decisive impact of Green's ethics on Nishida's formation as a philosopher. Inoue (2011) provides a more sober diagnosis showing that, while Green was unquestionably in the background of his thought, Nishida eventually came to find his work insubstantial. A more schematic comparison between Nishida and Green regarding self-realization can be found in Mizuno (2000).
5. Exceptions in the history of Japanese political thought can be found in Hane (1969). Literary examples are given in Walker (1979).
6. Take Ikegami (1995), who makes a detailed analysis of samurai culture to argue that individuality existed in the form of honor amongst individuals in a complex social setting. What this analysis can point us to is, specifically, the possibility that varying social structures provided a different kind of individualism in Japan in comparison with the West at large.
7. Due to a lack of space for sufficient detail, I am simplifying this gradual movement toward modernization. Keene (1969) has already shown that some Japanese scholars knew more of the West than we typically think. Jansen (1992) has also shown that other options (such as the foreign expulsion movements and proposals for a unified Asian bloc) were also presented as alternatives to Western learning.
8. As Inoue Katsuhito notes, Fukuzawa was not alone on this point. It seems almost all *early* enlightenment writers seem to have motivated individualism by appealing to the needs of the state (2011: 61, 73).

9   The most blatant evidence of this would be increasingly strict censorship laws which even led to a shutdown of the *Meiji Six* magazine in 1875. However, one more interesting anecdote from Blocker & Starling points out the fact that to combat early enlightenment tendencies toward liberalism, the Meiji government commissioned the translation of more government-friendly texts, such as Edmund Burke's *Reflections on the French Revolution* and *Appeal from the New to the Old Whigs*, as well as part of Hobbes's *Leviathan* (Blocker and Starling 2001: 122).
10 Gluck (1985: 102–27) goes into far greater detail regarding the ideology and rhetoric in the background of national morality than we can here.
11 The rescript specifically stated that "[o]ur Imperial Ancestors have founded Our Empire on a basis broad and ever-lasting, and had deeply and firmly implanted virtue. Our subjects ever united in loyalty and filial piety from generation to generation illustrated the beauty thereof. This is the glory of the fundamental character of Our Empire, and herein lies the source of Our education" (cited in Duke 2009: 348; see also Gluck 1985: 120–7 for greater analysis).
12 The common term during the Meiji era was *jiko jitsugen setsu* 自己実現説 or *jiga jitsugen setsu* 自我実現説, which both mean roughly "Theory of Self-Realization."
13 Thomas Hill Green was a British philosopher and teacher at Oxford University. While he is best remembered for resisting the naturalistically inclined accounts of morality popular among utilitarians or evolutionary theorists of his time, Green also weighed in on several political discussions, including the temperance movement in Victorian England. A detailed account of Green's metaphysical claims on self-realization can be found in Tyler (2010). The political and practical implications of Green's theories are well documented in Nicholson (1990).
14 Although this eternal consciousness is often referred to as God, scholars like Colin Tyler have shown that it is not difficult to take his notion of an eternal consciousness as meaning something akin to a "universal human spirit" without any serious misreading. What this means is that Green's interpreters had some freedom in terms of how they ought to deal with the religious aspects of generating moral ideals (Tyler 2010: 80–3).
15 Also keep in mind that the 1890s specifically saw fierce debates concerning what has been called the conflict between religion and state. In particular, Inoue Tetsujirō's harsh response to the Christian thinker Uchimura Kanzō's (内村鑑三, 1861–1930) failure to bow properly before the emperor's image sparked a great deal of controversy. Inoue believed that (even if Shintoism, Buddhism, and Confucianism were not troublesome) Christianity was a danger to national morality, and hence inherently conflicted with the state of Japan's needs to find moral consistency. This disagreement between thinkers like Inoue and Christian authors was a major background for all parties discussing self-realization (Paramore 2009: 130–60).

16 This seeming lack of awareness of Green's political philosophy may be at least partially because only the *Prolegomena to Ethics* was translated into Japanese, although it is also possible to imagine that this potentially inconvenient aspect of his thought was ignored, or at least sidestepped, to avoid potential backlash from the public or government (Hirai 1979: 122–3).

17 Green seemed to take the common good to refer to the capacity to ensure that all members of society had *equal opportunity* to pursue the good life and realize the full extent for the sole purpose of improving themselves and their moral capacities, *regardless* of instrumental concerns (see Green 1883/1997: 221–3). While it is not always clear what this amounts to for Green, one thing is clear that he was not advocating any conception of the individual only realizing their own good by strengthening the nation.

18 The relation between self-realization and the family-state is discussed in Hirai (1979: 116–25). One example of this is the Tokyo University scholar Yoshida Seiichi (吉田静致, 1872–1945), who argued that (even if other morals are valuable as well) the base of all morality is in loyalty and filial piety. Yoshida states the following: "The true self is a self that is a member of society. Thus, those who cannot do anything for themselves cannot do anything for society […] In other words, perfect individual morals match with perfect family morals, and moreover perfect social and national morals are in harmony with them as well" (Yoshida 1908: 377).

19 Some scholars have pointed out that the period in which Onishi's writings were written and the small number of direct references to Green ought to make us question if Green was actually in the background of his work. Thus, although Onishi's compatriot Tsubouchi Shōyō (坪内逍遥, 1859–1935) stated clearly that Green was the base for Onishi's theories about self-realization, there is still doubt about the level of Green's influence on Onishi. We shall forego trying to solve this problem for now on the grounds that we are more interested in the topics of self-realization and moral idealism than we are in the historical process of scholarship on Green in Japan (Katayama 2013: 125–6).

20 It is worth mentioning that *The Origin of Conscience* was published posthumously in 1914. Although the book is mostly completed and parts of it had been published in various journals, Onishi had been tinkering with it until his death in 1900 and never seemed to reach its full completion. See Kosaka (2013: 151–3, 167–8) for an outline of Onishi's life and speculation on why *The Origin of Conscience* was never published.

21 Onishi's critiques are far too detailed to enter into here, but good summaries can be found in Kosaka (2013: 177–85) and Hirade (2020: 353–5). Note that the core component of all of them is simple: Our consciousness of duty or sense of right and

wrong can neither be reduced to anything else (e.g., pain/pleasure), nor could any such reductive view ever explain where good and evil come from.

22 We should note that it is more difficult to criticize Green himself on this point. In his previously mentioned political philosophy, Green asked questions concerning the limits of individual freedoms, rights, and social resistance that would require more time to criticize than the less nuanced statement of many Japanese scholars that the self-realization of the individual benefits the whole of society.

23 "In sum, the theory I have proposed here does not necessarily presuppose what is usually called theism. Even so, my theory is not without its metaphysical suppostions. In other words, I believe must suppose that the various individual phenomena that make up the phenomenal world [i.e., reallity; 法界] must all have their own purpose [目的]." (OHS I: 151).

24 More specifically, Onishi refers consistently throughout the back half of *The Origin of Conscience* to the moral ideal as "our fated purpose (定めある目的)" or "true nature (本真の性)." As for what exactly this fated purpose or true nature of humanity is (or how we could discuss it as more than a postulate), Onishi himself seemed to recognize that this was an unfinished project. While Onishi argued that we must accept the existence of this teleological drive to fulfill our ideal form in *some* way, Hirayama (1989: 196–202) points out that he himself was not content to remain agnostic on this matter and intended to provide more details before his untimely death at thirty-six. If we were to attempt to fill in the holes in his theory, the most expedient answer to this question would be to say that the Christian Onishi is assuming a Green-ian framework in which we all recreate the form of God or the Eternal Mind within ourselves. With that said, in his shorter writings, like "The Grounds of the Moral Ideal (道徳的理想の根拠)," he also seems to imply that insofar as "[t]he various individuals that constitute the phenomenal world [法界] are not all independent of one another, but rather are all interrelated," they all have a complex relationship of "seeking fulfilment in the whole that they constitute" (OHS I: 370), and, thus, the ideal form of humanity we strive for is dependent upon our interrelations with the other individuals in this universe and the overarching purpose of the whole which we comprise together. While Onishi did not flesh out this view well enough for us to draw any further conclusions about his philosophical system from it, it is worth noting that there is a connection between his ideas and what we will refer to as the "organic worldview" discussed in the next chapter (see also Mizuno 2001 for how Onishi tried to ground this moral ideal).

25 See Mushiaki and Yukiyasu (1981: 94–5) for a more extensive explanation of Tsunashima's religious thought and its place in Japanese history.

26 Additionally, there is a view among some previous commentators that Nishida's major achievement in ethics was fusing Onishi's precise and logical arguments about the foundation of moral consciousness with Tsunashima's quasi-phenomenological

account of meeting with God. While there are no problems with this view from my perspective, we should be careful to avoid implying that Nishida inherited concerns about self-realization from only these two. See Hirayama (1997: 189–204).

27 Goto-Jones (2005) might disagree with this statement, arguing that there are concrete and important political ramifications to the entirety of Nishida's philosophical career, even going back to *Inquiry*.

28 Nishida's writings on Green are recorded in his complete works (NKZ 11: 3–22).

29 "Personality, which is both the unifying power of consciousness and the unifying power of reality, is first actualized in individuals. At the base of one's consciousness exists unanalyzable individuality. All activities of consciousness are an expression of this individuality: each person's knowledge, feeling, and volition possess qualities unique to the person. This individuality does not manifest itself only in phenomena of consciousness; it also emerges in each person's appearance, speech, and behavior" (IG: 136–7).

30 Nishida begins his discussion of ethics by first critiquing other alternatives: the "intuitive theory," "authority theory," "rational or intellectual theory," and the "hedonistic theory." Because these critiques are not crucial for achieving our goals in this chapter, we will not address them here. However, it is worth noting that the categories that Nishida made (and many of the critiques he leveled against them) were derived from Onishi's lectures on ethics. See Hirayama (1997: 194–7).

31 This possibility to derive any potential political message one wants to from *Inquiry* is a point I dive into in much more detail in Stone (2023).

32 Keep in mind that this is not a slight on Onishi or Tsunashima. Indeed, the two spent most of their adult lives in poor health and passed away quite young (at ages 36 and 37, respectively), thus denying them the time to work out their theories with the same degree of rigor as Nishida, forty-one years old when *Inquiry* was finally published, had been allowed to do.

33 "*Fundamentally, then, things themselves contain nothing evil.* Evil arises from the contradictions and conflicts of the system of reality. If someone asks about the origin of these conflicts, we can answer that they are based on the differentiating activity of reality and are a necessary condition for the development of reality" (IG: 171, emphasis added by the author of this book).

34 Consider the possibility of one who has been trained since birth to quickly and quietly assassinate anyone who dares to stand against her masters. One swoop of a knife would end conflicts with ease. The techniques employed could be mastered such that that no thought is needed to end a life and the motions themselves could be quite elegant. So, why would this form of mastery not count as pure experience?

35 Now, Green himself seems to have anticipated a position like Nishida's and already has a critique in place: "It may come to be thought that the only freedom is to be found in a life of absolute detachment from all interests; a life in which the pure

ego converses solely with itself or with a God, who is the same abstraction under another name. This is a view in which both saints and philosophers have been apt to fall. It means practically, so far as it means anything, absorption in someone interest with which the man identifies himself in exclusion of all other interests, which he sets over against himself as an influence to be kept aloof" (Green 1886/1997: 310). To reiterate, Green himself takes religious freedom found in unity with Self or God apart from society to be a form of aloofness, giving the individual an excuse to avoid engaging in social issues that would otherwise inconvenience him or her.

36 See Takeuchi (1970) for a defense of the claim that Nishida created a "romantic" notion of ethics. Now, it is worth noting that Nishida does not often mention any romantic authors directly in his notes and that any connections between him and the "romantic" tradition seem to be found purely in the zeitgeist of his era and proximity to writers like Takayama Chogyū (高山樗牛, 1871–1902) in Tokyo Imperial University. In this sense, it is important to clarify that even if Nishida was not a romantic author himself, there seems to have been enough common sources between the two to enable research like Takeuchi's to take place.

Chapter 4

1 Keep in mind that this does not mean that the notion of the true self in *Inquiry* has been ignored. Just to name a few important contributions, Nishitani Keiji (1991), Hisamatsu Shinichi (1971), and many others have tackled the issue of selfhood in *Inquiry*.

2 "This attitude [...] probably arose from the fact that those who embraced it still had the tradition of the spirit of the East as their base" (Nishitani 1991: 8). For clarity's sake, Nishitani did not mention any specific names of other Eastern authors or go into great detail when making this claim.

3 An interesting observation from authors like Inoue Katsuhito (2016) and Sako (1995) is that the matter of emphasizing the individual proper or a universal personality became divided among national lines. Those who emphasized the individual tended to insist upon the importance of English philosophy, while those who prioritized the universal aspect sided with German personalists.

4 Kiyozawa is far too complex to have his philosophy labeled outright as organic in spirit and even denies that his philosophy of spiritual activism can be reduced to an Idealist relation between small and great selves (Kiyozawa 1901/2015: 33–4). However, this does not mean that tendencies to describe the relation between the individual and the whole universe as part and whole of an absolute spirit/ great self were not present in his philosophy. The basis for this claim lies in the

basic "truth" that things (or our individual self) do not exist out of relation to one another: "As the truth of the universe, even when we are not aware of it (それを覚知しない間も), this [fact] is always operating above us. We likely think of the air, the sunlight, mountains and streams, trees, birds and beasts, and [even] other persons as things that exist separately of us as external things (外物). However, we cannot survive without air, nor can we survive without sunlight. While mountains, streams, trees, birds, beasts, and other persons may not be in relation [to us] directly in the same way as air and sunlight, they all provide necessary materials for us. One thing might provide us with materials for food and drink. Another might provide us with materials for shelter. It goes without saying that we would not be able to survive without such things. Furthermore, speaking on our 'spiritual world', much of the knowledge and thoughts we have within our spiritual world come from persons other than ourselves, and would not exist if it had not been for that person. In this way, the truth of the world is always active above us" (Kiyozawa 1901/2015: 7–8).

5. More specifically, Tsunashima relies on the language of finding a union between himself and God in the moment (刹那) of religious ecstasy, as evidenced by the fact that all three of his examples in "My Experience of Seeing God" seem to explore the notion of having lost himself in the moment or in the background that he happens to be seeing. More information is available in Mushiaki and Yukiyasu (1981).

6. Indeed, Tsunashima Ryōsen's response to Inoue's denial of a personal God can elucidate what many writers were aiming for by using the word "personality." As a brief summary, Inoue attempted to question the Christian notion of a personal God, assuming it to be both unscientific and harboring the assumption that God "is" somewhere. In place of this unfulfilling notion of a personal God, Inoue attempted to offer his notion of a "moral religion" as a substitute. On this view, the "smaller self (小我)" of the individual would find religious fulfilment in their agreement with the "great self (大我)" of society. In response, Tsunashima did not actually question the formulation of a smaller self and a greater self, instead pointing out that Inoue's own conception was just as personal as the Christian position he aimed to critique. More specifically, Tsunashima states that he agrees with the line of reasoning that Inoue takes, but wonders how Inoue's notion of a Great Self is any more scientific than a personal God, asking "[i]s not the professor's so-called voice of Great Self (大我)—the voice of *a priori* content (先天内容)—something that enacts its own laws [...] beyond the causal laws of natural phenomena?" From this standpoint, Tsunashima asks if—in the end—Inoue's replacement of the personal Christian God with a Great Self does not instead end up precisely as "a concept we should see in religion" (Tsunashima 1922: 63).

7. While his efforts to argue that the many positive traits of the Japanese people were directly a result of their environment is as peculiar as it was influential on

Japanese philosophy, we cannot afford to give it any substantial space here. Some explications of his thoughts on Japanese essence and the environment can be found in Pyle (1969: 61–3; 151–6).

8   We will refer to Miyake's *Uchū* (宇宙) as *The Cosmos*. This is not entirely in line with Miyake's wishes. As Miyake explains, his conception of *Uchū* includes both the notion of the "Universe" as the expanse of space we are floating in and the notion of the "Cosmos" as the underlying order and regularity that dictates how everything moves. Hence, my translation is imperfect. However, given no better option and noticing Miyake's tendency to stress the cosmic order of things, I have decided to translate the title as *The Cosmos,* even if some nuances are lost in English.

9   It is noteworthy that, starting from the early stages of his career, this "analogy" was not just an observation for Miyake so much as it was a methodology of sorts. To use a familiar phrase from Chapter 1, it was Miyake's "starting point" (Miyake 1892/1967: 245–8).

10 As the ever-present critic of Meiji philosophy, Onishi Hajime, publicly displayed, there are severe issues with this line of reasoning. Is the "death" of the body actually analogous to the "death" of the universe? Can the universe "die" at all? Why does Miyake start from dreaming consciousness when dreams utilize resources from our wakeful perceptions? (OHS 2: 233–62) We will leave these early methodological issues alone for the time being on the grounds that we are merely interested in reading Miyake's philosophy at its full strength in *The Cosmos* for the sake of comparison with Nishida.

11 Likely in the background of this orderly view of the universe is interest and familiarity with the Wang Yangming school of Confucian thought (陽明学). Miyake seemed to have a particular affinity for Itō Jinsai (1627–1705) and Oshio Heihachirō (1793–1837). While I have no time to justify myself here, my suspicion is that when Miyake refers to either a "will" or the "order" of the cosmos, he has in mind Confucian concepts of the Way as a pervading rational force in the universe which we ought to follow. An introduction to Miyake's writings on Japanese Neo-Confucianism is available in Morita (2015).

12 Here it is once again interesting to note the relation between Miyake's ontology and his politics. In lockstep with the trend discussed in the previous chapter, Miyake utilized this inter-connectedness between individual and community to argue that individual cultivation should be pursued for the sake of common interests (see Nagatsuma 2012: 37–41). Now, what is perhaps more interesting here, though, is that this "organic" conception of the universe was also crucial to Miyake's claims that many of Japan's better traditions and customs were clearly based on the relationship between the Japanese people, their biological makeup, and their geographical circumstances, insofar as the two were part of one inseparable organism. We will not contemplate the matter here, but we will note that further

research on how this line of metaphysical reasoning may have influenced later Japanese thinkers like Watsuji Tetsurō (和辻哲郎, 1889–1960) is certainly worthy of consideration.

13 It has been argued that Miyake did not properly have any sense of religion in his philosophy and this difference in attitudes does *seem to* separate his philosophical project apart from Nishida in important ways. Indeed, while Nishida discussed religion as a fundamental demand inherent in pure experience, Miyake took it as a necessary step in developing a more complete view of the universe (see Miyake 1909: 452). However, keeping in mind that Miyake seems to use religion to refer to a set of doctrines and dogmas, what Nishida describes as religion would probably fall under the category of "religion that is closer to philosophy" for Miyake's purposes and—keeping this in mind—I would like to leave open the possibility that they are more interested in a difference in terminology than anything.

14 This insistence upon all conscious organisms in the universe leads us to one crucial difference between Miyake and Nishida that we cannot analyze here fully. In contrast to Nishida's tendencies to glorify human life, Miyake was a fierce critic of anthropocentrism, almost to the point of diminishing human consciousness as "valueless" in opposition to the greatness of the universe and potential different forms of consciousness that are more advanced than our own (Miyake 1909: 506–7).

15 Reference made to Godart (2017: 145) when translating this quotation. For clarity's sake, I believe it would be best to note here that I have found no explicit reference to Nietzsche in Miyake's use of this word. Rather, the word "superman" in Miyake's context seems to be closer to a "great person" or someone who has surpassed the limits of their current era.

16 The most direct evidence to this point comes in part 2, where Nishida states "Expressed metaphorically, each person's spirit is simply one cell of the social spirit" (IG: 62). As this is, as Nishida clearly states, a metaphor, it is hard to use it as definitive evidence that Nishida would sympathize with a literal organic theory in the way we have described Miyake's philosophy. Additionally, while not direct enough to comprise strong evidence for an organic reading of Nishida's philosophy in its own right, the following passage is at least worthy of recognition: "Individual consciousness of course has a foundation called the body, and in this respect it diverges from social consciousness. But the brain is not a simple material object—it is a collection of cells. This is no different from the fact that society is made up of the cells called individuals" (IG: 139).

17 Emphasis added by the author.

18 Emphasis by the author of this book.

19 I say this keeping in mind the fact that Nishida does not delve into this matter in *Inquiry* and also explicitly denies any relation between his method and analogy

in his research notes, noting that analogical reasoning is a matter related to reflective reasoning and that the facts of pure experience stand prior to such acts of reflective reasoning (NKZ 16: 94). Put otherwise, an act of analogy can only be made outgoing from—and thus presupposes—a direct intuition of the facts of experience.

20 Consider that even those who adopt this view often end up unable to answer these questions. One such reader, Robert Wilkinson, starts by lauding Nishida's discovery of the true self in the loss of the individual self, but then admits that "[p]recisely how the individual self arises from the non-dual—if not undifferentiated—state of pure experience is not made clear in this book," claiming that it was left as a problem Nishida only dealt with as his career went on. Indeed, assuming that such a dual unity is actually in play, then this seems to be the only correct conclusion one could draw about the nature of the individual person in pure experience (see Wilkinson 2009: 57).

21 Tanabe explains: "Is this not precisely the same as how Plotinus conceives of three hypostases coming successively from the One? They differ from one another only in that there is a strong noematic tendency present in the whole of Plotinus' philosophy, while in Professor Nishida's work, the transcendence of noesis, which is his unique and profound thought, acts as its basis. [...] What I doubt is only whether or not philosophy as a religious philosophy (in the sense that Plotinus' philosophy was religious philosophy) might lead us to abandon philosophy, insofar as we are constructing a final inaccessible universal and interpreting actual existence through its own self-determination" (Tanabe 1930/2020: 286–7).

22 For example, Funayama 1959/1965, See Wargo 2005 as well.

23 Now, we *can* speculate about if there is an individuated soul-like substance or a greater macro-self in the background of pure experience. Crucially, though, this would indeed be mere speculation, given that these assumptions are neither empirically verifiable nor necessary for explaining the functions of the self. In this sense, we can follow Taguchi's (2019: 29–33) arguments for a "zero-person perspective" and claim "metaphysical neutrality" for pure experience regarding whether there actually exist a soul or macro-self.

24 This is what I think he is getting at when he states that "[t]he life of an individual is the development of consciousness that constitutes such a single system" (IG: 61).

25 Additionally, Kopf (2001) seems to me to have a similar view of personhood in Nishida's philosophy, as demonstrated by his comparison of it with Merleau-Ponty (1908–61) and Sartre (1905–80).

26 To provide more context, I think there are two points that deserve attention. First, Nishida's earliest writings—i.e., his graduation paper at Tokyo Imperial University—was indeed on Hume, meaning that it is not too out of place to assume that some latent influence remained in the background. Second, I make this

comparison insofar as the notion that one's self is nothing more than the hub which accumulates experiences into a coherent system is not too distant from Hume's assertion that we need no concept of self aside from the "bundle" of perceptions we happen to have aggregated up to this point (see Hume 1739/2000: 1.4.6.3). However, the fact that Nishida separates himself from those like Hume in that he views a Humean Bundle Theory of selfhood as a gradual and *passive* collection of thoughts is instructive for our purposes. As we have established here, Nishida's conception of self *actively* pursues the systematic organization of experiences: "According to one school of psychology, the self is simply a union of ideas and feelings apart from which there is no self. This view neglects the side of unity and entails consideration of the self from the side of analytical distinctions only. [...] Things are established by a unity, and ideas and feelings are made into concrete reality through the power of a unifying self" (IG: 76).

27 One issue that the early Nishida seems to avoid addressing explicitly is the notion that there are potentially multiple systems that count as their own reality that *cannot* be reconciled. Nishida avoids such a conclusion by introducing the universal principles at the base of experience that theoretically make it possible to reconcile any differing set of beliefs. Thus, Nishida assumes that while differing experiences may present contradictions, they will ultimately be resolvable by appealing to an underlying unity between conscious experiences. Yet, this strikes me as potentially unsound insofar as it too easily dismisses the following two possibilities. First, Nishida does not account for the possibility that different systems operate on entirely irreconcilable premises or principles. Insofar as Nishida explicitly states that the standards for truth are internal to their system, it appears difficult to explain how a claim from one system could be conceived of as favorable to the other without adding another criterion for truth. Additionally, there is no consideration of the possibility that two different systems never meet with one another. One could argue that it is enough that they be reconcilable with one another *in theory*, even though there are likely multiple fragmentary systems *in practice*. However, this raises questions as to what it means to call pure experience the sole reality. Is it referring to an ideal state of unity necessary to discuss pure experience? If that is the case, how do we overcome the previous problem of irreconcilable differences? Would it perhaps not be better to consider a multi-world theory like the one proposed by Nelson Goodman (1906–98) in his later years? Although these questions would need to be answered to actively argue in favor of my reading of *Inquiry*, we do not have time to tackle them here and—more importantly—they are not necessary to accomplish our main goal.

28 "When our spirit is in a state of completion, a state of unity, we experience pleasure, and when it is in an incomplete state, a state of disunion, we experience pain. As I said, spirit is the unifying activity of reality, and contradictions and conflicts

necessarily accompany this unity. We always experience pain when these contradictions and conflicts occur, and the infinite unifying activity immediately attempts to rid itself of them and to achieve an even greater unity" (IG: 78).

29 Example: "God is the greatest and final unifier of our consciousness; our consciousness is one part of God's consciousness and its unity comes from God's unity" (IG: 161).

30 A thorough and text-based demonstration of Nishida's "mystical" tendencies and how they developed over the course of his career can be found in Leonardi (2011).

Conclusion

1 With that said, as I have mentioned in Stone (2022), I think there is a path available to a consistent reading of *Inquiry* if we appeal to contemporary neurophenomenology to help fill in some gaps between Nishida's vision of self as a state of consciousness and as the originary activity present in every facet of individual moments of experience.

2 This interpretation is explained well by Nitta (2009/2018: 199), who claims that "Nishida's conception of pure experience served the fundamental role of the ground for explaining all knowledge. Yet this theory of pure experience faced a barrier. That is, as that which is both the liveable unity of the pre-distinction between subject and object (*shukyaku mibun*, 主客未分) as well as that which divides and develops itself (*bunka hatten*, 分化発展), it necessarily required a structure of self-relation within itself. This self-relating function could not be made outgoing from an externally formed hermeneutic formula. It needed to be capable of maintaining this self-relational structure within the self itself. Nishida called this function self-awareness. Self-awareness, as it is referred to here, is not formed externally. It is a function which transcends the Ego, is present throughout the Ego, and is thus witnessed within the Ego."

3 Regarding why Nishida emphasized the will, my view is that he believes all forms of contemplation, reflection, or any other form of understanding experience fundamentally required some form of primal activity at their base. As Nishida reminds us in "On What Is Directly Given" (toward the end of his period of fascination with the notion of an Absolute Will), "true self-awareness must be our experience of the will itself. [...] The true I is not the knowing I but the acting I. [This is because] knowing is a form of acting. Seeing, listening, and thinking, are all acts of the I. [...] The I is the unity of these acts [作用]" (NKZ 3: 267).

4 NKZ 2: 9; As for what made this book so mystical, the answer seems to be the aforementioned notion of An Absolute Will as a vital force pervading experience with which we join when possible.

5 Maraldo (2019: 72) provides an account of this "mirroring" or "reflexivity" in Nishida, stating "[i]n Nishida, reflecting or mirroring is the natural activity of consciousness or awareness. Consciousness projects (*utsusu* 映す) itself and is reflected back so that it is able to 'see itself' and be 'self-luminous.' The self (自己) that 'intends' or mirrors itself within itself, that is self-aware, names the unity of this activity." Crucially, Maraldo clarifies that this reflexivity does not imply the total deletion of any "phenomenological" or "pre-reflexive" self-awareness. Instead, it means that this primitive self-awareness is only capable of (in our words) contextualizing itself as it reflects back on itself from the world.

6 Nishida's theory rests upon a key distinction between "knower" and "known" or "consciousness that is conscious (意識する意識)" and "consciousness we are conscious of (意識される意識)." Thus, attempts to reflect upon or objectify "knowing consciousness" will inevitably end in abstraction, given that this objectified vision of consciousness must be presented before something (presumably, the knower itself). Nishida's ultimate point from *Inquiry* onward thus seems to be that this knowing consciousness can never be found through a higher-order act of reflection (i.e., the objectification of the knowing self), but is only available to us as it projects itself and is reflected back in its actions within this world.

7 With regard to space: "Universal and particular are not mutually heterogeneous in the same way that things and space are. The particular is a part of the universal and moreover it is its [reflected, mirror] image [*eizo*]. However, for the particular, the universal carries no sense of being at all. It is completely nothing" (Nishida 1926/2012: 62; translation modified from NKZ 3: 429); With regard to time: "If we are to speak from the side of the universal, subsumption means the development-of-differentiation itself. Needless to say, although I speak of a process whereby the universal particularizes itself, this does not immediately signify an event appearing in time" (Nishida 1926/2012: 63).

8 In response to Nishida's perceived decision to take religious self-consciousness as the end point of philosophy in his early and middle periods, Tanabe remarks that should "philosophy take[s] religious truth as its own content, it is no longer *philosophia* (love of wisdom/knowledge 愛知). Instead, it becomes [mere] *sophia*" (Tanabe 1930/2020: 287; translation slightly adjusted). Tanabe clarifies that, although *sophia* has its own place in philosophy, to do away with our love for pursuing dynamically changing truths and stop at religious consciousness loses sight of a core element of philosophical praxis. Philosophy must pursue "infinitesimal" knowledge, mediated and dynamically morphing throughout history in our accordance with our pursuit of it.

9 It cannot be overstated how crucial Tanabe's critique was for urging Nishida to engage in more concrete analyses of how we, as embodied and historical subjects living in a particular social or cultural sphere, live, work, and die. While problems

of historicity and embodiment were left out of our considerations in this work (and much of the first half of Nishida's career), Sugimoto (2013: 84–6) provides a succinct summary of Tanabe's critique and how it awakened Nishida to the irrationalities of history.

10 In this regard, Maraldo's (2017; 2022) idea of "trans-lation" is, in my view, complementary to what I say here. Trans-lation is demarcated by "between-ness" as it "transforms textually embedded problems, methods and terminologies both across and within natural languages" (Maraldo 2022: 125). Maraldo himself seems to recognize in Nishida a role similar to what I am describing here, stating that he "stands at the crossroads of modern and pre-modern" (2022: 117), even if he does not seem as friendly toward continuing to refer to Nishida as modern Japan's first philosopher. Now, I do not think that one necessarily must agree with what Maraldo says about trans-lation to accept what I am arguing for in this conclusion, but I will note that our findings are complementary to Maraldo's position.

References

Abbreviations and Completed Works

NKZ 『西田幾多郎全集』 [Collected Works of Nishida Kitarō]. Tokyo, Iwanami shoten, 2003–9, 24 vols.

IES 『井上円了選集』 [Selected Works of Inoue Enryō]. Tokyo, Toyo University Press, 1987–2004, 25 vols.

OHS 『大西祝選集』 [Selected Works of Onishi Hajime]. Tokyo, Iwanami bunko, 2013, 3 vols.

Altobrando, Andrea (2016), "Kitarō Nishida and the Essence of Individuality: A Contribution from Eastern Asia to a Transcultural Understanding of the Meaning of Individualism," in Gilles Campagnolo (ed.), *Liberalism and East Asian/Chinese Economic Development: Perspectives from Europe and Asia*, 111–31, New York: Routledge.

Bernasconi, Robert (2003), "Ethnicity, Culture, and Philosophy," in Nicholas Bunnin and E. P. Tsui-James (eds.), *The Blackwell Companion to Philosophy* (second expanded edition), 567–81, Oxford: Blackwell.

Blocker, H. Gene and Christopher L. Starling (2001), *Japanese Philosophy*, Albany: State University of New York Press.

Brecher, W. Puck (2012), "Useless Losers: Marginality and Modernization in Early Meiji Japan," *The European Legacy*, 17: 803–17.

Davis, Bret W. (2020), "What Is Japanese Philosophy?" in Bret W. Davis (ed.), *The Oxford Handbook of Japanese Philosophy*, 1–80, Oxford: Oxford University Press.

Davis, Bret W. (2022), "The Kyoto School," Edward N. Zalta, ed., *The Stanford Encyclopedia of Philosophy*, accessed March 28, 2023.

Duke, Benjamin (2009), *The History of Modern Japanese Education: Constructing the National School System, 1872–1890*, Rutgers, NJ: Rutgers University Press.

Fujita, Masakatsu 藤田正勝 (2007), *Nishida Kitarō–Ikiru Koto to Tetsugaku* (Nishida Kitarō: Life and Philosophy), Tokyo: Iwanami Shoten.

Fukuzawa, Yukichi (1872/2013), *An Encouragement of Learning*, trans. David A. Dilworth, New York: Columbia University Press.

Fukuzawa, Yukichi (1875/2009), *An Outline of a Theory of Civilization*, trans. David A. Dilworth and G. Cameron Hurst III, Tokyo: Keio University Press.

Funayama, Shinichi 船山信一 (1959/1965), *Meiji Tetsugakushi Kenkyū* (Research on Meiji Philosophy), Kyoto: Minerva Shobo.

Gallagher, Shaun (2012), "On the Possibility of Naturalizing Phenomenology," in Dan Zahavi (ed.), *Oxford Handbook of Phenomenology*, 70–93, Oxford: Oxford University Press.

Gallagher, Shaun and Dan Zahavi (2007), *The Phenomenological Mind*, London: Routledge.

Garfield, Jay and Brian W. Van Norden (2016), "If Philosophy Won't Diversify, Let's Call It What It Really Is," *New York Times*, May 11, 2016.

Gluck, Carol (1985), *Japan's Modern Myths: Ideology in the Late Meiji Period*, Princeton, NJ: Princeton Paperbacks.

Godart, Gerard Clinton (2004), "Tracing the Circle of Truth: Inoue Enryō on the History of Philosophy and Buddhism," *The Eastern Buddhist*, XXXVI (1/2): 106–33.

Godart, Gerard Clinton (2017), *Darwin, Dharma, and the Divine: Evolutionary Theory and Religion in Modern Japan*, Honolulu: University of Hawai'i Press.

Goto-Jones, Christopher (2005), *Political Philosophy in Japan: Nishida, the Kyoto-School and Co-Prosperity*, New York: Routledge.

Green, Thomas Hill (1883/1997), *A Prolegomena to Ethics*, Peter Nicholson (ed.), *Collected Works of T. H. Green* 4, London: Thoemmes Press.

Green, Thomas Hill (1886/1997), "On the Different Senses of 'Freedom' as Applied to Will and to the Moral Progress of Man," in Peter Nicholson (ed.), *Collected Works of T. H. Green*, Vol. 3, 308–54, London: Thoemmes Press.

Hane, Mikiso (1969), "Early Meiji Liberalism: An Assessment," *Monumenta Nipponica*, 24 (4): 353–71.

Heck, Richard G. (2000), "Non-conceptual Content and the Space of Reasons," *Philosophical Review*, 109: 483–523.

Heisig, James W., Thomas P. Kasulis, and John C. Maraldo, eds. (2011), *Japanese Philosophy: A Sourcebook*, Honolulu: University of Hawai'i Press.

Heisig, James W. (2001), *Philosophers of Nothingness*, Honolulu: University of Hawai'i Press.

Hirade, Kiyoe 平出喜代恵 (2020), "Onishi Hajime ni okeru Kant Juyō no Ariyō" (How did Ohnishi Hajime Receive Kant's Philosophy?), *Journal of East Asian Cultural Interaction Studies*, 13: 349–62.

Hirai, Atsuko (1979), "Self-Realization and Common Good: T. H. Green in Meiji Ethical Thought," *The Journal of Japanese Studies*, 5: 107–36.

Hiraishi, Noriko 平石典子 (2012), *Hanmon Seinen to Onna Gakusei no Bungakushi—"Seiyō" wo Yomikaete—*(The Literary History of Troubled Young Men and Female Students—Re-Reading the "West"), Tokyo: Shinyosha.

Hirayama Yō 平山洋 (1989), *Onishi Hajime to sono Jidai* (Onishi Hajime and His Time), Tokyo: Nihon Tosho Sentā.

Hirayama Yō 平山洋 (1997), *Nishida Tetsugaku no Saikōchiku—sono Seiritsu Katei to Hikaku Shisō* (A Reconstruction of Nishida's Philosophy—Its Formative Process and Comparative Thought), Kyoto: Minerva.

Hisamatsu, Shinichi (1971), *Zen and the Fine Arts*, trans. Tokiwa Gishin, Tokyo: Kodansha.

Howland, Douglas (2001), *Translating the West: Language and Political Reason in 19th Century Japan*, Honolulu: University of Hawai'i Press.

Hume, David (1739/2000), *A Treatise of Human Nature*, David Fate Norton and Mary J. Norton (ed.), Oxford: Oxford University Press.

Ikegami, Eiko (1995), *The Taming of the Samurai: Honorific Individualism and the Making of Modern Japan*, London: Harvard University Press.

Inoue, Katsuhito 井上克人 (2011), *Nishida Kitarō to Meiji no Seishin* (Nishida Kitarō and the Spirit of the Meiji Era), Osaka: Kansei Daigaku Shuppanbu.

Inoue, Katshito (2016), "The Philosophical World of Meiji Japan," trans. Takeshi Morisato, *European Journal of Japanese Philosophy*, 1: 10–30.

Inoue, Tetsujirō (1894/2011), "Fragments of a Worldview," in James Heisig, Thomas P. Kasulis, John C. Maraldo (eds.), *Japanese Philosophy: A Sourcebook*, 611–17, Honolulu: University of Hawai'i Press.

Inoue, Tetsujirō 井上哲次郎 (1897/2003), "Genshō-soku-Jitsuzairon no Yoryō," in *Inoue Tetsujiro Shū Dai 9 Kan* (Inoue Tetsujiro Collection, vol. 9), Tokyo: Kuresu Shuppan.

Inoue, Tetsujirō 井上哲次郎 (1900), *Nihon Yōmeigaku no Tetsugaku* (The Philosophy of the Japanese Yang Ming School), Tokyo: Fuzambo.

Itabashi, Yūjin 板橋勇仁 (2004), *Nishida Tetsugaku no Ronri to Hōhō—Tetteiteki Hihyōshugi to wa Nani ka?* (Logic and Method of Nishida Philosophy: Nishida, Fichte, and Neokantians), Tokyo: Hosei Daigaku Shuppankyoku.

James, William (1890/1983), *The Principles of Psychology*, Cambridge: Harvard University Press.

Jansen, Marius B. (1992), *China in the Tokugawa World*, Cambridge, MA: Harvard University Press.

Josephson, Jason Ānanda (2006), "When Buddhism Became a 'Religion': Religion and Superstition in the Writings of Inoue Enryō," *Japanese Journal of Religious Studies*, 33 (1): 143–68.

Junichi, Katayama 片山純一 (2013), *Onishi Hajime: Tatakau Tetsugakusha no Shōgai* (Onishi Hajime: The Life of a Fighting Philosopher), Tokyo: Kibito sensho.

Keene, Donald (1969), *The Japanese Discovery of Europe, 1720–1830*, Stanford, CA: Stanford University Press.

Kiyozawa, Manshi 清沢満之 (1901/2015), *Seishinshugi* (Spiritual Activism), Hashimoto Mineo (ed.), *Seishinshugi, hoka* (Spiritual Activism and More), Tokyo: Chuko Classics.

Kopf, Gereon (2001), *Beyond Personal Identity: Dogen, Nishida, and a Phenomenology of No-Self*, London: Routledge.

Kopf, Gereon (2013), "The 'Modern Buddhism' of Inoue Enryō," *International Inoue Enryō Research*, 1: 25–36.

Kosaka, Kunitsugu 小阪国継 (1995), *Nishida Kitarō—sono Shisō to Gendai* [Nishida Kitarō—His Thought and the Present], Tokyo: Minerva Shobo.

Kosaka, Kunitsugu 小阪国継 (2013), *Meiji Tetsugaku Kenkyū—Nishi Amane to Onishi Hajime* [Studies in Meiji Philosophy: Nishi Amane and Onishi Hajime], Tokyo: Iwanami Shoten.

Kosaka, Masaaki 高坂正顕 (1969/1999), *Meiji Shisōshi* (Meiji Intellectual History), Minamoto Ryoen (ed.), Tokyo: Toeisha.

Krueger, Joel W. (2022), "James, Nonduality, and the Dynamics of Pure Experience," in Lee A. McBride III and Erin McKenna (eds.), *Pragmatist Feminism and the Work of Charlene Haddock Seigfried*, 193–216, London: Bloomsbury.

Krummel, John W.M. (2015), *Nishida Kitarō's Chiasmatic Chorology: Place of Dialectic, Dialectic of Place*, Bloomington, IN: Indiana University Press.

Kurata, Hyakuzō 倉田百三 (1912/2016), *Ai to Ninshiki to no Shuppatsu* (Departing with Love and Knowledge), Tokyo: Iwanami Bunko.

Kurata, Hyakuzo (1912/2020), "Looking for One's Self in the Opposite Sex," trans. Richard Stone, in Takeshi Morisato and Roman Pasca, *Asian Philosophical Texts*, Vol. 1, 259–80, Milan: Mimesis International.

Leonardi, Andrea レオナルディ・アンドレア (2011), "Nishida no Shinpishugi to Kami no Gainen no Henka—Bannen no Nishida Shūkyō Tetsugaku he no Hihan" (Nishida's Mysticism and Changes in His Concept of God—A Critique of the Later Nishida's Religious Philosophy), in Fujita Masakatsu 藤田正勝 (ed.), *Zen no Kenkyū no Momotose: Sekai he/Sekai kara* (100 Years of *An Inquiry into the Good*: To the World, From the World), 164–82, Kyoto: Kyoto Daigaku Gakujutsu Shuppankai.

Lotman, Miikael-Adam (2020), "The Problem of Meaning in Nishida's Early Writings," *Tetsugaku*, 4: 70–83.

Maraldo, John C. (2017), *Japanese Philosophy in the Making 1: Crossing Paths with Nishida*, Nagoya: Chisokudo Publications.

Maraldo, John C. (2019), "Nishida and the Phenomenology of Self-Awareness," in Shigeru Taguchi and Andrea Altobrando (eds.), *Tetsugaku Companion to Phenomenology and Japanese Philosophy*, 57–76, Cham, Switzerland: Springer.

Maraldo, John C. (2022), "A Response in Turn," *European Journal of Japanese Philosophy*, 7: 116–69.

McVeigh, Brian J. (2017), *The History of Japanese Psychology: Global Perspectives, 1875–1950*, London: Bloomsbury.

Mead, George H. (1932). "The Present as the Locus of Reality," in Arthur Murphy (ed.), *The Philosophy of the Present*, 1–31, London: The Open Court Company.

Mitsuhara, Takeshi (2015), "Nishida and Husserl between 1911 and 1917," *Journal of Japanese Philosophy*, 3: 95–116.

Mitsuhara, Takeshi 満原健 (2018), "*Zen no Kenkyū* to Shinrishugi" (*An Inquiry into the Good* and Psychologism), *Nishida Tetsugakkai Nenpō*, 15: 159–73.

Mitsuhara, Takeshi (2021), "Nishida's *An Inquiry into the Good* and Japanese and German Thought in the Late Nineteenth Century," *European Journal of Japanese Philosophy*, 6: 7–33.

Miura, Setsuo 三浦節夫 (2014), "Inoue Enryō no Yōkaigaku" (Inoue Enryō's Mystery Studies), *International Inoue Enryō Research*, 2: 285–311.

Miyajima, Hajime. 宮島肇 (1960), *Meijiteki Shisōka no Keisei—Nishida Tetsugakushi to Shisōshi Hohoron no Mondai* (The Formation of the Image of Meiji Thinker: On the Establishment of Nishida Philosophy and the Problem of Methodology in Intellectual History), Tokyo: Miraisha.

Miyakawa, Tōru 宮川徹 (1962), *Kindai Nihon no Tetsugaku* (Modern Japan's Philosophy), Tokyo: Keiso Shobo.

Miyake, Setsurei 三宅雪嶺 (1909), *Uchū* (The Cosmos), Tokyo: Seikyosha.

Miyake, Setsurei 三宅雪嶺 (1967), *Miyake Setsureishū* (Miyake Setsurei Collection), Yanagita Izumi (ed.), *Meiji Bungakushū* 33, Tokyo: Chikuma Shobo.

Miyazoe, Ikuo みやぞえ郁雄 (2013), *Nishida Kitarō: Shogakukan Gakushu Manga* (Nishida Kitarō: Shogakukan Learning Manga), Scenario by Taira Takahisa 平良隆久, Overviewed by Nishida Kitarō Museum of Philosophy, Tokyo: Shogakukan.

Mizuno, Tomoharu 水野友晴 (2000), "Nishida Kitarō to T. H. Green: Jiko Jitsugen no Genri ni Chumoku shite" (Nishida Kitarō and T. H. Green: On the Principle of Self-Realization), in Nihon Tetsugakushi Forum (ed.), *Nihon no Tetsugaku: Tokushū Nishida Tetsugaku Kenkyū no Genzai* (Japanese Philosophy: A Special Edition on the Present State of Nishida Philosophy), 58–75, Kyoto: Showado.

Mizuno, Tomoharu 水野友晴 (2001), "Meiji Kōhanki ni okeru Risōshugiteki Jinkaku Jitsugen Setsu no Seiritsu ni tsuite" (On the Formation of the Moral Idealist Theory of Personal Realization in the Later Meiji Period), *Shūkyo Tetsugaku Kenkyū*, 18: 61–73.

Morita, Yasuo 森田康夫 (2015), *[Hyoden] Miyake Setsurei no Shisōzō* (Legacy: The Image of Miyake Setsurei's Thought), Osaka: Waizumi Sensho.

Motora, Yūjirō (1905A). "Conflict of Religion and Science: From a Japanese Point of View," *The Monist*, 15 (3): 398–408.

Motora, Yūjirō (1905B/2015). "Idea of Ego in Eastern Philosophy," in Oyama Tadashi et al. (ed.), 『元良勇次郎著作集第10巻』 (Writings of Motora Yūjirō, vol. 10), 5–43, Tokyo: Kuresu Shuppan.

Motora, Yūjirō 元良勇次郎. (1915), *Shinrigaku Gairon* (An Outline of Psychology), Tokyo: Teimatsu Shuppansha.

Mushiaki Tadashi虫明凱 and Yukiyasu Shigeru 行安茂 (1981), *Tsunashima Ryōsen no Shōgai to Shisō* (The Life and Thought of Tsunashima Ryōsen), Tokyo: Waseda Daigaku Shuppanbu.

Nagai, Hitoshi 永井均 (2018), *Nishida Kitarō: Gengo, Kahei, Tokei no Seiritsu no Nazo he* (Nishida Kitarō: Facing the Mystery behind the Formation of Language, Currency, and Time), Tokyo: Kadokawa.

Nagai, Michio (1954), "Herbert Spencer in Early Meiji Japan," *The Far Eastern Quarterly*, 14: 55–64.

Nagatsuma, Misao 長妻三佐雄 (2012), *Miyake Setsurei no Seiji Shisō: Shinzenbi no Yukue* (Miyake Setsurei's Political Thought: In Search of The True, The Good, and The Beautiful), Kyoto: Minerva.

Nakajima, Yūta中島優太 (2011), "Nishida [Rinrigaku Shoan Daiichi] ni okeru ishi no jiyu to kyarakutaa – Wundt, Green, Hoffding no Bunmyaku ni oite" (Free-will and Character in Nishida's "Ethics First Draft" – Put in the Context of Wundt, Green, and Høffding), in Fujita Masakatsu 藤田正勝 (ed.), *Zen no Kenkyū no Momotose: Sekai he/Sekai kara* (100 Years of *An Inquiry into the Good*: To the World, From the World), 144–63, Kyoto: Kyoto Daigaku Gakujutsu Shuppankai.

Nakamura, Hajime (1964), "Consciousness of the Individual and the Universal among the Japanese," *Philosophy East and West*, 14: 333–51.

NHK (2019), "Producer A no Omowaku—10 gatsu no meicho: *Zen no Kenkyū*" (Producer A's Thoughts—October's Famous Book: *An Inquiry into the Good*), hosted on NHK website, accessed April 6, 2023, https://www.nhk.or.jp/meicho/famousbook/92_nishida/index.html.

Nicholson, Peter (1990), *The Political Philosophy of the British Idealists: Selected Studies*, Cambridge: Cambridge University Press.

Nishida, Kitarō (1911/1990), *An Inquiry into the Good*, trans. Masao Abe and Christopher Ives, New Haven and London: Yale University Press.

Nishida, Kitarō (1926/2012), "Basho," in John W. M. Krummel and Shigenori Nagatomo (trans.), *Place and Dialectic: Two Essays by Nishida Kitarō*, Oxford: Oxford University Press.

Nishitani, Keiji (1991), *Nishida Kitarō*, trans. Yamamoto Seisaku and James W. Heisig, Berkeley and Los Angeles: University of California Press.

Nitta, Yoshihiro 新田義弘 (1988) "Inoue Enryō no Genshō-soku-Jitsuzairon" (Inoue Enryō's Theory of Phenomena-soku-Reality), in Saito Shigeo (ed.), *Inoue Enryō to Seiyō Shisō* (Inoue Enryō and Western Thought), 79–102, Tokyo: Toyo Daigaku Inoue Enryō Kenkyū Dainibukai.

Nitta, Yoshihiro (2009/2019), "Self-awareness as Transcendental Mediationality," in Shigeru Taguchi and Andrea Altobrando (eds.), *Tetsugaku Companion to Phenomenology and Japanese Philosophy*, 185–206, Cham, Switzerland: Springer.

Noë, Alva (2004), *Action in Perception*. Cambridge: MIT press.

Okada, Masahiko (2005), "Revitalization Versus Unification: A Comparison of the Ideas of Inoue Enryo and Murakami Sensho," *Eastern Buddhist*, 1 (37): 28–38.

Okubo, Ryō 大久保遼 (2018), "Kankaku no Riron to Shakai no Riron – Nihon Shakaigakushi ni okeru Motora Yūjiro," (A Theory of Sensations and a Theory of Society: Motora Yūjirō in the History of Japanese Sociology), *Shakaigaku Hyōron*, 69 (2): 179–95.

Onishi, Hajime 大西祝 (1921), "Kokkashugi no Kaishaku" (Interpretations of Nationalism), in 『大西博士全集第6巻』 [Complete Works of Professor Onishi, vol. 6], Tokyo: Keiseisha.

Paramore, Kiri (2009), *Ideology and Christianity in Japan*, London: Routledge.

Pyle, Kenneth B. (1969), *The New Generation in Meiji Japan: Problems of Cultural Identity, 1885–1895*, Palo Alto: Stanford University Press.

Sakamoto, Rumi (2008), "Confucianising Science: Sakuma Shōzan and *wakon yōsai* Ideology," *Japanese Studies*, 28 (2): 213–26.

Sako Junichirō 佐古純一郎 (1995), *Kindai Nihon Shisōshi ni okeru Jinkaku Gainen no Seiritsu* (The Development of the Concept of Person in Modern Japanese Thought), Tokyo: Chōbunsha.

Sansom, George (1984), *Japan in World History*, Tokyo: Charles E. Tuttle.

Schultzer, Reiner (2019), *Inoue Enryō: A Philosophical Portrait*, New York: SUNY Press.

Shikano Masanao 鹿野正直 (1991), *Kindai Nihon Shisō Annai* (A Guide to Modern Japanese Thought), Tokyo: Iwanami Shoten.

Shimomura, Toratarō 下村寅太郎 (1990), *Nishida Tetsugaku to Nihon no Shisō* (Nishida Kitarō and Japanese Thought), Tokyo: Misuzu Shobo.

Shirai, Masato 白井雅人 (2012), "Inoue Enryō *Tetsugaku Issekiwa* to Nishida Kitarō" (Inoue Enryō's *An Evening of Philosophical Conversation* and Nishida Kitarō), *Journal of International Philosophy*, 1: 101–8.

Snodgrass, Judith (2003), *Presenting Japanese Buddhism to the West: Orientalism, Occidentalism, and the Columbian Exposition*, Chapel Hill, NC: The University of North Carolina Press.

Staggs, Kathleen (1983), "Defend the Nation and Love the Truth: Inoue Enryō and the Revival of Meiji Buddhism," *Monumenta Nipponica*, 38 (3): 251–81.

Stone, Richard (2018), "Independence and Self-Realization: The Historical Background of the Early Nishida's Individualism," *European Journal of Japanese Philosophy*, 3: 31–56.

Stone, Richard (2021), "The Middle Path and Pure Experience: A Re-evaluation of the 'Beginning'" of Modern Japanese Philosophy," *The Journal of East Asian Philosophy*, 1: 15–29.

Stone, Richard (2022), "Nishida Kitarō's Two True Selves: Revisiting Self, Meaning, and Method in *An Inquiry into the Good*," *Journal of Japanese Philosophy*, 8: 47–71.

Stone, Richard (2023), "The Politics of Pure Experience: Individual and State in *An Inquiry into the Good*," *Asian Studies*, 11 (3): 177–202.

Stone, Richard and Andrea Altobrando (2023), "Pure Experience Revisited: A Critical Reassessment of Nishida Kitarō's Radicalization of William James' Empiricism," *The Philosophical Forum*, 54 (1–2): 43–60. https://onlinelibrary.wiley.com/doi/10.1111/phil.12333.

Sugimoto, Koichi 杉本耕一 (2013). *Nishida Tetsugaku to Rekishiteki Sekai: Shukyo no Toi he* (Nishida Philosophy and the Historical World: Towards Questions of Religion). Kyoto: Kyoto Daigaku Gakujutsu Shuppankai.

Taguchi, Shigeru (2019), "Extreme Obviousness and the 'Zero-Person' Perspective," *Metodo: International Studies in Phenomenology and Philosophy* (Special Issue 1.3): 15–37. https://metodo-rivista.eu/pub-229641.

Takahashi, Satomi 高橋里美 (1912/2001), "Ishiki Genshō no Jijitsu to sono Imi—Nishida-shi cho *Zen no Kenkyū* wo Yomu" (The Facts of Conscious Phenomena and their Meaning—Reading Mr. Nishida's *An Inquiry into the Good*) in Noe Keiichi (ed.), *Zentaisei no Genshōgaku* (Phenomenology of the Whole), 296–331, Tokyo: Toeisha.

Takano, Choei (1835/1972), "Seiyō Gakushi no Setsu. The Theories of Western Philosophers," translated by Gino K. Piovesana, *Monumenta Nipponica*, 27 (1): 85–92.

Takasuna, Miki (2007), "Proliferation of Western Methodological Thought in Psychology in Japan: Ways of Objectification," *Integrative Psychological and Behavioral Science*, 41: 83–92.

Takemura, Makio (2013), "On the Philosophy of Inoue Enryō," *International Inoue Enryō Research*, 1: 3–24.

Takeuchi, Yoshitomo 竹内良知 (1970), *Nishida Kitarō* (Nishida Kitarō), Tokyo: Tokyo Daigaku Shuppankai.

Tanabe, Hajime (1930/2020), "Requesting the Guidance of Professor Nishida," in Morisato Takeshi and Roman Pasca (eds.), Richard Stone and Morisato Takeshi (trans.), *Asian Philosophical Texts*, 1, 281–308, Milan: Mimesis International.

Tanabe, Naoki 田邊尚樹 (2021), "Motora Yūjirō no Kagaku to shite no Jinkakuron to Shūyōron: 20 Seiki Shotō no Kokkashugiteki na Risōshugi to Kagaku Bannōshugi to iu Mondaiken ni Chakumoku shite" (Yūjirō Motora's Theory of Personality and Cultivation (*Shūyo*) as Science: Focusing on the Problematic Regions of Nationalist Idealism and Scientism in Early 20th Century Japan), *Kyōikugaku Kenkyū*, 88 (4): 585–96.

Tsunashima Ryosen 綱島梁川 (1922). *Tsunashima Zenshū dai 4 kan* (Tsunashima Complete Works Vol. 4), Ed. Tsunashima Kai 綱島會. Tokyo: Shunjusha.

Tyler, Colin (2010), *The Metaphysics of Self-realisation and Freedom: Part 1 of the Liberal Socialism of Thomas Hill Green*, Luton: Andrews, U.K.

Wakabayashi, Bob Tadashi (1986), *Anti-foreignism and Western Learning in Early-Modern Japan: The New Theses of 1825*, Cambridge, MA: Harvard Univ Asia Center.

Walker, Janet (1979) *The Japanese Novel of the Meiji Period and the Ideal of Individualism*, Princeton, NJ: Princeton University Press.

Wargo, Robert J. J. (2005), *The Logic of Nothingness*, Honolulu: University of Hawai'i Press.

Watabe, Kiyoshi 渡部清 (1998), "Bukkyō Tetsugakusha to shite no Hara Tanzan to 'Genshō-soku-Jitsuzairon' to no Kankei" (Hara Tanzan as a Buddhist Philosopher and His Relation to Theories of Phenomena-qua-Reality), *Philosophical Studies*, 24: 89–113.

Wilkinson, Robert (2009), *Nishida and Western Philosophy*, London: Routledge.

Yoshida, Seiichi 吉田静致 (1908/1911), *Jissen Rinrigaku Kōgi* (Lectures in Practical Ethics). Tokyo: Dobunkan.

Yukiyasu Shigeru 行安茂 (2008), *Kindai Nihon no Shisōka to Igirisu Risōshugi* (Modern Japanese Thinkers and British Idealism), Tokyo: Hokujo Shuppan.

Yusa, Michiko (2002), *Zen & Philosophy: An Intellectual Biography of Nishida Kitarō*, Honolulu: University of Hawai'i Press.

Index

A

Abe Jirō 阿部次郎 91, 93
Absolute Contradictory Self-Identity 絶対矛盾的自己同一 7
Aesthetics xv, 83, 89–91, 93, 103, 138 n. 11
Aizawa Seishisai 会沢正志斎 xi–xii 6, 139 n. 13
Anthropocentrism 107, 161 n. 14
Aristotle 153 n. 3
Association (of ideas) 52, 57–9, 149 n. 21
Awakened Mind/Awakening 47, 100, 106

B

Berkeley, George 45, 143 n. 17, 146 n. 30, 149 n. 21
Bernasconi, Robert 139 n. 12
Bible 22
Body 50–1, 84, 100–2, 143 n. 17
Bowen, Francis xv
Buddhism 21–7, 39–40, 48, 140 n. 21, 141 n. 2 and n. 5, 142 n. 8 and n. 12
    Buddhist Meditation 2
    Buddhist Philosophy 20, 40, 140 n. 22, 141 n. 3
    Zen Buddhism 2, 48, 133, 135, 137 n. 5, 150 n. 27, 154 n. 15
Burke, Edmund 154 n. 9

C

China xv
    Chinese 9, 150 n. 24
    Chinese-English Dictionary 136 n. 1
Christianity xi, xiii, xv 2, 20, 22–3, 79, 81, 141 n. 2, 142 n. 8, 154 n. 15
    Christian xi, xiii, xv 6, 22, 48, 79, 80, 142 n. 7, 154 n. 15, 156 n. 24, 159 n. 6
    Wicked Learnings 邪宗 xi
Civilization xiii, xv 80
    Civilized xv 9, 76
Clark, William xiii
Cohen, Hermann 132
Complete Experience 自全経験 50, 52–3
    Incomplete Experience 不全経験 43, 50–3, 149 n. 17
Comte, Auguste xiii
Confucius 孔子 5, 89
    Confucianism 5, 9, 48, 73, 140 n. 21 and n. 23, 154 n. 15, 160 n. 11
Conscience 良心 79–81, 155 n. 20, 156 n. 24
Constitution (Meiji Constitution) xiv 1, 76
Cousin, Victor 143 n. 17

D

Descartes, Rene 134
    Cartesian 34, 125
Dictionary (Japanese to English) 2, 136 n. 1
    Philosophical Dictionary 哲学字彙 xiv
Direct Experience 直接経験 19, 33–5, 41–4, 47, 49–50, 54–6, 58, 60, 63, 65–8, 112–13, 129, 144 n. 25, 147 n. 3, 149 n. 16, 150 n. 24 and n. 27
    Indirect Experience 間接経験 49–50, 55–6, 149 n. 20
Discrimination 差別 29–30, 35, 44, 64–5, 100
    Non-discrimination 無差別 29–30, 100
Dōgen 道元 5–6, 138 n. 11 and n. 12
Doshisha English School 同志社英学校 xiii
Dualism 19, 49, 124–5, 143 n. 17, 145 n. 26

E

Ebina Danjo 海老名弾正 xv
Emperor xiii–xiv, 1, 72, 76, 154 n. 15
Empiricism 45–6, 57, 62, 143 n. 17
    Radical Empiricism 69, 84, 149 n. 18
Energetism 87
Enlightenment 73, 75–6, 82, 153 n. 8, 154 n. 9

Epistemology 11, 68, 92, 132, 146 n. 32
   Epistemological 64, 84, 92–3, 95, 103, 108, 117
Eternal Consciousness 77, 79, 82, 154 n. 14, 156 n. 24
   See also Divine-Mind
European Countries xi–xii, 6
   See also European Forces
European Imperialism xi
European Traditions 72
Evil 89, 131, 156 n. 21, 157 n. 33

F
Fenollosa, Ernest xiii–xiv
Fichte, Johan Gottlieb 143 n. 17
Freedom xv, 72, 82, 91, 100–1, 108, 125, 126, 131, 142 n. 8, 154 n. 14, 156 n. 22, 157 n. 35, 158 n. 36
Fukurai Tomokichi 福来友吉 48
Fukuzawa Yukichi 福澤諭吉 13,13, 72–6, 79, 83, 94, 136 n. 1, 153 n. 8
Fumie 踏絵 xi
Funayama Shinichi 船山信一 140 n. 24, 143 n. 13, 144 n. 23, 162 n. 22

G
Gallagher, Shaun 149 n. 14
Germany xiv, 138 n. 10
   German Idealism 142 n. 6
God 14, 23, 27, 77, 81–2, 86, 96–8, 103–4, 106–7, 109–10, 113, 115–18, 120, 126, 142 n. 8, 154 n. 14, 156 n. 24, 157 n. 26, 158 n. 35, 159 n. 5 and n. 6, 164 n. 29
Good, the 善 70, 84, 86–9, 100, 103, 104, 106, 153 n. 1 and n. 3
   Common Good 76–79, 91, 155 n. 17
Goodman, Nelson 163 n. 27
Great Self 大我 14, 98–9, 103–4, 106–8, 110, 112, 114–15, 117, 120, 130, 158 n. 4, 159 n. 6, 162 n. 23
   See also Big Self
   Small Self 小我 14, 96, 99, 100–1, 103, 104–5, 108–9, 115–17, 119–21, 126, 129, 130, 155 n. 19, 158 n. 4, 159 n. 6
Greater Japan Society 大日本協会 148 n. 10

Greek (Philosophers) 138 n. 9
Green, Thomas Hill xv, 70–1, 76–9, 82–3, 86, 90, 96–7, 126, 153 n. 4, 154 n. 13 and n. 14, 156 n. 16 and n. 17 and n. 19, 156 n. 22, 157 n. 27 and n. 35

H
Hall, Granville Stanley 48
Hara Tanzan 原坦山 xiv, 23, 143 n. 13
Hegel, Georg William Friedrich xiv 5, 57, 143 n. 17
   Hegelian 26, 57, 125
Hisamatsu Shinichi 久松真一 158 n. 1
Hobbes, Thomas 154 n. 9
Høffding, Harold 153 n. 3
Holland xii, 6, 136 n. 2 and n. 4
   Dutch Traders xi
Human Life 人生 34, 38, 161 n. 14
   Beautiful Life 89–90
   Inner-life 91
   Problem of Life 人生の問題 16, 34, 38, 40–41
   Rebirth 39, 116, 128
   True Life 116
Hume, David xv, 112, 143 n. 17, 162 n. 26

I
Ideal 理想 71, 77–8, 80–3, 85–8, 126–7, 154 n. 14, 156 n. 24, 164 n. 27
Idealism 19, 21, 26, 29–30, 108, 140 n. 24, 142 n. 6, 143 n. 17, 145 n. 26
   Moral Idealism 79, 81, 86, 88, 98, 127
   Personal Idealism 98
Independence 72, 74–5, 125
Individualism 13, 72, 74–5, 82–3, 87, 91–3, 153 n. 6 and n. 8
Inoue Enryō 井上円了 xiv, xv, 4, 8, 10, 12, 15, 20–35, 37–41, 101, 125, 133, 140 n. 22, 141 nn. 1–5, 142 nn. 7–12, 143 n. 13, 143 n. 16 and n. 17, 144 n. 21 and n. 23, 145 n. 26
Inoue Tetsujirō 井上哲次郎 xiv–xv, 4, 8, 12, 15, 20, 80, 99, 125, 140 n. 23, 141 n. 3, 143 n. 13, 144 n. 22 and n. 23, 145 n. 26, 152 n. 38, 154 n. 15

Intuition 37, 119–20, 129–30, 162 n. 19
    Action-Intuition 行為的直観 7, 144 n. 24
    Intellectual Intuition 知的直観 37, 144 n. 25
Itō Jinsai 伊藤仁斎 160 n. 11

J

James, William 5, 12, 19, 43, 45, 47, 50, 52, 54–55, 57, 112, 147 n. 5, 148 n. 7 and 13, 149 n. 18
Janes, Leroy Lansing xiii
Japanese Identity 9
Japanese Philosophy vi–viii, 3–6, 8–9, 16, 19, 21, 37, 123–4, 132–4, 138 n. 11, 139 n. 12, 141 n. 25
Japanese Thought 5–6, 9, 16, 71, 92, 98, 128, 139 n. 12
Japanist 日本主義 148 n. 10
Judgment 35–7, 41–7, 49, 51, 53–7, 59, 61–6, 70, 84, 87, 130–1, 145 n. 25, 147 n. 2 and n. 4, 150 n. 25, 152 n. 34
    Judgmentive experience 42

K

Kant, Immanuel 5, 143 n. 17
Katō Hiroyuki 加藤弘之 136 n. 2
Kiyozawa Manshi 清沢満之 4, 12, 15, 20, 98–99, 141 n. 3 and n. 4, 158 n. 4
Kuhn, Thomas 134
Kūkai 空海 5
Kumamoto School for Western Studies 熊本洋学校 xiii
Kurata Hyakuzō 倉田百三 70–1, 91–4, 138 n. 10
Kyoto School vi, vii, 70, 136 n. 5
Kyoto University xvi

L

Lask, Emil 132
Leibniz, Gottfried Wilhelm 143 n. 17
Liberalism 75–6, 154 n. 9
    Liberal Authors 74
    Liberal Tradition 72
Liberty 自由 72
Locke, John 143 n. 17
Logic xiv, 72, 100, 106, 161
    Logic of Place 場所の論理 10, 128
    Logic of Soku 45
    Logicism 64 n. 45

M

Marxist 108, 140 n. 24
Materialism 19, 21, 26, 29–30, 143 n. 14 and n. 17
Mead, George Herbert 43, 50, 149 n. 19
Meiji Six xiii, 73, 154 n. 9
Merleau-Ponty, Maurice 162 n. 25
Metaphysics xiv, 22, 33, 128, 146 n. 32, 148 n. 7
Methodology 12, 16, 20–1, 34–8, 41, 43, 47, 59–60, 84, 97, 101, 108, 112, 115, 128, 131, 135, 138 n. 11, 160 n. 9
Mill, John Stuart xiii, 74, 136 n. 2
Mind 20, 23, 25–33, 37, 41, 48–51, 100–1, 125, 142 n. 12, 144 n. 19 and n. 25, 145 n. 26, 149 n. 14, 151 n. 30
    Divine Mind 77
    Mind-Body Dualism 143 n. 17
    Mind-independent world 28, 37, 108, 143 n. 13
    See also Mind-independent objects
    Other minds 2, 92, 114
Miyake Setsurei 三宅雪嶺 xiv, 12, 14, 20, 97, 99–110, 115, 118–21, 138 n. 10, 141 n. 3, 146 n. 33, 160 nn. 8–12, 161 nn.13–16
Modernity viii, 135
Modernization xvi, 40, 137 n. 8, 153 n. 7
Monism 28, 124–5, 145 n. 26
Mori Arinori 森有礼 73
Motora, Yūjirō (元良勇次郎) xiv, 4, 12–13, 43, 47–59, 64, 69, 125, 148 nn. 8–14, 149 nn.17–22, 150 n. 24 and n. 25, 150 n. 27
Mysticism 129
    Mystical Unity 130
    Mystical Experience 101, 107

N

Nakae Chōmin 中江兆民 3, 15, 140 n. 21
Nakajima Rikizō 中島力造 xiv, 76, 83
Nakamura Hajime 中村元 72
Nakamura Keiu 中村敬宇 xiii, 136 n. 2
National Morality 国民道徳 76, 80, 154 n. 10 and n. 15
Nationalism 80, 148 n. 10
Natorp, Paul Gerhard 132
Natsume Soseki 夏目漱石 93

Naturalism 143 n. 17
Nature 自然 87
Neo-Kantianism 7, 132
Nietzsche, Friedrich 161 n. 15
Niijima Jo 新島襄 xiii
Nishi Amane 西周 xiii–xiv, 2, 6, 73, 134, 136 n. 2, 137 n. 6, 139 n. 16
Nishimura Shigeki 西村茂樹 73
Nishitani Keiji 西谷啓治 91, 93–5, 158 n. 1 and n. 2
Nitta Yoshihiro 新田義弘 144 n. 21, 164 n. 2
Noe, Alva 152 n. 30
Nominalism 60, 146 n. 30, 149 n. 21
Nothingness 68, 130

O
Okakura Tenshin 岡倉天心 xv
Onishi Hajime 大西祝 xiv–xv, 4, 8, 10, 32, 70, 80–81, 83, 90, 126, 133, 144 n.23, 153 n. 3, 155 n. 20 and n. 21, 156 n. 24, 157 n. 30, 160 n. 10
Ontology 4, 15, 27, 32–3, 35, 87, 123, 142 n. 13, 146 n. 31, 160 n. 12
  Ontology of Meaning 12
  Ontology of Patterns 60
Opium War xii, 6
Organism 有機体 14, 99, 102–7, 114, 120, 126, 151 n. 30, 160 n. 12, 161 n. 13
  Organic (philosophy) 14, 96–7, 100, 103, 105
Originality viii, 3–4, 10, 12, 16
Originary Activity 30, 128, 164 n. 1
Oshio Heihachirō 大塩平八郎 160 n. 11

P
Perry, Commodore Matthew, xii, 1, 3, 6, 72, 138 n. 9
Personality 人格 14, 48, 86, 96–7, 106, 113–14, 116, 157 n. 29, 158 n. 3, 159 n. 6
  Macro-Personality 81–2, 96
  Personal God 115
Phenomena-*soku*-Reality 現象即実在論 12, 20, 27, 142 n. 6 and n. 13, 144 n. 22, 145 n. 26

Phenomenology 7
  Neurophenomenology 148 n. 14, 164 n. 1
  Phenomenological (Views) 92, 98, 156 n. 26, 165 n. 5
Place 場所 7, 128, 130–2
Platonism 59
Plotinus 162 n. 21
Psychology xiv, 11, 45, 47–8, 57–8, 60, 123, 148 n. 7, 148 n. 13 and n. 14, 163 n. 26
Psychologism 58–9, 150 n. 26
Psychologistic 13, 43, 59, 64, 150 n. 26

R
Rationality 22–4
  Rational Egoism 92
  Rational Form 理体 25
Reason 理性 88, 127
Reid, Thomas 143 n. 17
Reflection 反省 34–5, 37, 45, 56, 70, 86, 90, 108, 120, 129, 145 n. 25, 146 n. 1, 164 n. 3, 165 n. 6
  Pre-reflective experience 45, 46, 85, 89, 130
  Reflective Consciousness 12, 42, 44, 46, 55–6, 70, 89, 92, 129–30, 145 n. 25, 147 n. 5
Religion xi–xii, xv, 11, 14, 21–6, 42, 58, 63, 68, 79, 103, 105–7, 110, 115–18, 123, 131–2, 142 n. 8, 147 n. 2, 154 n. 15, 159 n. 6, 161 n. 13
  Philosophical Religion 21–3
  Religious Consciousness 82, 96, 115–18, 128, 165 n. 8
Rescript (Imperial Rescript on Education) xiv–xv, 76, 79–80, 154 n. 11
Rights 権利 1, 72, 79, 86, 90–1, 156 n. 22
Romantic (Ethics) 90, 158 n. 36
Russia xi, 137 n. 3
  Russo-Japanese War xv 2, 90

S
Sakoku 鎖国 xi, 6, 139 n. 13
Sakuma Shōzan 佐久間象山 xii, 139 n. 15
Sapporo Agricultural College 札幌農学校 xiii
Sartre, Jean Paul 162 n. 25

Schelling, Friedrich Wilhelm
    Joseph 143 n. 17
Schopenhauer, Arthur 101, 120
Science 22–3, 25, 102–3, 141 n. 1 and n. 5,
    142 n. 12, 148 n. 8 and n. 14
    Neuroscience 62
    Social Sciences 48
Seikyōsha 政教社 20, 99, 141 n. 2
Self-awareness 自覚 116, 120, 129–30,
    164 n. 2, 165 n. 5
Self-consciousness 45–6, 77, 110, 117,
    147 n. 6, 165 n. 8
Selfhood 4, 69, 95–6, 107, 109–10, 112,
    114–15, 119, 131, 158 n. 1,
    163 n. 26
Shintoism 154 n. 15
Shogunate xii–xiii, 1, 139 n. 13 and n. 16
Sincerity 至誠 89
Smiles, Samuel xiii, 136 n. 2
Sōda Kiichiro 左右田喜一郎 132
Solipsist 92
Spencer, Herbert xiv, 80, 102, 143 n. 17
Spirit 49, 78, 87–8, 106, 153 n. 1, 158 n. 4,
    161 n. 16, 163 n. 28
    Absolute Spirit 98, 158 n. 4
    Eastern Spirit xii, 158 n. 2
    National Spirit 108
    Spiritual Truths 23, 25
    Universal Human Spirit 81–2, 106, 110,
        154 n. 14
    Western Spirit xiv
Statist Educational Theory 81
Substance 25, 46, 117, 120, 162 n. 23
Suchness 真如 25
Supermen 超人 104, 161 n. 15
Suzuki Daisetsu (D. T.) 鈴木大拙 136 n. 4,
    148 n. 7

T
Taisho Period 大正時代 40, 91, 93
Takahashi Satomi 高橋里美 13, 43,
    64–7, 99, 131, 138 n. 10, 151
    n. 31 and 32, 152 nn. 34–36
Takano Chōei 高野長英 xi–xii, 137 n. 9
Takayama Chogyu 高山樗牛 158 n. 36
Tanabe Hajime 田辺元 i 108, 132, 162
    n. 21, 165 n. 8, 166 n. 9
Tetsugaku 哲学 xiv, xv, 2–3, 6, 9, 73,
    137 n. 6 and n. 8, 140 n. 23

Theory of Self-Realization 自己実現説
    13, 71, 76–9, 82, 84, 89, 91, 93,
    154 n. 12
Thought/Thinking 思惟 34–5, 37, 44, 55–7,
    59–60, 62, 67, 88, 106, 108, 111,
    152 n. 39, 153 n. 1, 164 n. 3,
    159 n. 4
Tokugawa Ieyasu 徳川家康 xi
Tokyo University xiii, xiv, xv, 2–3, 23, 48,
    143 n. 13, 158 n. 36, 162 n. 26
Tomonaga Sanjuro 朝永三十郎 98
Tosaka Jun 戸坂潤 132
Trans-lation 166 n. 10
True Self 真の自己 13, 42, 95–7, 106–8,
    110, 112, 116–17, 120, 126,
    129–30, 158 n. 1, 162 n. 20
Truth, Good, and Beauty 真善美 100, 103
Tsubouchi, Shōyō 坪内逍遥 155 n. 19
Tsuda, Mamichi 津田真道 xii, 6, 136 n. 2,
    139 n. 16
Tsunashima Ryōsen 綱島梁川 4, 82–3,
    98–9, 126, 156 n. 25 and n. 26,
    157 n. 32, 159 n. 5 and n. 6

U
Uchimura Kanzō 内村鑑三 xv, 154 n. 15
Unifying Activity 36, 57, 106, 117,
    163 n. 28
Universal 一般者 57, 59–60, 62–3, 66–8, 98,
    109–11, 114–15, 117, 119, 131,
    145 n. 26, 146 n. 30 and n. 31,
    151 n. 30, 162 n. 21, 165 n. 7
    Abstract universal 146 n. 30
    concrete universal 13, 43, 57, 62–3, 68,
        131
    Universal Human Spirit 82, 108,
        154 n. 14
    United States of America xii, 6,
        148 n. 12
    American xiii, 6, 72, 139 n. 12, 150
        n. 24
Universe, the 宇宙 14, 27, 28, 34, 39, 41–2,
    69–70, 87, 97, 99–104, 106–8, 110,
    114–17, 120, 126, 129, 131, 156
    n. 24, 158 n. 4, 160 n. 8 and n. 10,
    160 n. 11 and n. 12, 161 n. 14
    Cosmic Activity 85, 101
    Cosmic Biology 102
    Cosmic Order 103, 160 n. 8

V
Van Koeber, Rafael xiv
Vissering, Simon xii 139 n. 16
Volition 70, 118, 145 n. 25, 157 n. 29

W
Wang Yangming School 陽明学 140 n. 23, 160 n. 11
Watsuji, Tetsurō 和辻哲郎 161 n. 12
Western Learning xi–xii 73, 146 n. 33, 153 n. 7
Western Philosophy xi–xii, xiv 2, 4, 9–10, 21–2, 26, 40, 133–4, 137 n. 5, 138 n. 11, 140 n. 22, 141 n. 3 and n. 4, 143 n. 17
Will 意志 33, 35, 37, 70, 79, 101, 106, 111, 120, 129, 131, 153 n. 1, 160 n. 11, 164 n. 3
  Absolute Will 120, 129, 164 n. 3 and n. 4
Wolff, Christian xii 138 n. 9
Wundt, Wilhelm 12, 43, 47, 49, 54, 57, 148 n. 13, 149 n. 16

Y
Yokoi Tokio 横井時雄 xv
Yoshida Seiichi 吉田静致 155 n. 18

Z
Zahavi, Dan 149 n. 14

www.ingramcontent.com/pod-product-compliance
Lightning Source LLC
Chambersburg PA
CBHW052120300426
44116CB00010B/1748